Books by Mich

and publis
The Write Thought

Under the "Hardboiled-Noir" imprint:

The VICAP series featuring FBI agents Flynn and Tanner:

Blood Sport
Slay Ride
The Necro File
Head Games
Road Kills
Black Lace
Wet Work
Jigsaw
Dead Heat

Thrillers:

Cat and Mouse
Korea Kill
Child of Blood
China White

True Crime:

Silent Rage: Inside the Mind of a Serial Killer

From the Classic Wisdom on Writing Series:

How to Write Action Adventure Novels
Armed and Dangerous: A Writer's Guide to Weapons

Silent Rage

Inside the Mind of a Serial Killer

BY

MICHAEL NEWTON

Hardboiled-Noir
An imprint of The Write Thought, Inc.
Sanger, California

The Write Thought, Inc.
1254 Commerce Way
Sanger, California 93657
559-876-2170

Info@TheWriteThought.com

9781618092021   K
9781618092038   ePub
9781618092045   POD

For Gary. Long time passing.

CONTENTS

Every society gets the kind of criminal it deserves.
—Robert F. Kennedy

The car is parked in such a way that it conceals them from the street. Cole doesn't know whether it's locked or not, but his prey makes it easy, leaning back against the door and reaching for him. "Waste of time to wait," she says.

Cole agrees. As she flows into his arms for an embrace, his fingers lock around her throat.

With a practiced move, he cuts the legs out from under her and takes her down …

PROLOGUE

The tavern starts to clear by half past one o'clock. An old man nursing whiskey at the far end of the bar, a clink of glasses as the barkeep washes up. Slim pickings for the hunter as he lights another cigarette and sips his beer.

The barroom smells like smoke and sweat and wasted dreams. A country-western groaner on the jukebox, emphasizing failure, just in case late drinkers fail to get the point.

The hunter thinks he may have lost an evening, mostly sitting by himself and waiting for his luck to change. A pickup game of eight-ball with some rednecks he may never see again. No women in the place for hours.

Some nights, waiting serves to heighten his anticipation. Other times, the weariness creeps in and leaves him feeling empty.

Like tonight.

Still half an hour to closing time, but what's the point? Already low on cash, he doesn't need another beer to make him stagger on the walk back to his seedy rented room. Despite the hour and the neighborhood, he has no fear of being mugged along the way.

A slogan from a pop-art military poster comes to mind and makes him smile. *Yea, though I walk through the valley of the shadow of death, I shall fear no evil ...for I am the baddest motherfucker in the valley.*

Damn right.

He is resigned to leaving when the door swings open, new arrivals laughing louder than they need to, moving toward a corner booth. Three men, all Mexican, surround an Anglo woman in her early thirties. Blond, not bad to look at, round breasts straining at the fabric of her blouse.

The hunter takes points off for choice of company, imagining the four of them together in an old, low-rider Chevy. Three on one, the wetbacks getting what they've always wanted most, the white slut getting paid in cash or all the liquor she can handle. Anything to make her come across.

And, then again, she may be one of those who takes to slumming. The perverse excitement of it, like a taste of some forbidden fruit. Not sweet, exactly— often quite the opposite—but still invigorating, in a twisted kind of way.

Like sudden death.

A sweet-sick taste the hunter knows from long experience.

But there is nothing for him here.

He palms his bankroll, wishing there was more of it to go around. Another day or two, at most, and he will have to look for work. Whatever pays enough to rent a bar stool for the night, and if he has to lose the crummy room, so be it. He can always find himself another place to sleep.

About to put his money on the bar, he sees the blonde get up. Tight jeans to emphasize her ass and legs, a mental image of the denim down around her ankles while she services the wetbacks. Do they wait in line, he wonders, or attempt to take her all at once, wherever they can find an empty hand or hole?

The hunter frowns as she approaches him. A new expression on her face, not laughing now.

"You mind if I sit down?"

"Free country."

He can smell her as she settles on the stool. Perfume and perspiration, with an undertone of musk. Familiar odors.

"I was wondering," she says, "if you could help me out."

"How's that?"

"These guys I'm with, they've had a lot to drink. I mean, we *all* have, but it's getting out of hand, okay?" "You want to ditch them."

"Will you help me?"

Three on one is sucker odds. He glances at the barkeep, rinsing glasses, wondering how much the man has seen, or if he has enough invested in the place to give a damn. Some like to settle problems on their own, while others leave it all to the police.

The hunter doesn't need police tonight.

Across the room, the Mexicans have picked up on her act by now. One of them is on his feet and bitching to the others. Heated Spanish, the machismo kicking in with a tequila booster. All three moving toward the bar now, just a tad unsteady on their feet.

"You got a problem, ese?"

Turning slowly on his stool, the hunter looks their self-appointed mouthpiece up and down. "No problem I can see."

"You better get your eyes checked, man. The lady came with us."

An old, familiar chill inside the hunter now. Prepared for anything, and screw the odds. He smiles.

"That doesn't mean she's leaving with you, Pancho."

"Hey, *pendejo,* how about we fuck you up?"

He has one hand around the sweaty Lone Star bottle, calculating its trajectory and what will follow, when a sound like giant knuckles rapping on the bar distracts him. The proprietor is scowling at his latest customers and tapping on the bar top with a leaded baseball bat.

"Nobody's fucking anybody up in here unless I do the fucking, get it?" Waiting for the punks to take it in before he adds, "It's time to say good-bye."

The wetbacks calculating now, deciding that an Anglo *puta* isn't worth the risk of broken bones and time in jail. They exit muttering, same slouching walk that every young Latino seems to learn at puberty, one of them spitting on the floor. A puny parting shot.

The blonde has found her smile again. "You saved my life."

"I doubt it."

"Anyway, I owe you one."

In case the hunter doesn't get her point, she takes his hand and places it between her legs, thighs trapping him. He lets his fingers do the walking, makes her squirm against the stool.

"You have a name?"

He nods. "Most people do."

"Is it a secret?"

"Eddie"

"Pleased to meet you, Eddie." Squeezing with her thighs. "I'm Wanda."

"Want a drink?"

She licks her lips. "Why not."

He pays the tab one-handed, hoists his beer the same way. Heat communicated from the woman to his fingers, knowing if he slipped his hand inside her panties, he would find her wet and waiting.

Halfway through her drink, the woman says, "It's past my bed-time. Have you got a car?"

"Sure thing." A lie, but what the hell.

"Why don't we go someplace a little bit more private?"

"Did you have a place in mind?"

That hungry smile again. "I might."

The alcohol kicks in once she is on her feet. The floor starts playing games. She takes his arm and leans against him, giggling as they move in lock-step toward the door.

A glance in each direction, up and down the street, assures him that the Mexicans are gone. No ambush waiting in the shadows. They are all alone.

She stumbles on the threshold, but he catches her. More giggling, as he homes in on the only car still sitting in an open lot beside the bar. He steers her toward it, crunching gravel underfoot.

"Tha's yours?"

"You guessed it."

"Hey, I'm good that way. Good, period."

She gropes him in the darkness, feeling his erection, teasing him. "Oh, my."

The car is parked in such a way that it conceals them from the street, once they have reached the driver's side. He doesn't know if it is locked or not, but Wanda makes it easy, leaning back against the door and reaching for him.

"Waste of time to wait," she says, and then she can't talk anymore, their tongues entwined. She helps him with the buttons of her blouse, no bra confining luscious breasts that fill his hands, the nipples swelling at his touch. She moans into his mouth and grinds against him, one hand dropping to his fly.

And freezes, as his fingers lock around her throat.

The first reaction is surprise, a short step into full-blown panic, but a long night's boozing has deprived her of coordination, sapping any strength she might have had when sober. With a practiced move, he cuts her legs from under her and takes her down, the gravel sharp against his knees.

It isn't like the movies, squeezing for a second till the eyes roll back and everything goes limp. Not clean and easy, like they write it up in Hollywood. He straddles her and puts his weight behind the effort, Wanda wriggling underneath him in a parody of intercourse that almost gets him off.

Almost.

It seems to take forever, and his hands begin to ache. A new condition for the docs to write up in their journals: strangler's cramp.

He rocks back on his haunches, takes a chance releasing her. Dry, rasping sounds as straining lungs suck wind. He tugs his belt off, looping it around her neck to form a noose, and pulls it tight.

Much better. Still not quick, but getting there.

A final tremor rippling through her body, starting at the shoulders, working downward to her feet. He rides it out and keeps the pressure on a few more minutes, making sure. Her cheeks are mottled with congested blood, her swollen tongue protruding in a rude expression that would piss him off, if she were still alive.

The best part over, but he isn't finished yet.

A sound of footsteps on the gravel, and he freezes, sitting on a corpse. Perhaps the rightful owner of the car returning, yards away from stumbling on a homicide in progress. Swallowing his sudden fear, the hunter isn't sure if he has strength enough to take a man, right now. His hands and forearms tingle from the strain of snuffing out a life; his legs are almost numb, from too much alcohol and squatting over Wanda's prostrate body. If he has to fight or run . . .

The footsteps veer away before they reach the car, retreating through a nearby gate. The hunter spends another moment waiting, listening, at last deciding he is too exposed. Thigh muscles cramping as he lurches to his feet and looks around for cover.

Like the lady said, someplace a little bit more private.

Several yards away, a fence divides the lot from an adjacent rooming house. All dark at this time of the morning, no one to distract the hunter from his prey.

He drags the woman by an arm, heels scraping on the gravel, through the open gate. A driveway cast in shadow, good enough to suit his purpose. Bending down, he strips her jeans and panties off, the woman more attractive to him now that she is limp and still. The ritual is not complete until he spreads her legs and rams himself into her unresisting flesh, debasing her in death.

Recoiling from the sudden stench, he wrinkles up his nostrils, cursing. She has soiled herself, the anal sphincter letting go as consciousness and life escape. He cannot bring himself to touch her now.

A goddamn waste.

He leaves her there, spread-eagled in the driveway, drops her clothing in some bushes several yards away. No fingerprints on fabric. The police will have to earn their money, for a change.

He hopes for better luck, next time around.

The blonde is not his first. She will not be *the* last.

ONE

Aside from blind domestic beefs, the D.B. calls are worst. You never know about dead bodies, going in. Assuming that the call-in wasn't bogus to begin with—a deliberate hoax, a transient sleeping on the sidewalk, or a drunk who never made it home, for instance—it could still mean anything.

Dead bodies get that way by different means. A sudden stroke or heart attack. Old age. An accidental overdose or suicide. A hit-and-run.

Or murder.

People kill each other every day with knives and firearms, baseball bats and steam irons. Poison. Power tools. The family car. An argument turns deadly and dissolves in blood. A crying child is battered into silence once too often. Starry-eyed romance blurs into green-eyed savagery. More times than not, the killing stems from friendship, love affairs, or family ties.

With any luck, the killer is dismayed, consumed by grief and guilt. He lingers at the scene until police arrive, or leaves sufficient evidence behind to keep the manhunt brief.

And then again . . .

Like any other law enforcement agency, police in Dallas, Texas, have their share of unsolved homicides on file. Gang shootings, where the triggermen are known but evidence is insufficient to support a case in court. A contract killing, nice and clean. The random holdups, sexual assaults, and muggings that are part of urban life around the world.

But every now and then, you run across a freak. No motive evident, or else the crime is so bizarre and brutal it defies apparent logic. Psychopaths who kill repeatedly, as if to entertain themselves, selecting total strangers as their prey.

By 1980, clinical psychologists and federal agents had begun to speak of these as "serial killers," drawing a distinction between the chronic repeaters and simple "mass murderers," who run amok in public, shooting everyone in sight. More to the point, some authorities describe their elusive prey as "recreational killers," and Texas has produced her share in modern times.

Joe Ball, the Elmendorf nightclub owner and amateur herpetologist, who fed at least a dozen women to his alligators in the 1930s.

Johnny Meadows, the Odessa strangler, sentenced to life imprisonment for one of his half-dozen murders, committed between 1968 and 1972.

Dean Corll and Elmer Henley, homosexual torture-slayers of twenty-seven young men and boys around Houston, in the early 1970s.

Henry Lucas, convicted of ten murders and suspected of dozens more, who suddenly recanted his confessions in the spring of 1985, leaving befuddled lawmen to pick up the pieces.

The names are infamous because they were identified and brought to justice, of a sort ... but what of those who get away? By 1980, national statistics showed that one in four American homicides remained unsolved forever, and solution rates were even worse in larger cities, where police are overrun by gangs, the homeless, transient drifters. In an average year, at least 5,000 killers walk away, scot-free, to recreate their crimes if they are so inclined. According to the FBI's best estimate— admittedly conservative, at that—a minimum of thirty-five active serial killers are known to be at large in the United States on any given day.

A Dallas P.D. operator logged the call at 5:15 A.M. on Wednesday, November 12, 1980. Details were sparse, the caller breathless. He had found a woman's body in the 4100 block of Bryan Street, an inner-city neighborhood of honky-tonk saloons, cheap lodgings, greasy spoons. No further information was available.

The uniforms come first, dispatched by radio to check it out before the lab technicians and detectives are disturbed. The corpse in question is discovered in the driveway of a shabby rooming house at 4136 Bryan, adjacent to a gravel parking lot with trees and weeds on the perimeter. The cruiser's spotlight picks her out, a pale discarded mannequin.

The uniforms approach on foot, to verify the fact of death. The corpse is definitely female, naked from the waist and braless underneath the open blouse. Blond hair. Brown eyes, still open, looking more like dusty marbles now. Up close, the flashlights pick out mottled bruising on her throat, a crust of blood around the silent lips.

Another call, this time official. There is ample reason to suspect a homicide, perhaps with sexual assault involved.

Detective Gerald Robinson, representing the Dallas P.D.'s Crimes Against Persons division, was on the scene by 6:00 A.M., followed closely by a police photographer, a team from the forensics lab, and an assistant Dallas County medical examiner. It is the M.E.'s task to supervise collection of forensic evidence and hazard a suggestion on the cause of death. In this case, there appears to be no mystery. The verdict: strangulation. Any further details, as to rape or secondary injuries, will have to wait upon a visit to the morgue.

At first glance, from the placement of the corpse, Detective Robinson surmised the victim had been strangled elsewhere, then discarded by her killer at the present site. The theory lasted all of fifteen minutes, shattered when a searcher found the victim's slacks behind a clump of trees, some twenty feet away. The garment had been ripped, in rage or haste, and soiled by the release of sphincter muscles at the point of death.

Nearby, some partial tracks and drag marks indicated how the body had been moved to where it lay. Abrasions on the victim's legs and buttocks verified that she was dragged across the dirt and gravel like a sack of laundry, after she was killed and stripped.

Examining the ruined slacks, Detective Robinson turned out the pockets and retrieved a driver's license, identifying the victim as Wanda Faye Roberts, age thirty-two. Her home address was listed as 4607 Bryan, five blocks north of where she died.

The autopsy report on Wanda Roberts confirmed manual strangulation as the cause of death, revealing no evidence of rape or other sexual activity. The victim's blood-alcohol level suggested she was drinking heavily before she died, a pointer that would give Detective Robinson his last, best hope of plotting out her movements prior to death.

Armed with photos from the morgue, Robinson returned to Bryan Street, working the bars for two blocks on either side of the murder scene, questioning bartenders and cocktail waitresses along the way. At Pauline's Bar, a short block north of where the body was discovered, employees identified Wanda Faye as a regular. She had been drinking in Pauline's the night she died, and hung around until the mandatory closing time at 2:00 A.M. The bartender could not be certain, but he thought that Wanda might have left the tavern with another semiregular named Eddie. No last name, but over several weeks of idle conversation, Eddie had described himself as living at a halfway house for ex-cons on parole.

It was a start, but nothing more. Assuming Eddie No-Name wasn't spinning bullshit yarns to make himself sound tough, the Dallas-Fort Worth area was rife with halfway houses catering to former inmates, drug and alcohol abusers, even mental patients making the adjustment from an institution to the streets. Without a face or name attached, the lead was going nowhere, fast.

And there was still a problem of geography for Robinson to solve. The victim had been found a block south of Pauline's, although her home address was four blocks *north* on Bryan, from the bar. To understand why she had died, it would be necessary to discover why a drunken woman turns away from home at 2:00 A.M., when all the bars and liquor stores are closed.

If she was traveling with Eddie No-Name, then the problem solved itself. A proposition over drinks, a short walk back to his place, but the lady never gets there. Death is waiting, on the way.

Removing Eddie No-Name from the picture raised two further possibilities that Robinson would have to deal with and eliminate, before he made his case. If Wanda Faye had left Pauline's alone, there was an outside chance she could have been disoriented for a moment, walking south on Bryan till she caught herself— or someone caught her—at the gravel parking lot. And, then again, she could have left the bar with someone else, or even met some unknown man outside.

Considering his list of options, Robinson already knew that he was on the clock. Statistically speaking, a murder unsolved after forty-eight hours was likely to remain unsolved forever, a grim fact of life for detectives working the homicide beat. The two days passed on Wanda Faye, became two weeks, and Robinson was still without a decent clue to the identity of her assailant.

He would need a lucky break, and soon, if Wanda Faye was not to join the city's growing list of "open" murder files.

*****

Near midnight on November 30, a Sunday, Sally Thompson's two sons brought a girlfriend home to visit at her Rawlins Avenue apartment. Lights were burning in the living room, the television playing, but the door was locked, and neither of the boys had thought to bring a key. They started knocking, alternately rattling the knob, but several minutes passed before a stranger opened up the door. The man was slender, average height, with dark hair and a thin mustache. His breath was eighty-proof and he appeared disoriented, but he offered no resistance as the boys brushed past him, looking for their mother.

The living room was piled with packing cartons from a recent move, but it did not obstruct their view of Sally Thompson lying on the floor, facedown beside the couch, her jeans and panties wadded up around her ankles. Frightened now, the boys retreated, banging on a neighbor's door and calling out for help.

Inside, the stranger walked back to the couch and sat, apparently befuddled, with the prostrate body of the forty-three-year-old legal secretary stretched out at his feet.

The neighbors came, took one look at the eerie scene, and ran to telephone police. A nervous guard was posted at the door, in his pajamas, but the silent stranger sat, immobile, staring at the television with his eyes half-closed.

The uniforms arrived, confirmed the lady of the house was dead, and slipped a pair of handcuffs on the silent stranger's wrists. He seemed to come around as they began to question him, the fog of alcohol retreating as he focused on their words.

The suspect gave his name as Carroll Edward Cole, his address barely two blocks distant, at 4038 Lemmon Avenue. As Cole recalled the evening, he encountered Sally Thompson in a nearby bar, the Club DeVille, and after several rounds of drinks she had invited him to share her bed. Once back at the apartment, they had settled down to business on the couch, and Cole was in the process of disrobing her when Thompson suddenly collapsed, apparently unconscious. He was trying to revive her when the unexpected visitors turned up, distracting him.

A team of paramedics rolled in moments later, reaffirming death and checking out the corpse for signs of violence. None were visible, and while the paramedics could not specify a cause of death, the symptoms pointed to an overdose of drugs or alcohol.

Reluctantly, the officers removed Cole's handcuffs, but they were not finished with their questions, yet. Outside, a growing crowd of neighbors watched the shrouded stretcher disappear, immediately followed by the pair of uniforms with Cole in tow.

It is a four-mile drive from Rawlins Avenue to the Police and Courts Building at Main and Harwood, downtown. Light traffic in the predawn hours of a Monday morning, and the officers were in no hurry, switching off the colored lights that had been flashing since they parked outside of the apartment complex. Sally Thompson was well on her way to the morgue, and Carroll Edward Cole was going nowhere till the officers had checked his story out in greater detail.

At the station, Cole smoked and worked his way through several cups of coffee, running down his story from the top. No change. The lady had been willing, if a trifle drunk, and he could not explain her sudden lapse into unconsciousness and death.

In time, the word came down. The M.E. had conducted his postmortem, and the cause of death was filed as "indeterminate." No clearcut signs of violent trauma on the corpse; no drugs or poison in the blood or tissue to account for her demise. An elevated blood-alcohol count supported the tentative verdict of an accidental, alcohol-related death.

Case closed.

With no grounds for detention or a charge against him, Cole was driven back to Lemmon Avenue and dropped off near the address he had listed as his home. The officers dismissed him from their minds before he wandered out of sight.

*****

Sometimes, coincidence can break a case when legwork and persistence fail. The fact embarrasses detectives, but they take what they can get. In Queens, New York, the "Son of Sam" neglects to read the street signs when he parks his car and goes in search of human prey; a traffic cop writes out the ticket and forgets about it, until homicide investigators start to run a list of license plates. In Hollywood, the "Skid Row Slasher" drops his driver's license at a crime scene, and the rest is history.

Detective Gerald Robinson began his Monday morning shift with a review of weekend crime reports. The death of Sally Thompson hardly seemed to qualify, but something caught his eye. He went back. Started from the top.

The suspect's name was Carroll *Edward* Cole; a friend might call him Eddie, over drinks. On top of that, his address rang a bell. A moment's consultation with the Rolodex told Robinson that 4038 Lemmon

Avenue was the address of the Way Back, a halfway house for felons on probation or parole. A rough two blocks from Sally Thompson's place on Rawlins, the Way Back stood within two miles of Bryan Street, where Wanda Roberts met her death.

So far, so good.

Robinson telephoned the halfway house and spoke to head counselor Linda Bishop, digging for some background on his man. He learned that Cole's most recent fall had been for violating terms of his probation on a four-year-old mail-theft conviction, a federal rap originating out of San Diego. Released from the federal hospital in Springfield, Missouri, on October 6, Cole hit Dallas two days later and settled in at the Way Back. He had some trouble with the rules, specifically including abstinence from alcohol, and by the last week of October he was missing nightly lock-outs, sleeping where he could. Cole left the halfway house November 3, but called back and negotiated for a grudging readmission on the twelfth.

The day that Wanda Roberts died on Bryan Street.

From Linda Bishop, the detective learned that Cole was readmitted to the house with strict provisions that included counseling, no liquor, and a curfew that would get him off the streets by ten o'clock at night. If Sunday night was any indication, Cole had found his way around the curfew and had fallen off the wagon in the process. He was working lately, at a warehouse— Toys "R" Us, the big pre-Christmas rush—but he was sullen, uncommunicative. Bishop was convinced that he had something preying on his mind.

Encouraged by his findings, so far, Robinson reached out for background information on his suspect from the Federal Bureau of Investigation. A quick scan of FBI file No. 160-613-D gave Robinson a feeling for his man and reassured him he was on the right track, after all.

Born in May 1938, in Sioux City, Iowa, Cole moved to northern California with his family at age three. He joined the navy in early 1957 and was bounced a year later with a bad-conduct discharge, the result of stealing two pistols from a shipboard armory. His juvenile record was sealed under California law, but the adult arrests dated back to September 1958, when he was picked up for burglary and auto theft in San Diego. Over the next two decades, Cole averaged two arrests per year, his tracks spanning California, Nevada, Texas, Missouri, and Oklahoma.

The charges ranged from drunk driving and petty theft to more serious counts, including a 1965 arson conviction in Dallas that earned him two years in state prison. In 1967 Cole was convicted of felonious assault with intent to ravish an adolescent girl in Missouri; his five-year sentence was commuted in the spring of 1970. Serving federal time on the 1976 mail-theft charge, Cole was twice released and twice rearrested for violating probation before he finally turned up in Dallas.

And the women started dying.

Apart from his violent criminal record, Cole also boasted a history of mental quirks. The psychiatric record listed a suicide attempt in Dallas, along with voluntary self-committals to state hospitals in California and Nevada, where he regaled staff doctors with his tales of a compelling urge to rape and strangle women.

Close enough.

The doctors weren't convinced, but Robinson was getting there. If nothing else, he had already satisfied himself that Cole deserved a closer look.

*****

Near closing time on Monday afternoon, Detective Robinson entered the Toys "R" Us warehouse, asking the foreman for directions to Eddie Cole's work area. At first glance, his slender, well-groomed subject did not look the part of a compulsive killer but Robinson knew well enough that looks could be deceiving. He approached the stranger cautiously, prepared to cope with flight or physical resistance if the ex-con tried to cop an attitude.

Cole saw him coming, recognized the new arrival as a lawman, but he made no move to break away. The suspect's manner was respectful and reserved as Robinson displayed his badge, requesting Cole to join him for another ride downtown.

No sweat.

If Cole was nervous, it had not begun to show.

Outside, the unmarked car was wall-to-wall detectives, two men in the back, a driver at the wheel. They put Cole in the back seat, wedged between two suits, with Robinson up front, beside the driver. It was cramped inside the car, but they were only six or seven minutes from their destination, and they made the drive in silence, Cole almost invisible between his burly escorts.

At the station, three of the detectives split, Robinson and a companion steering Cole toward the Crimes Against Persons division. They left him in a small interrogation room, two chairs facing each other across a narrow table, and Robinson came back moments later with two cups of coffee, taking the empty seat across from Cole.

The questions started off with a warning, read from a Miranda card. You have the right to remain silent. Consult an attorney. Have counsel appointed in cases of poverty. Anything you say . . .

Cole waived his rights, a man with nothing to hide. He had already told the Sally Thompson story twice, and he was not about to change it now.

Robinson surprised him with the name of Wanda Roberts. Did Cole know the lady, by any chance? Had they left Pauline's together in the early morning hours of November 12? Did Cole, perhaps, remember strangling her and stripping down the corpse before he dumped it like a broken doll on Bryan Street?

The suspect grudgingly admitted meeting Wanda Roberts at Pauline's the night she died. In fact, they *had* walked out together, but a tall, slim stranger waited for them on the sidewalk, accosting Wanda in familiar tones. After a boozy exchange of words, Wanda brushed Eddie off, casting her vote for the competition. Cole had last seen Wanda Roberts, he recalled, as she had walked away down Bryan Street and left him feeling like a fool.

Without missing a beat, Robinson shifted back to the Thompson case, eliciting the same account of her sudden, inexplicable collapse during foreplay. By now, the story had begun to sound rehearsed.

Again, Cole spurned the offer of a lawyer. Would he sit down for a polygraph exam, to clear the whole thing up? Cole thought about it for a moment, finally shrugged, indifferently. Why not?

A rapping on the door distracted Robinson, one of his colleagues drawing him into the corridor. They had a new squeal on an officer-involved shooting, and Homicide was shorthanded at the moment. Could Robinson leave his suspect long enough to cover the scene?

Back in the interrogation room, Robinson took a chance, informing Cole that they were out of time. The interview was over. Cole was bound for booking on suspicion of murdering Wanda Roberts.

The suspect blinked. "We shouldn't quit right now," he said. "I've still got things to tell you. It could take a while."

What kind of things?

"About a murder. I'll need coffee and some smokes, before we start."

Robinson escorted Cole to the cigarette vending machine, standing by while his suspect fed coins into the slot and made his selection. Returning to the cubicle, he buttonholed another officer and passed the shooting on. No time for interruptions, when he had a live one on his hands.

"Okay," he said, when he was seated facing Cole, "tell me what happened."

"I can tell you right now," Cole answered, "that I need some help. It's like I'm with a woman, having drinks, and then something comes over me. I have to kill her."

Robinson could feel the short hairs rising on his nape. "Go on."

Without further hesitation, Cole launched into a description of a typical incident. Sunday afternoon in Charlie's Bar, at Carroll and Gaston, drinking with a woman he had never seen before. The invitation to her home was no surprise. An easy walk, and they were sitting on the couch, still drinking beer and watching television with the front door open. Suddenly, in place of lust, a new sensation like "a foggy haze" enveloped Cole.

"I grabbed her around the throat and pulled her behind me on the couch," he recalled, "so hard her wig slipped off. I was choking her a few seconds before I remembered the open door, then I lifted her into a sitting position, laying my head on her shoulder for appearances, while I kept up the pressure on her throat. It was easy, no struggle at all. At one point, a Mexican passed by the door and looked in at us, but he figured we were making out and kept on going."

Finally satisfied that she was dead, Cole rose and shut the door. Returning to the couch, he stripped his victim, carrying her naked body to the bedroom. She had soiled herself in death, and he retrieved a washcloth from the bathroom, cleaning her and pausing once to vomit from the stench. That done, he raped the corpse and fell asleep beside it, waking several times for intercourse throughout the night.

Alarm bells were going off in Robinson's head. Aside from the graphic details of murder and necrophilia, there was something . . .

"The next morning," Cole went on, "I took her key and locked the apartment before I went out drinking. That night, I came back and slept with the body and screwed her several times. The second morning I left and never went back."

It struck Robinson then. Cole was describing a *different* murder, of which the detective was totally ignorant. Stunned, Robinson interrupted Cole and excused himself for a moment, rushing down the hall to check for any records of a case he somehow might have missed.

A Sunday in November narrowed down the possibilities. If Cole spent two nights with his victim, it would have to be November 9, when he was AWOL from the halfway house.

Short moments later Robinson was scanning a report on the death of Dorothy King, age fifty-two, found in the bedroom of her apartment on Tuesday, the eleventh of November. A worried friend dropped by to check on King, after she missed work two days in a row. The medical examiner's report attributed her death to natural causes, linked to chronic alcohol abuse.

A lot like Sally Thompson, right.

Back in the interrogation room, Robinson knew he was on to something, his suspect confessing to one murder, circumstantially linked with at least two more. He had to bring some order out of the confusion, try to get his questions back on track.

"Now about this girl in the bar," Robinson began, starting over from scratch. "Tell me about her."

Cole frowned, apparently confused.

"Which one?"

TWO

Cole's litany of death consumed the afternoon and evening of December 1. Detective Robinson took notes by hand, to start with, trying to keep up. Stenographers could wait.

With Dorothy King disposed of, Cole returned to Wanda Roberts, altering his story of the night she died. Instead of losing Wanda to an unknown man outside Pauline's, they walked together, south on Bryan, to the gravel parking lot, where Wanda leaned against a car and they began to grapple in the dark, Cole's hands inside her blouse.

"She got mad for some reason and started screaming," he told Robinson. "I got scared and she started struggling, so I put my hands on her neck. I asked her what was the matter and kept squeezing her neck. I just couldn't stop."

When Wanda ceased to struggle, going limp in death, Cole tugged her slacks off, tearing them. He meant to rape her body, but the smell of feces repulsed him.

"Afterward," he said, "I walked around and called the halfway house and asked them if I could move back in."

It didn't help, and by November 30 he had begun to prowl again. That Sunday night, while he was drinking beer and watching football at the Club DeVille, he first met Sally Thompson.

"She told me she was lonely," Cole recalled, "and said that I looked like I was lonely, too. She came right out and said she was looking for a man to live with her."

The prospect put Cole off, but with a few more drinks inside him, he returned with Thompson to her Rawlins Avenue apartment. They were barely settled on the couch, when he was overcome with second thoughts.

"I remember thinking, 'Why don't these goddamn whores leave me alone?' "Cole shook his head, disgusted and confused. "I turned around and grabbed her by the neck and started choking her."

It was enough for Robinson, but Eddie wasn't finished yet. The Dallas women weren't alone. In fact, there had been six before them in the past nine years. All drunken sluts, by Cole's account. All strangled. Some of them molested after death.

In San Diego he remembered three. The first was Essie Buck, a tavern owner, strangled, stripped, and dumped outside the city limits back in May 1971. Another San Diego victim, Bonnie Sue O'Neil, had been a working prostitute. Cole throttled her and left her naked body in an alleyway behind the small appliance shop where he was employed during August 1979. A month later his alcoholic wife Diana fell victim to his homicidal rage, her body wrapped in blankets and secreted in a closet of their home while Eddie hit the road.

Las Vegas was another city where the drifter spent considerable time, and he had claimed two victims there. Part-time hooker Kathlyn Blum was naked when detectives found her lifeless body in a residential alley, during May 1977. More than two years later, in November 1979, victim Marie Cushman had been strangled and left in the bed she briefly shared with Cole at the Casbah Hotel.

The final victim on Cole's list was Myrlene Hamer, nicknamed "Tepee" and described by Eddie as a half-breed Indian. Strangled and dumped in a field outside Casper, Wyoming, her body was recovered by authorities in August 1975.

When he ran out of names and corpses, Cole was finally booked into City Jail on three counts of first-degree murder, his pockets turned out and searched for the first time since Robinson braced him at the Toys "R" Us warehouse. By that time, word of his long-playing confessions had leaked to the Dallas media, and television camera crews were backing up outside the station house.

Cole's first stop in the lockup, after fingerprints and mug shots, was a one-man cage with nothing but a telephone for furniture. He had no one to call, and in a little while his keepers moved him to a holding pen with three more inmates. Eddie went in braced for trouble, but the others had their own concerns and left him to himself.

Time passes. Fitful dozing on the noisy cell block; starchy meals delivered and removed on plastic trays. The morning does a fade to afternoon, before a uniform arrives and escorts Cole to the visiting room, to meet his court-appointed lawyer. They are introduced through double layers of heavy glass and stout wire mesh.

Doug Parks is skilled in criminal defense, but there is little he can do in light of Cole's confessions and the waivers of his right to silence. Even so, he cautions Cole to keep his mouth shut in the presence of a figure called by inmates "Dr. Death"—one James P. Grigson, a psychiatrist and jailhouse regular, so dubbed by criminal defendants for the frequency of his appearance as a prosecution witness in capital cases.

Cole knows psychiatrists; he takes the sage advice to heart.

That night, a grinning deputy stops by the cage and holds a copy of the evening paper out to Eddie, asking for his autograph.

*****

COLE'S MARATHON CONFESSIONS WEREN'T ALL GRAVY for the prosecution. He had cleared three cases, but the only one officially recorded as a homicide was Wanda Roberts. Dorothy King and Sally Thompson were still down on the books as natural causes, related to chronic alcoholism. Both women were drunk when they died, and King's blood-alcohol level, at .30, was three times the legal limit for intoxication. In light of Cole's statements, Dr. Charles Perry, Dallas County's medical examiner, had no qualms about amending his original verdict in both cases.

"It doesn't take much to strangle someone under those circumstances," Perry told the press, "and there may well not be any marks at all." Concerning the initial postmortem results, he explained, "This is not an infrequent finding, really. The circumstances of death and the scene examination are very important, so an autopsy is only one tool used in determining the manner of death."

While local authorities were putting their paperwork in order, news of Cole's confessions was crackling on the wire from coast to coast. Aside from jurisdictions where their prisoner admitted homicides, Dallas police had issued a general alert to any police departments with unsolved murders that appeared to fit the lethal drifter's modus operandi.

*****

In Las Vegas, Nevada, Detective Joe McGuckin took the call and caught a flight to Dallas on December 3. The first detective on the scene when Kathlyn Blum was found in 1977, McGuckin had been waiting three and a half years for a break in the case. Another year of wasted effort since a maid at the Casbah Hotel found Marie Cushman strangled in bed. He kept his fingers crossed on Eddie Cole, aware that it could just as easily go sour, blow up in his face, and leave him holding squat.

At the Police and Courts Building, downtown, McGuckin was met by Gerald Robinson, guided to an interrogation room, and introduced to his suspect. Robinson left them alone, and McGuckin started off by reading Cole his rights from the familiar Miranda card.

No fencing. Both men knew why they were there.

McGuckin led with questions, having Cole describe Kathlyn Blum, her general appearance, and the clothing she wore on the night she died. That done, he laid a fan of photographs in front of Cole, and Eddie picked the victim out in two of them. The story, once begun, was brief and to the point.

Cole said he first met Kathlyn Blum a week before he killed her, idling in a Vegas bar. They drank together off and on, the next few days, until the night of May 14. They left a bar called Dan and Ray's together, and he steered her toward an alley backing Cleveland Street, where he choked the victim unconscious with his hands and finished the job with her own brassiere, then stripped and raped her corpse.

Moving on to Marie Cushman, McGuckin repeated his stock performance, having Cole describe the woman and her clothes before he laid the photos down. Another hit. With the preliminaries covered, Cole spun out another tale of death.

The first time he laid eyes on Cushman, Eddie said, had been November 4. The night she died. They were together in the Casbah Bar and drinking heavily, when Cushman's husband suddenly confronted her, demanding she come home. Marie laughed in his face, berating him until he finally retreated to escape her acid tongue. A short time later Eddie and Marie adjourned to the hotel next door. He paid the bill, and Cushman showed her gratitude by going down on Eddie in the bathtub, subsequently taking him to bed. When they were finished, Cole began to dress, but she kept grabbing at him, wanting more. In sudden, blinding rage, he turned upon her, choking her barehanded for a while, before he reached inside his pocket for a piece of rope he'd picked up on the street the day before.

Cole's memory for detail and concise description of the murder scenes convinced McGuckin he was looking at the man responsible for both the Blum and Cushman homicides. On Thursday he returned to Vegas with the word that both his open cases had been solved.

*****

AUTHORITIES IN SOUTHERN CALIFORNIA did their talking to the press. When a reporter for the *San Diego Union* questioned Cole's confessions, the reaction was emphatic—even hostile—and unanimously negative.

Speaking for the coroner's office, Deputy Coroner Jay Johnson told newsmen, "It's just my personal opinion, but I don't believe there's anything to it. Maybe he knew these women. Maybe they drank at the same bars and he was aware of the circumstances of their deaths."

While the 1971 autopsy report on Essie Buck was inconclusive, the cause of death undetermined, official verdicts on the other two reputed victims seemed to bear out Johnson's skepticism. Despite the fact that she was found nude in an alley, her clothes missing from the scene, a postmortem examination of Bonnie O'Neil attributed her death to Laennec's cirrhosis, an ailment linked with chronic, long-term alcoholism. As for Diana Cole, with a toxic blood-alcohol level of .42, the cause of death was listed as liver failure and ethyl alcohol poisoning.

If the coroner's office was skeptical, San Diego police were openly scornful of Cole's confessions. For the record, Lt. John Gregory—chief of the city's homicide division—announced that his detectives had no interest in Cole, no plans to check his statements out.

"All things considered," Gregory declared, "it is obvious he had knowledge and knew they were dead, and apparently he had a history of mental instability and a background of criminal activity. The coroner conducted thorough autopsies, and the man would have to have been some sort of expert to have strangled these women without leaving any bruise marks. Some of these confessions could be the product of a sick mind."

However, there was one piece of information Lt. Gregory appeared not to know. The last night Essie Buck was seen alive, she left the bar she owned on El Cajon Boulevard in the company of a man whom several witnesses identified as Carroll Edward Cole. Two days later, when her naked body was recovered from suburban Poway, county sheriff's officers were assigned to the case, which fell outside city police jurisdiction. Homicide investigator Robert Ring had questioned Eddie Cole in jail, that July, while Cole awaited sentencing on a conviction for passing fraudulent checks, and the interview proved enlightening. Cole admitted taking Essie Buck to a motel, and waking up next morning with her lifeless body in the bed, beside him. Panicking, he stuffed her in the trunk of his car and spent the whole day driving aimlessly, before he dropped her off in Poway after dark. Pleading loss of memory, Cole stopped short of confessing to murder on that occasion, but he remained the only suspect in the case.

By December 1980, however, Robert Ring had found himself a new job, as investigator for the San Diego district attorney's office. If he was cognizant of Cole's confessions at the time, Ring kept it to himself, allowing the chorus of denials to stand unopposed. Another four years would elapse before the ex-detective got involved in the case again.

*****

The case of Myrlene Hamer, in Wyoming, was more straightforward. Detective Art Terry, of the Natrona County sheriff's office, flew into Dallas on December 10, and took his turn with Cole that afternoon in the interrogation room. Once more, the recitation of Miranda rights, before Cole launched into his story of the victim's final hours.

As Eddie recalled it, he had gone out barhopping with "Tepee" Hamer, living it up on the night of August 4, 1975. They decided to go for a ride in Cole's car, cruising without direction for a while, until they passed the bentonite plant where Cole was employed. He pulled into the deserted parking lot and shut the engine off. Overcome by a sudden urge to strangle Hamer, he attacked her on impulse, garroting her with the cord of an electric table lamp he carried in the car. As often seemed to happen, murder left him drowsy, and he dozed with Tepee dead beside him, on the seat. When he awoke, Cole drove into the sandy foothills north of town and hauled her body from the car. He stripped the corpse, then paradoxically went back to fetch a sleeping bag and covered her before he left the scene.

With Dallas—and, potentially, Las Vegas—lining up to prosecute their several counts of Murder One, a formal charge in Casper was superfluous, but Terry left the station house convinced that he had cracked his case. Of nine reputed victims, Cole was clearly good for six, and the dissenting votes from California —where condemned prisoners were more likely to die from old age than lethal gas—were of no immediate concern.

A scattering of other agencies with unsolved homicides on file sent officers to question Eddie Cole, but he was done with show-and-tell. In retrospect, it seems like a rehearsal for the controversial case of Henry Lucas, three years later, but the names and photographs meant nothing to Cole, and his visitors went home disappointed. In time, when no new victims were appended to the list of dead, the circus atmosphere began to fade.

The word came down for Cole's removal to the county lockup overlooking Dealy Plaza. His assignment—"for protection"—was a tiny strip cell, one of ten adjoining the infirmary. No heat, no bed, no blankets, with a blower pumping the December chill inside, around the clock. He went in naked, but was finally allowed a jailhouse uniform.

Cole's neighbors on the isolation wing were a mixed bag. One prisoner had knifed his roommate to death, afterward cutting out and devouring the victim's heart. Another had gunned down his girlfriend in a burst of fire that also toppled several bystanders. Yet another inmate was already familiar to Cole from the Way Back. Lately paroled on a conviction for strangling an elderly woman, Cole's acquaintance had shown up at a house-warming party high on Quaaludes, slipping away from the bash with a cute fourteen-year-old whom he strangled, afterward jamming a tree limb into her vagina.

Old home week.

Cole spent a month in isolation before Attorney Edgar Mason, teamed with Parks for the defense, stepped in and got him moved to the infirmary. TV. A mattress. Room to breathe. It felt like the Ritz after lockdown, but the respite was short-lived. The next transfer shifted Cole to a regular cell block, where word of his crimes and confessions had begun to filter down. A battle-scarred veteran of life in the joint, Cole quickly made friends with the inmates that counted, de facto rulers of the block, and settled in to wait for his impending trial.

On February 5 the mail brought notice of divorce proceedings, from Las Vegas. Sharla Cole had filed for dissolution of their marriage after fourteen months, the bulk of which had seen Cole locked away for violating his probation on the federal mail theft charge. As a resident of Nevada, she was entitled to a divorce within six weeks, unless Eddie contested the suit.

Cole retreated into silence, ignoring the summons, allowing the action to proceed. A Las Vegas court found him in default when he had not responded by March 10. The final decree of divorce was issued two weeks later.

Caged in Dallas, Eddie had a chance to contemplate his first unselfish act in more than thirty years.

*****

Before the wheels of justice rolled on Eddie Cole, both sides were bent on pinning down his state of mind. What sort of man admits to murdering nine women in as many years, sometimes enjoying sex with their remains? With the confessions down in black and white, attorneys Parks and Mason staked their hopes for saving Eddie's life on an insanity defense. The prosecution, meanwhile, pledged to see him dead or locked away for life, was equally intent on proving Cole was sane, and thus responsible for all his acts.

The first step in appraising Eddie's mental state was taken by the medical director of the Dallas jail infirmary. On December 8 Dr. Elliot Salenger wrote to the Medical Center for Federal Prisoners at Springfield, Missouri, requesting copies of Cole's psychiatric records. The sluggish response, dated December 30, acknowledged the existence of three such reports, compiled in July and August, but declined to release them on grounds that their "confidentiality must be protected." Springfield was still stalling on January 20, when a Dallas subpoena was served on R. A. Truesdale, the facility's chief records officer, demanding surrender of pertinent records on Cole. Six days later, Truesdale responded with the curious advice that "We are unable to identify this individual." He suggested that Dallas prosecutors double-check their information, to discover whether Cole had been confined at Springfield under an alias. On January 28, the district attorney's office fired back with Cole's FBI booking number and a terse offer to supply any further information needed for an expeditious settlement. In Springfield, the bureaucratic fog began to lift.

Oh, *that* Carroll Edward Cole. Why didn't you *say* so?

Eddie's psychiatric records from the federal lockup, cleared at last on February 3, were hardly worth the wait. A report from clinical psychologist Daniel Taub, dated July 22, noted that Cole's responses to a

Rorschach test "suggest a character disorder, not a psychosis." Dr. Taub recommended Cole's transfer out of MCFP "as not requiring hospital care," but the move was delayed, pending further analysis.

On August 15 a staff psychiatrist, Dr. Theodore Trusevich, wrote: "There is no evidence of psychosis or neurosis in Mr. Cole. Diagnostically he may be described as a character disorder. It is unlikely that major personality changes will occur. He does not appear motivated for any sort of treatment at this time."

Returned to the general prison population with a diagnosis of "passive-aggressive personality," Cole rated one more report, on August 29. Case manager E. L. Horton and psychologist M. A. Conroy concurred that "Subject has a long history of emotional maladjustment and has experienced at least 3 or 4 hospitalizations for in-patient psychiatric care. Diagnosis has vacillated between sociopathy with anti-social personality and undifferentiated schizophrenia. As suggested earlier in this report, for many years, he has manifested severe emotional aberrations with overtures of violence in some form or another."

Despite those findings, inasmuch as he had caused no problems for the Springfield staff, Cole's early release was approved in October 1980, with four months off for good behavior. The paperwork on his release recommended neither hospitalization nor outpatient treatment to resolve his long-standing problems with women and society at large.

*****

While Springfield and the D.A.'s office were engaged in their peculiar minuet, the local doctors had a crack at Cole. He sat for interviews with Dr. Grigson and another psychiatrist, Clay Griffith, whom he unaccountably mistook for a member of the defense team. (In fact, Cole's lawyers publicly complained that they could find no doctors willing to consult with the defense.)

The Griffith interview took place on January 30, in the Dallas County jail. Cole sketched his background for the doctor, noting that he started drinking at the age of twelve and committed his first criminal offense at fifteen, stealing beer from a Richmond, California, liquor store. Fueled by hatred for his mother, violent fantasies began to dominate his life, prompting two suicide attempts in 1961 and '62. The first time he leapt from a highway bridge in front of a passing car, but escaped serious injury; the next attempt, with pills, was no more successful.

Still, as he explained to Griffith, "The thoughts of hurting someone were bothering me." Voluntary hospitalization in California brought no relief, and Cole made his first attempt to strangle a woman in 1963, frustrated when her screams drove him off.

In recounting the Dallas murders for Griffith, Cole began backing off from his original confessions, pleading loss of memory. Dorothy King had invited him home on November 9, but the rest of it was a blank, Cole said, until he woke up Monday morning with her corpse in bed beside him.

"Did you think it unusual," Griffith asked, "to wake up in bed with a dead woman?"

"No," Cole replied. "It's happened before."

With Wanda Roberts, Cole remembered leaving Pauline's Bar and strolling south on Bryan Street. "We walked to a car and tried to get in," he recalled, "but it was locked. Then, she turned around and wanted to make love to me on the ground. She took off her clothes, and we were kissing. She pulled me down on the ground, then she seemed to change, acting like she was going to scream. She let out a yell, and I put my hand over her mouth. The next thing I remember, it was the next morning. I was behind an apartment house, in a hallway where I had slept. I got up and walked out to the driveway. She was lying there, and I kept on going. I didn't know if she was dead."

There had been no blackout with Sally Thompson, but "I did get hazy before I strangled her." In reference to the other cases, Cole was vague in the extreme. His longest blackout, surrounding the 1979 murder of his wife, had erased two full days from Cole's memory, and he appeared uncertain of his final body count. Under questioning from Dr. Griffith, he admitted, "I don't know if I have killed a man," suggesting that "There may have been other times I had memory losses," beyond the nine slayings he had already confessed.

Concerning the women he remembered, Griffith asked, "Did you have intercourse prior to killing them?"

"Yes, some of them."

"Did you have intercourse *after* killing them?"

"Yes."

"Why?"

Cole shrugged. "I had occasionally slept with dead women before."

Throughout the grim exchange, Griffith noted no change of expression or signs of remorse in his subject. There was a show of fear, however, with Cole complaining of his keepers, "I think they have put something in my food here in jail, to give me cancer like they did Jack Ruby." In the margin of his notes, Griffith dismissed the remark with a terse observation: *"Faking."*

Winding down with some general knowledge questions, Griffith learned that Cole thought there were fifty-two states in the Union; he drew a blank on the number of U.S. senators and stripes in the American flag, answers that placed him on a par with the average high school graduate. In parting, Dr. Griffith solicited Cole's opinion of his own sanity.

"Is there any reason why you can't go to trial?"

"No," Cole replied.

"Any reason why you think you were insane when the murders occurred?"

"I couldn't control myself." Reaching the heart of the matter.

"How do you know?"

Another hopeless shrug. "I don't."

*****

By the first week of April, both sides were ready for trial before District Judge John Mead. Opposing Doug Parks and Ed Mason, Assistant District Attorneys Mary Ludwick and Andy Anderson were teamed for the prosecution. Cole's involvement in three local murders was never contested, but his plea of innocent by reason of insanity required a jury's verdict to decide if he would be confined to prison or a mental hospital.

The first hurdle was jury selection, no simple task in an atmosphere charged with emotion and fueled by incessant publicity. Several potential jurors were excused from duty after frankly admitting prejudice against Cole, and one young woman fled the court in tears, before a panel of twelve jurors was finally seated. Betty Smith was elected foreman of the panel charged with judging Eddie Cole.

The trial began on Monday, April 6, with opening statements from each side. Assistant D.A. Ludwick sketched the bare facts of her case, stressing the state's intention of proving Cole both guilty and sane.

Cole's lawyers countered with the outline of an insanity defense, citing their client's long history of treatment in mental hospitals as evidence that his crimes stemmed from a deep-seated, irrepressible compulsion to kill.

Prosecutors get first crack at the evidence in American courts, and the Dallas team appeared to have copious ammunition against Cole. Detective Robinson was called to relate the circumstances of Cole's arrest and confessions, after which Eddie's December statements were read to the jury. Doctors Griffith and Grigson rounded off the prosecution's case, concurring in their diagnosis of Cole as a classic sociopath. Simply stated, they regarded Cole as an antisocial chronic offender, perhaps sexually deviant, but fully capable of understanding and controlling his behavior.

Desperate for a second (or third) opinion, Parks and Mason petitioned the court for a new psychiatric evaluation of Cole, and Judge Mead ordered yet another session—with Dr. Griffith. Cole's second interview with Griffith took place on Tuesday morning, April 7, in a conference room adjacent to the judge's chambers. Edgar Mason was on hand, for the defense, and Griffith filled three more pages with notes as Cole repeated his story of an abysmal home life, violent fantasies, fruitless hospitalization, and random homicide. Wrapping up the interview, Cole said, "I want to die. I want the death penalty, or else to spend the rest of my life in a mental hospital."

When the public trial resumed that afternoon, Parks and Mason put their only witness on the stand. Cole's testimony led the cringing jurors through his ruined life—the hatred for a mother who abused him, masturbating over photographs of murdered women in detective magazines, years wasted in prisons and nearly a dozen mental institutions. The women he murdered reminded him of his drunken, adulterous mother. "I think," he told the panel, "I've been killing her through them."

Addressing himself to the Dallas slayings, Cole clung to his new amnesia story. His description of Dorothy King's death was typical: "It's pretty foggy. It seems like a haze. I took the cigarette out of her hand, and the next thing I realize, she's dead." After raping her corpse, Cole recalled, "I felt very disgusted and scared and sorry as hell it happened. I was disgusted with myself."

The first surprise in Eddie's testimony came when he addressed himself to crimes outside of Dallas. Rather than the six murders described in his December confessions, Cole now admitted nine, for an even dozen since 1971. He had omitted the other three from previous statements, Cole explained, because he didn't know the victims' names.

The revised tally included two more dead in San Diego, one of them reportedly an illegal alien, and a woman killed in Oklahoma City on Thanksgiving 1977. "This one is almost a complete blank," he told jurors of the Oklahoma victim. "I don't remember her name, but she had black hair and was about thirty or thirty-five years old."

Once more, he had no recollection of the crime itself, but woke to find his rented room in disarray. "I had gotten out of bed and I was in the kitchen making coffee," he testified. "Evidently, I had done some cooking the night before. There was some meat on the stove in a frying pan and part that I hadn't eaten on a plate, on the table. It looked like round steak. I had gone to the bathroom and found her in my bathtub, and part of her buttocks was missing. The feet were gone, the hand, and the arm. I found them in the refrigerator."

Thinking fast, Cole took a hacksaw and cut the body into smaller pieces, stuffing them in plastic garbage bags and dropping the parcels in a nearby Dumpster. "I don't think they ever found any of the parts," he said, "and I never heard anyone say she was missing. I guess nobody will ever know who she was."

On Wednesday, April 8, it was Mary Ludwick's turn to cross-examine Cole. Rather than dispute his public confession to a dozen homicides, she challenged his alleged memory lapses and uncontrollable desire to kill.

"Do you feel the urge to kill anyone right now?" she asked Cole.

"I've got all this in me," he replied. "It's always with me. Right now, it's even directed ... I could even say it's directed at you."

"Why haven't you killed me, then?"

"Well, this is a controlled situation," he answered, stating the obvious. "And I can control it to a certain extent."

With that, there was nothing left to hear but the summations. Mary Ludwick dismissed Cole's twenty-year odyssey through the mental health system as an elaborate, carefully thought-out charade, looking forward to the day when he would need an insanity defense to save his life. "He's not insane," she told the jury. "He knows exactly what he's doing. He knew exactly what he was doing every time he picked up a victim."

Nor, Ludwick suggested, should squeamish jurors be swayed toward a finding of insanity by lurid admissions of necrophilia and cannibalism. Concerning the nameless Oklahoma victim, Ludwick told the court, "I think he has a tendency to grossly exaggerate. I find it strange that he just happens to have a hacksaw on hand to dismember a body. It sounds like he read it in a detective magazine."

Defenders Parks and Mason took turns dissecting the "sociopath" diagnosis from Doctors Griffith and Grigson, dismissing the tag as a lazy psychiatrist's way of ignoring an illness, writing off Cole and others like him as untreatable. "Can you call all of this antisocial conduct?" Mason challenged the jury. "Can you buy that? Murder? Necrophilia? Cannibalism? The doctors who decided he was not a danger to himself or others should shoulder the blame. They could have stopped him."

Parks hammered on the same theme, characterizing Cole as "a mighty sick man who was a victim of the Texas psychiatric system. Carroll Cole has been asking for help for twenty years and has yet to receive it. The evidence screams out: This is a sick man!" Parks lamented that jurors were "placed in the position of cleaning up twenty years of bungling" by various psychiatrists, but he asked them to go the extra mile and find Cole insane, thereby sparing his life and mandating confinement to a state hospital.

Judge Mead had the last word, instructing jurors in the rule of law concerning an insanity defense. Bound, like most American states, by the nineteenth-century "McNaughten rule," Texas law demands that a criminal defendant be considered sane unless "at the time of the committing of the act, the party was laboring under such a defect of reason, from disease of the mind, as to not know the nature and quality of the act he was doing, or, if he did know it, that he did not know he was doing what was wrong."

It took the jurors barely twenty-five minutes to convict Cole on all counts, finding him sane and responsible under prevailing law. Cole waived his right to have the jury fix his penalty, and the court was adjourned pending Judge Mead's pronouncement of sentence on Thursday.

Leaving the court, jurors and counsel alike ran the media gauntlet.

Foreman Betty Smith told newsmen that the insanity argument didn't sell at all, torpedoed by Cole's admission to Mary Ludwick that he could control himself whenever he wanted. Juror Victor Powell spoke for the rest of the panel when he told reporters, "There is no doubt that the man needs help. We agreed that there should have been some help given the man a long time ago. But no matter how we feel about it, the legal charge was pretty clear. We had to find him guilty."

Facing the microphones one last time, Ed Mason deplored the fact that Doctors Griffith and Grigson held a virtual monopoly on criminal psychiatry in Dallas, habitually turning up in court as prosecution witnesses. "We don't have any psychiatrists who will come down here and dispute them," Mason complained.

Too late.

On April 9 Cole stood before Judge Mead to hear his sentence handed down. Sparing the defendant's life, Mead sentenced Cole to three life terms in prison, two of them to run concurrently. The sentence precluded parole before the year 2005 A.D., when Cole would be sixty-seven years old.

As he was led away in chains, the killer seemed relaxed. At ease.

Twenty-five years? No problem.

Eddie had been doing hard time all his life.

THREE

WHAT EVENTS CONSPIRE TO SHAPE A HUMAN MONSTER in the mold of Eddie Cole, Ted Bundy, John Wayne Gacy, and their ilk? Authorities may quibble over details, but they universally agree—*The Bad Seed* notwithstanding—that compulsive killers are not born; they are, in essence, manufactured by a series of events and circumstances starting virtually at the moment of birth.

Since World War II, repeated studies have confirmed that battered children tend to pay the violence back in kind. Most child molesters were, themselves, molested at an early age. Prospective rapists learn contempt for women years before they understand the raw mechanics of a sexual assault. And would-be killers bide their time.

Surprised by the rapid escalation of serial murders in the 1970s, the FBI's Behavioral Science Unit conducted a four-year survey of sex slayers confined in American prisons. The results of that study, concluded in 1983, are both instructive and disturbing.

Of thirty-six killers who agreed to sit for interviews, 74 percent reported some form of psychological abuse in childhood; nearly half had suffered physical or sexual abuse. Seventy-two of the respondents recalled a negative relationship with their fathers or male caretakers, while 66 percent described their mothers as the dominant parent. Forty-six percent related histories of family sexual problems, and 73 percent had witnessed sexually traumatic events.

The final products of that grim assembly line were children who experienced a sense of isolation (73%) and responded with rebelliousness (72%). They were assaultive toward adults (86%) and other children (44%), often practicing extreme cruelty toward animals (36%). Once these children reached adolescence, their deviant behavior included chronic lying (68%), theft (56%), and compulsive masturbation (81%).

Behind the raw statistics, though, each killer is an individual, with private demons of his own. We cannot chart the course of a polluted stream, without beginning at its source.

*****

The soil of Iowa is steeped in blood and history. Two hundred years of brutal conflict with the native Indians; admission to the Union as a part of the Missouri Compromise; deserved honors as the birthplace of the Republican Party. Along the way, the Hawkeye State produced a crop of famous sons, including Herbert Hoover, Buffalo Bill Cody, Glenn Miller, John Wayne, and Billy Sunday.

Not to mention Carroll Edward Cole.

His name will not be found in any literature extolling Hawkeye virtues, but he owns a piece of history regardless, bought and paid for with the currency of blood and pain. Denying Eddie's roots will never make him go away.

Cole's father was a product of the North Dakota flatlands, born and raised in Fargo, near the Minnesota line. LaVerne Cole's early life remains a vacuum prior to his arrival in Sioux City, Iowa, where he pursued and won the hand of Vesta Odom, settling down with his new bride to raise a family. Vesta Cole was timid on her wedding night, a fact thrown up to her with laughter at successive family gatherings, but she performed her wifely duty in the end. The couple's first child, Richard Keith, was born in 1933; a daughter, Nancy, followed two years later, with the Great Depression near its worst. A second son, named Carroll Edward, was delivered in Sioux City on the ninth of May, in 1938.

It took the new arrival years to learn this much about his parents, storing bits of information gleaned from conversations, chance remarks, the fallout of domestic arguments. "Thinking about it," he wrote from death row, "I know nothing about them, which is strange ... or significant, however you see it."

We know that one or both of them were Roman Catholic, because they packed their children off to catechism class when it was time, but neither one apparently took religion much to heart. Eddie lived with the impression that his father quit school in the seventh grade to work for pay, though this fact was never documented. LaVerne maintained this habit throughout his life. In retrospect, Cole would describe his father as "a good provider in practically everything"—but the addition of the qualifier told another tale, for those with eyes to see.

The hindsight worked with Vesta Cole, as well. Despite the bawdy jokes about her honeymoon, implying near-hysterical virginity, by adolescence Eddie saw his mother in a vastly different light, being aware of her adulterous liaisons with other men.

Founded in 1853 and incorporated four years later, Sioux City bills itself as "the best known and best advertised city in the United States." Its major industry is agriculture, a reliance on the soil that spelled disaster for a generation in the 1930s. Oklahoma may have been the Dust Bowl, but farmers everywhere were stricken by the crash on Wall Street and its aftermath. In Iowa, farm prices plunged to their lowest point in a half-century, with corn selling for ten cents a bushel and hogs going to market at three cents a pound. Around Sioux City, dairy farmers launched a milk strike to improve their lot with artificial shortages, but the results were marginal at best. Foreclosures followed, driving many of the homeless onto vacant land along the east bank of the wide Missouri River, where they built a shantytown and planted small subsistence gardens for their families. Some others fled the state entirely, echoing the sentiments expressed by one John Peirce when he decamped a generation earlier. "Goodbye, Sioux City," Peirce had written in an open letter to the town, "perhaps for aye. You are at once the birthplace of all my ambitions and the graveyard of all my hopes."

That spring, LaVerne Cole gathered up his wife, four children (with Patricia, born in 1939), and his assorted in-laws, moving west. Their goal was San Francisco, give or take, but they would settle for the next best thing. The looming threat of global war had done what good intentions never could, recalling a depressed economy from grim disaster to a semblance of vitality. Henry Kaiser had five shipyards running 'round the clock in northern California, and he advertised for labor nationwide. "Help Wanted!" screamed the ads on billboards and in daily papers. "Male or Female, Young or Old, Experienced or Inexperienced" —to which one wag appended "Dead or Alive!!!"

For some, it was uncomfortably near the truth.

The Cole and Odom clan touched down in Richmond, where the Kaiser yard employed 100,000 workers, turning out a new Liberty Ship every ten hours, seven days a week. Nicknamed "California's War Baby," Richmond would see its population grow fivefold within a decade, new arrivals crowding into cheap apartment houses, huddled close around the San Francisco suburb's sixty factories.

The Coles were fortunate enough to find a small three-bedroom home on Fifth Street, in a neighborhood of houses overshadowed by apartment buildings. Modern California guidebooks make the point that

Richmond has "no prestigious residential district," but at least a house ensured some marginal degree of independence from the neighbors. If three bedrooms meant sharing, there was still a spacious yard, with room enough to plot a baseball field. Beneath the house, young Eddie found himself a private place with access from a crawlspace underneath the porch, flattening cardboard boxes to pave and insulate a "fort" that ran the full length of the house, from front to back.

His early memories of life in Richmond were confined to playing underneath the house or jostling with his brother in the yard by daylight, huddled under blankets in the darkness as a creaking door announced the latest episode of *Inner Sanctum,* broadcast on the radio. At Christmas, family members gathered at the clubhouse of a golf course Vesta's parents managed for the owners, hoisting glasses to the season, dropping coins into illegal slot machines that flanked the bar. For all their gaiety, however, it was still a tarnished celebration of the holidays, for Eddie's father had been called to military service. He was leaving soon, and he would not return until the European war was won.

The turning point of Eddie's life—as for the world at large—was 1943. Outside his narrow universe, Benito Mussolini was deposed and jailed, while Allied forces fought their way up the Italian boot; the Wehrmacht was repulsed by Russian troops, and Allied forces bagged a quarter-million German prisoners in northern Africa; across the vast Pacific, island-hopping brought a modern warlord named MacArthur closer to fulfillment of a promise in the Philippines. At home, Cole's newest sibling—sister Linda—was a babe in arms, and Vesta Cole was growing restless in the home that had become a crowded cage.

One afternoon, while Eddie marched toy soldiers through their paces in the garden, he was interrupted by his mother calling from the porch. Reluctantly, he left his game and went inside the strangely silent house. No children's voices echoing around the walls, with Nancy and his brother off at school, Patricia and the baby likewise absent—placed with relatives or neighbors for the day. He found his mother waiting in the kitchen, with a curious expression on her face.

"Go get cleaned up. We're going visiting."

And so, with an innocuous remark, nightmares begin.

When he is washed and tidy to a mother's satisfaction, Vesta locks the house and leads him south on Fifth to Cutting Boulevard, exchanging smiles and greetings with acquaintances they pass along the way. At Cutting, they turn west in the direction of Point Richmond, till they reach a neighborhood of bleak apartments managed by the local Housing Authority, squat buildings, ill-maintained, with peeling paint and tenants matching every color of the human rainbow.

Eddie's mother seems to know where she is going, focused on a block of twelve apartments, six on six, with garbage strewn about the scruffy yard. His curiosity is tinged with apprehension as they climb a flight of dingy stairs and pause again, outside a numbered door. His mother stoops to brush a lock of hair back from his forehead, speaking to him in a new and unfamiliar tone of voice.

"Whatever happens, don't you *dare* tell *anyone,* you understand?"

A frown for emphasis before she knocks, her first try muffled by the sounds of blaring music from within. She tries again, and this time she is answered by a girl of roughly Eddie's age, stark naked save for panties and a layer of filth that seems to cover her from head to foot.

The girl stands mute, until a tall man brushes her aside and welcomes Vesta in. She steps into his arms and kisses him, their bodies pressed together, Eddie gaping as the stranger's hands slide down his mother's back and cup her buttocks, squeezing through her dress.

Inside, the door shut tight behind him, he counts three more couples in the small apartment's living room. The men all dress alike, in khaki pants and undershirts, while cast-off shirts with colored stripes and badges drape surrounding chairs. He does not recognize the military uniforms on sight, too much for any five-year-old to fully understand.

At one end of the sagging couch, a woman has her blouse unbuttoned, suckling an infant. Close beside her, busy with themselves, another couple grapples playfully, oblivious of Eddie looking on, the soldier fondling his partner's breast. Cole turns in time to see a bedroom door just closing on his mother's shadow, locking her away.

He fastens on a passing stranger, tugging at her skirt, disoriented, asking for a drink of water. She escorts him to the kitchen, seats him at the table with a glass in front of him, and leaves him there. He loses track of time, the party noises amplified by flimsy walls, retreating to a quiet place within himself.

At length, Cole is distracted by a rolling, creaking sound, distinct and separate from the din of revelry. A door directly opposite the kitchen exit to the living room swings open to reveal a shriveled apparition in a wheelchair, swathed in blankets, with a middle-aged attendant pushing from behind. To Cole, the new arrival is a monstrous thing, queer mewling sounds escaping from between its shriveled lips.

The "thing"—in fact, a senile victim of a recent stroke—is trundling closer by the moment, when Cole's mother and her playmate suddenly appear. They recognize a small boy's desperate fright and burst out laughing at the spectacle. Instead of reassuring Eddie, Vesta scoops him up and forces him to kiss the wizened face, apparently delighted by his tears and cries for help.

The cruel game quickly loses its appeal, and Eddie is released to play outside. To his chagrin, the little girl pursues him, clothed by this time in a rumpled dress. He is bewildered as she starts to call him in a whiny, taunting voice.

"Carroll, oh, Carroll!"

Confusion and humiliation amplified as other children suddenly appear, as if from nowhere, moving to surround him. All of them are laughing at him, joining in the classic childhood sport of torturing the odd man out. Their voices ring in Eddie's ears, confusing him at first, until he grasps the message.

"Carroll is a *girl's* name! Carroll is a *girl's* name!"

The action swiftly escalates to shoving, Eddie jostled back and forth within the chanting circle. Someone trips him and he stumbles, skinning hands and knees. Hysterically, he lashes out at his tormentors, kicking, punching, sobbing in his fear and shame.

In time, the noise grows loud enough to rouse the party animals, upstairs. Cole's mother pushes through the ring of children, trailing soldiers in her wake, and snatches Eddie, fingers tightening around his slender arms. Her eyes and voice are furious.

"You started this! You're *always* starting trouble, damn you!"

Stony silence on the long march back to Fifth Street. Once inside the house, the storm breaks over Eddie, Vesta slapping him repeatedly and bending him across her knee to jerk his pants down, flailing at his naked buttocks with a belt. The raging accusations of a "ruined" afternoon are interspersed with furious demands for silence, where the family is concerned.

"You'll keep your mouth shut, if you know what's good for you!"

As further punishment for his offense, Cole is forbidden to set foot outside the house for seven days. A sympathetic Grandma Odom intercedes to get his sentence lifted after two days time, but Vesta's spite has other outlets. Eddie makes a beeline for the garden, where his tanks and soldiers wait ... to find that they have disappeared without a trace. He searches high and low, once glancing toward the house to find his mother watching from a pantry window, with an enigmatic smile. Days pass before he learns that she has gathered up his toys and given them away to neighbor children, down the street.

The covert outings are repeated time and time again in months to come, tall strangers pawing at his mother while the boy looks on or seeks out places he can hide, avoiding other children from the complex who delight in teasing him about his "sissy" name. At home, his mother follows Eddie with suspicious eyes, incessantly reminding him that he must keep her secret safe, the threats habitually accompanied by a pinch or slap, a whipping with the belt, sometimes a twisted arm. If he complains around the party house, the soldiers lend a hand with whippings, sometimes locking Eddie in the closet.

One of Vesta's "special" punishments assumed the form of a sadistic ritual, with Eddie forced to wear his sister's frilly dresses, while his mother summoned other housewives from the neighborhood for coffee, served by "Mama's little girl." The brutal "game" humiliated Cole, exacerbating sexual confusion at a time when he already suffered endless childish taunts about his "girlish" given name. Unable to perceive his mother's twisted motives, he was being taught to doubt his masculinity ...and he was also learning how to hate, firsthand.

It is impossible to say, at this remove, why Vesta Cole chose Eddie as an escort on her extramarital liaisons, while Patricia and the infant Linda were sequestered with obliging relatives or neighbors. Probably, it would have been too much for her to turn up on a lover's doorstep with a babe in arms and two more children on her heels, but it remains a mystery why Eddie was selected as a witness—and, by implication, an accomplice—to adultery. The first time may have been a simple, careless oversight ...but there were unexpected benefits. The helpless child became an outlet for her own frustration, pent-up anger, and regret at being saddled with a family that tied her down.

With time, the cycle of abuse begins to feed upon itself. Impulsive violence, first employed to guarantee a small boy's silence, soon becomes a self-fulfilling end. From blaming Eddie for the gibes against his name, it is a short step to deliberate humiliation and effacement of his sexual identity. So caught up in her private game is Vesta Cole by autumn 1944 that she holds Eddie out of school an extra year, defying California law to keep her plaything close at hand. In the confusion of a war to save democracy, with Richmond schools bogged down in triple sessions, Eddie tumbles through the cracks and is forgotten.

In self-defense, he starts to spend more time beneath the house, withdrawing from his few friends in the neighborhood. The musty darkness is a sacred refuge, stolen candles or a beam of filtered sunlight from the porch providing faint illumination for the tiny hermit in his cave. Sometimes, when Vesta calls him from the yard, he waits in silence and ignores her, cherishing the fragile secret of his hiding place.

With spring, another turning point. The family gathers for an outdoor banquet, celebrating the return of Eddie's father from the battlefront. Long tables are arranged outside, well stocked with finger foods and liquor, while the men dig out a pit for barbecue. Cole watches from the sidelines, ever conscious of his mother's scrutiny, unable to respond when smiling aunts and uncles question his morose behavior.

In the midst of the festivities, his father lifts a frosty beer and shares a smile with family. There is enough to go around, and when the neighbors turn up uninvited, they are urged to stay and help themselves. The children have a separate table of their own, plates heaping, but the burden of his silent guilt steals Eddie's appetite and leaves him trembling on the verge of tears.

"Dad must have noticed me and made some comment to my mother," Cole recalled, "because she came around and told me that she needed help with something, from the house."

Already clumsy on her feet from too much liquor, Vesta stumbles on the back porch steps and takes a moment to regain her balance, Eddie waiting as she hauls herself erect. Inside, she grips his arm and drags him through the house, her pretense of a simple chore forgotten as they reach the farthest bedroom from the crowded yard. More walls to muffle any inconvenient sound.

Before he can defend himself, Cole's ears are pinched and twisted painfully, tears streaming down his face. His mother towers over him, her features chiseled out of stone, a hateful mask.

"Shut up!" Her voice is like a whiplash in the silent room. "I know exactly what you're up to, pouting so you draw attention to yourself. Don't think that I'm not wise to all your little games. You want to ruin everything, upset your father on his special day."

He chokes on a denial, sobbing helplessly.

"I'm *telling* you to straighten up!" Familiar warning in the tone. "If *he* asks *anything,* remember what I said. You tell on me, I'll *really* punish you, no matter what!"

For emphasis, she grabs an arm and twists it high between his shoulder blades, exertion working up a sweat while Eddie screams. No answer from the yard, where merriment remains the order of the day.

"You stop that sniveling and wipe your face. We get outside, I want you acting *normal,* understand?"

He does his best, returning to the children's table, picking at the food in front of him until his parents are distracted by another round of drinks. Unseen, he ducks away and creeps around the house, to seek a dark and silent refuge underneath the floor.

LaVerne's more frequent presence in the home immediately terminated Vesta's "coffee afternoons" and scotched—however briefly—her excursions to the wrong side of the tracks. It also meant that, come September, Eddie would be going off to school.

*****

A year behind his classmates when he entered Nystrom Elementary, at Tenth and Florida, Cole was immediately tagged an "oddball," and "the kids made quite a thing of taunting me." Along with the expected jokes about his given name, one adversary—a Chicano girl named Evelyn Garcia—took to calling Eddie "Cabbage Head," because his mother sometimes packed a lunch including brussels sprouts. The childish nickname followed Cole for years, to junior high, and while it seems a trivial affront, his jaundiced view of females made the source—a sneering girl—especially significant.

In class, Cole spoke when spoken to and paid attention to his lessons when he felt the urge. His grades were satisfactory, but he was easily distracted, drifting into fantasy on cue whenever school announcements or the strains of "Peter and the Wolf" erupted from the P.A. system, speakers mounted on the classroom wall. At recess, Cole was learning to defend himself with fists and feet, already working on his reputation as a boy who took no shit from bullies.

On the side, away from Nystrom, there was catechism class at a local Catholic church near downtown Richmond. Eddie made the walk from home with sister Pat, dismayed to find himself in care of nuns who carried rulers in their fists and punished inattention with a stinging rap across the knuckles. Frequently distracted from the Scriptures by his troubled life at home, he came to know the rulers well. To Eddie's mind, it was another case of spiteful females dealing in the currency of pain. His confirmation, after months of stifled anger, meant no more to Cole than a reprieve from punishment.

At home, while physical abuse had tapered off somewhat, the tension Eddie felt between his mother and himself remained a constant source of mutual anxiety. "I felt the animosity," he later wrote, "withdrawing more and more into myself." His fortress was secure, beneath the house, and Eddie also looked for sanctuary at the movies, choosing "gruesome horror shows" and sitting through them several times, unmindful of the fact that he would catch hell from his mother when he came home late. One of the neighbors was a recluse who despised most children, chasing them away whenever groups would scale his fence and rob his trees of fruit, but Eddie Cole was always safe when he crept in alone, as if the hermit recognized a kindred soul.

Cole's introduction to the act of sex, albeit once removed, had been chaotic, even terrifying, soiled with rage and pain. The next encounter, when it came, would add another twist to Eddie's sad, inverted personality.

A lazy afternoon at home, with Eddie in the bathroom, standing at the toilet to relieve himself. The door swings open to reveal an older boy, one of his brother's friends. Instead of backing out with an apology, to wait his turn, the neighbor steps inside. The bathroom door is closed and latched.

As Cole recalled the childhood incident, "I must have been seven or eight years old at the time. Nothing unusual happened [!], *and I don't remember everything,* but I was taught the act of masturbation, something that became an everyday affair for the remainder of my life." The neat synopsis bears its own disclaimer, but it seems self-evident that Eddie Cole—already striking back against the classmates who reviled him as a "sissy" or a "little girl"—would not emerge unscathed from such a quasi-homosexual encounter. Claims of faulty memory aside, the bathroom incident inevitably helped confuse Cole's sexual identity, already blurred by months of Vesta's dress-up rituals.

However that may be, the lesson, once acquired, was put to frequent use, becoming a compulsive pastime. Eddie masturbated in the bathroom, in his cave beneath the house, and sometimes in the room he shared with Richard, sitting on his bed, the door wide open, with a clear view of the family room beyond. On one occasion, Vesta caught him at it, Eddie startled when she turned away and closed the bedroom door, without a word.

Perhaps, in retrospect, it was a kind of victory: the boy reduced to playing *with* himself, as *by* himself, deprived of normal interaction with the world outside. But Eddie still had much to learn.

Weeks later, Eddie playing with a female relative in the house, alone. On impulse, he suggests a game of "doctor" and persuades her to remove her panties, fondling her and probing with his fingers, finally attempting penetration. Foiled by age and ignorance, he comes away from the experience with guilt and something worse. A new conviction there is "something wrong" with him, that he will never be "a man."

If Eddie Cole went looking for a male he could respect, a model for his own behavior, he was out of luck at home. On the one hand, there was brother Richard, issuing a challenge to the local girls, proclaiming he could beat up any one of them who chose to face him in a stand-up fight. The very statement was embarrassing enough, but it had barely made the rounds before a spunky challenger called Richard's bluff and decked him in the middle of the street.

And on the other hand, there was LaVerne. One afternoon, a scuffle with the neighbors. Eddie finds himself outnumbered, beaten, racing home in tears. LaVerne adopts a macho pose, returning to the battleground with Eddie at his side, to find the bullies and their father waiting. Challenged to a fight, LaVerne first tries to reason with the other man, and then backs down, retreating to the sound of laughter. Eddie trails him at a distance, publicly humiliated once again.

"Our relationship wasn't much to speak of, anyway," Cole later wrote from prison, "but it went downhill from there. Thinking about it today, I realize that incident wasn't the real problem, though. The *real* reason I had lost respect for Dad was that, even though I never told him, he should have known about my mother, exonerating me for not telling and punishing her for her domineering ways. To me, he just wasn't a man."

There were appearances to be maintained, around the house, but Cole increasingly dismissed his father as a figurehead or puppet, going through the moves when Vesta pulled his strings. "My dad was always putting on a show of trying to be masterful," Cole said, "but when it came down to it, he always kowtowed to Mom. Oh, he would go full tilt when dealing with us kids, and the others could think what they would, but I knew the truth, and he *knew* I knew."

That understanding was reflected when it came to discipline at home. LaVerne would paddle Eddie's sisters, on occasion, and his punishment of Richard during later years would sometimes lapse from spanking into clenched-fist beatings, but his younger son enjoyed a virtual immunity. When Eddie needed whipping, it was Vesta's job, a tacit signal that the boy was hers, beyond an ineffective father's reach. To cross that line, LaVerne would have to force the issue, risk an airing of the dirty little secret the two of them (at least) already shared.

*****

In spite of everything, Cole nurtured the illusion of a normal life around the corner, somewhere. All he had to do was wait the bad times out. LaVerne might still wake up and prove himself a man, although the odds seemed more remote with every passing moment. Vesta might be magically transformed into a faithful, loving wife and mother. "There was still a chance to work things out," Cole wrote, "until the incident that I feel was the most degrading thing of all."

In the neighborhood, his nearest playmates were a boy and girl whom he has known for years. In Eddie's view, the girl is "an aggressive kid, a trait that irks me," and she seems to have a crush on Cole that he does not reciprocate. The afternoon in question, they are playing out in front of Eddie's house, Cole wrestling the girl, with the boy and the Coles' new puppy for an audience. As luck would have it, the girl is stronger, pinning Eddie on his back, her full weight on his chest. He

Michael Newton

struggles to unseat her, but his arms are trapped against his sides.

And suddenly, without a hint of warning, the girl lifts up her skirt, a flash of cotton panties as she sits on Eddie's face. Her chubby thighs grip Eddie like a padded vise, her crotch pressed tight against his mouth and nose. The musky heat is overpowering. Humiliation and arousal, helpless fear and anger, swirl together in his mind, survival paramount as Eddie fights to breathe. He dares not bite a girl "down there," but he is suffocating, drowning in her flesh.

At first, his mother's snarling voice seems distant, muffled, but a moment later the girl is snatched away. Instead of raging at the girl responsible for Eddie's torment, Vesta drags him to his feet and whips her open hand across his face, a stunning blow that knocks him backward, off his feet.

Behind him somewhere, car doors slamming, voices raised. Aunt Gladys and her husband Ernie, stopping by to visit, catching Vesta with her arm cocked for another swing. The brief diversion is enough for Eddie, lurching to his feet and dashing back around the house to reach his hidden sanctuary, Wriggling in the darkness like a wounded animal. The puppy follows him instinctively, more curious than frightened by the racket on the lawn.

The adults take their argument indoors, raised voices clearly audible in Eddie's cave, beneath their feet. A tearful Gladys pleading with her sister, offering to raise the boy herself if Vesta hates him so. Immediate agreement from her husband, with a warning that the pain inflicted now may be repaid in kind, someday. Cole's mother cursing them as meddlers, showing them the door with sharp reminders that they have no personal experience in raising willful, wicked children. The unspoken fact that she cannot afford to let him go, because of what he has experienced, the things he knows and might reveal.

Beneath the floorboards, Eddie huddles in a womb of darkness, trembling as he weeps hysterically, the puppy wriggling in his lap. Long moments pass before the dog is quiet, longer still before Cole realizes it is dead, its tongue and eyes protruding from the pressure of his hands around the fragile neck.

In time, he scratches out a shallow grave and plants the tiny corpse, smooth dirt and cardboard covering the spot. Outside, no sign of Mother as he breaks from cover, crossing yards and scaling fences in his flight to reach the local hermit's property. A silent figure watches from the house as Eddie climbs a fruit tree, perching in the lower branches, but he is not driven off.

"The real thought of revenge and strangling my mother—*any* woman—came to me right there," Cole wrote, "while I was sitting in that tree. The act of strangulation as a method of killing was born after, and because of, choking that pup. It was the most horrifying way of killing someone I could think of, later taking a different turn and becoming a sick obsession."

Stony silence in the house for days thereafter, with LaVerne pretending not to notice anything amiss. No one appears to understand that Eddie has been pushed across the line from suffering in silence to exacting retribution where and when he can. No outward sign betrays his resolution to defend himself by making others suffer in his place.

Another afternoon, days later, Eddie safe beneath the floorboards with his buried secret. Several boys stop by the house on Fifth Street, and he wriggles out to meet them, blinking in the light. He recognizes three of them as playmates from the neighborhood; the fourth, "an ass from school named Duane," is one of those who still rags Cole about his "sissy" name, from time to time.

The day is warm enough for swimming, and the boys ask Eddie if he wants to tag along. They have no money for admission to the nearby Richmond Plunge, but empty pockets make no difference at the harbor, down by Cutting Boulevard. The presence of Duane puts Eddie off, but after some discussion he agrees to join them for a while.

The walk down Cutting Boulevard takes Eddie past the drab apartments where his mother used to visit "friends," his mood already soured by the time Duane begins to tease him.

"How's it feel to have a *girl's* name, *Carroll?*"

Duane is as shocked as anyone when Eddie turns and drives a fist into his stomach, winding up to throw a roundhouse punch before the others rush between them, one of Eddie's neighbors telling Duane to knock it off. Uneasy peace returning as they straggle toward the harbor, Cole still furious but covering his rage.

The local yacht club shares facilities with various nonmembers and commercial craft, berths fashioned out of floating logs bound end-to-end. A favorite game and test of skill requires each boy to walk out on the logs as far as possible, maintaining balance while the others splash and try to spook him into falling off. The winner's prize is simple satisfaction.

Eddie Cole has visited the harbor many times before, but this trip is his last. He stays close to Duane, their spat apparently forgotten, trailing him around the far side of a ship at anchor while the others drift away.

They are alone at last, with Eddie in the water, Duane crouched on a nearby log, prepared to spring. He holds his nose and jumps, feet first, a splash before he disappears with bubbles trailing in his wake. Cole tracks his progress, shifting to be ready when his target tries to surface.

Now!

He clamps his legs around Duane to hold him under, palms braced on the nearest log to give him leverage. The water roils beneath him, making it appear that Cole is treading water, practicing his kick.

It is a game at first, the kind of thing boys do when they are "being boys." Who hasn't pushed a playmate underwater at a swimming party, even holding him— or her—beneath the surface for a careful moment, just to prove a point?

The difference lies in grim determination, when your prey decides the game is over and begins to fight for life. The water softens punches, but you can't avoid the desperate fingers scrabbling at your legs and naked back until they falter, trailing off. The spark extinguished. One last scattering of bubbles on the surface, there and gone.

"I held him under till I knew that he was dead," Cole wrote, remembering the moment after almost forty years. "And when I let him go, he sank."

The rest is history. Cole's playmates coming back and hardly noticing Duane is gone. The boys are halfway home before somebody thinks to ask about him, finally deciding that he must have gone back early, on his own. Discovery of the bloated body leads to questions, later, but authorities in Richmond have no time to spare on accidental drownings. No one bothers asking Eddie Cole if he has anything to share.

"When anyone would ask me if I wanted to go swimming at the harbor, after that," Cole said, "I turned them down. No way. I was afraid of the police—with reason, as I thought—but there was no remorse about Duane. I hated him, and I was glad I stood up for myself."

Silent Rage

Another deadline crossed. Doors closing in an eight-year-old assassin's mind, the tumblers falling into place. No turning back.

FOUR

AT BEST, THE THRILL DERIVED FROM MURDER IS A TEMPORARY FIX. Like any other powerful narcotic, homicidal violence satisfies and dulls the senses for a time, but the effect—that heady rush, the feeling of achievement—ultimately fades.

And when it does, a predator goes hunting.

"If I thought my life was going to improve," said Cole, "I was sadly mistaken. Neither at home or at school. I was getting meaner and meaner, fighting all the time in a way to hurt or maim, and my thoughts were not the ideas of an innocent child, believe me."

Increasingly, those thoughts turned toward a repetition of the act that brought him temporary peace. One early target was a playmate, Jimmy Whitney, who spent time with Cole on holidays and after school. A younger boy, and smaller, Jimmy was the perfect target for a plan already taking shape in Eddie's mind. "No reason to speak of," Cole recalled, "but the thought of killing him entered my head." He had experience with drowning, courtesy of Duane, and what worked once would surely work a second time.

Cole's favorite recreation spot, in those days—other than the cave beneath his house—lies on the other side of Cutting Boulevard. It is a swampy area, with cattails massed along the banks of green canals, and ponds that sometimes prove deceptive in their stagnant depth. One afternoon, at Eddie's urging, he and Jimmy build a raft from scraps of lumber, poling out into the middle of a sluggish stream. His friend is at the bow, imagining himself a bold explorer of the Congo or the Amazon, when Eddie lifts a piece of lumber, taking aim, a batter's stance. One blow to put his quarry in the water, and the rest is simple leverage.

A sudden thrashing on the bank distracts him, children crashing through the reeds in hot pursuit of frogs. Reluctantly, Cole lays his bludgeon down, already wise enough to know he must not strike in front of witnesses. He swallows bitter disappointment, feeling cheated, drawing consolation from the thought that there will always be another chance.

At Nystrom Elementary, Cole marked time to graduation, covering his darker urges when he could and putting on a "normal" face. Despite the schoolyard battles with his enemies, in sixth grade Eddie was selected as a student crossing guard, one of the chosen few whose uniforms included crimson sweaters, Sam Browne belts, and whistles for directing traffic after school. He loved the feeling of authority that came with his position, but the best part of the job was fantasy, imagining the carnage if he blew his whistle to release the flow of traffic with a group of students in the crosswalk. Standing on the curb and watching while they bled and died.

Cole never gave that signal, but his daydreams kept him occupied until a new diversion came along. That spring, the hottest toys around were Duncan yo-yos, and he spent the remnants of his Christmas money on a sleeper, practicing incessantly to learn the tricks he saw on television, getting ready for a scheduled contest at the school. He didn't feel the urge to maim and kill so much, when he was training, and he even slacked off masturbation for a while. An athlete needs his energy.

On contest day, he came in feeling strong and confident. Preliminary matches were a breeze, and Eddie made it to the semifinals, then the final face-off. It was one-on-one, with everybody watching ...and he lost. To make it worse, the winner was a popular, good-looking kid who automatically went down as "a conceited ass" in Eddie's book. Embarrassment and feelings of defeat blurred into anger, outrage, seething hatred.

But he knew enough to bide his time.

Comes summer, and the children who can't wait to get away from school all year are drawn back to the grounds compulsively, like filings to a magnet. South of Nystrom Elementary, a giant playground offers swings and slides and jungle bars, but the attraction on this Sunday afternoon is a hulking piece of road-grading equipment parked on a slope near the school. Boys scramble over it like monkeys, no one thinking twice when Eddie takes the driver's seat. Below him, standing near the massive treads, his nemesis. Cole understands momentum and mechanics, from experimental sessions in his father's car. He waits until a small hand slips between the tread and sprocket, kicks the gearshift once, and leaves the rest to gravity. All blood and screams, like music in his ears.

No yo-yo trophies coming up for the conceited ass.

That fall, Cole entered seventh grade at Roosevelt Junior High School, a gloomy brick pile that consumed a whole block, the adjacent lot fenced off for playing fields, flanked by separate, individual classrooms. Roosevelt reminded Eddie of a boiler room or haunted castle, with its dingy walls, blind windows, gloomy corridors.

It felt like jail.

Cole did his best, all things considered, winding up his first year at the new school with a B average in attitude, more a tribute to his acting skills than any change of heart. Academically, he churned along in the D+ range, with poor grades in gym and arithmetic pulling down solid C's in his other subjects. At that, he did better than anyone had a right to expect, considering he turned up absent one day out of every five.

The first semester of eighth grade looked more promising. Cole earned no grade below a C, with solid B's and an occasional A in English, social studies, and art. It seemed that Eddie was about to turn his slump around …and then, the roof fell in.

Fresh back from Christmas break in early January, Eddie took exception to a bully's prodding in the gym. They came to blows, a coach stepped in, and Eddie wound up visiting the dean. In those days, schoolyard discipline involved a leather strap, before the California legislature got around to banning corporal punishment. The dean prepared to whip both boys impartially, a no-fault kind of settlement, but Eddie saw things differently. If anybody laid a hand or strap on him, he told the dean, they should prepare to die.

As luck would have it, Eddie's family was about to move in any case, a short hop to Richmond's Florida Avenue and a new school district. His expulsion from Roosevelt got lost in the shuffle, with none of the heat he expected at home. He was starting from scratch at Harry Ells Junior High, on McDonald Avenue, adjacent to Nichols Park and the YMCA.

At first, the change of scene brought mixed results. Achievement tests administered in February 1953 showed Eddie reading at grade level but two years behind in arithmetic, this despite a tested "genius" IQ level of 152. His grades in attitude had slipped to C's and D's, perhaps a function of abrupt displacement, and he scraped by that semester with a D+ average overall.

On the flip side, moving was a boon to Eddie's social life. "From practically the first day," he recalled, "I was accepted, mostly by the girls. I went to all the school affairs and parties, and I pretty well played the field with this girl or that." With all new faces, nothing of his "oddball" reputation dogging Cole, a part of him felt fresh, reborn. He dropped his hated given name and introduced himself as Eddie when he had the chance. In ninth grade, he displayed improvement, even though his tested reading skills declined. His absentee rate fell below his halfway mark of what it was at Roosevelt. It seemed like things were looking up.

But there would always be Duane, the urge to kill again.

Some nights, he would accompany schoolmates to a skating rink, near Alvarado Park, but Eddie didn't spend much time on wheels. He liked to slip away, outside, and stalk the darkened footpaths of the park, in search of female prey. "I fantasized about finding some unsuspecting girl and killing her," he later wrote. "I also prowled around Nichols Park, by our house, acting like some kind of animal seeking an unwary victim. Screwy, huh?"

His luck—or that of his intended prey—was holding. Eddie never met a girl out by herself on his nocturnal prowls, and finally he gave it up.

Cole's social life at Harry Ells, while much improved, was not risk-free by any means. In ninth grade, Eddie began "messing around" with a girl two years younger, feeling confident enough in their relationship to drop by her home one evening, on Richmond's "Snob Hill." Her father met Cole at the door and warned him off in no uncertain terms. He did not fit their "type," and never would. Humiliated and dejected, Eddie snubbed the girl at school next day and started shopping for a playmate from his own side of the tracks.

At that, most of Cole's new friends were female. The sole exception was a gangly loner, Valance Briggs, who had earned the nickname "Beetle Brows" from his most prominent feature. The two boys were close for a while, cruising the popular Uptown Theater for girls until Eddie decided that Briggs cramped his style. They would remain in touch through high school, but Cole was bent on going his own way.

For a time at Harry Ells, Cole managed to avoid the fights that were his trademark back at Roosevelt. One afternoon, as class adjourned, he joined a crowd to watch a fight between "a real good-looking kid" named Sherwood and a Chicano "delinquent-type" called Chico. The combatants had barely squared off when a hoodlum friend of Chico's, Donnie Moss, tossed a board to his sidekick, and Chico hammered Sherwood to his knees. The crowd was stunned, nobody moving as Moss waded in, aiming a kick a Sherwood's bloody face.

In retrospect, it was a bonehead play, but Eddie Cole saw red, the vicious two-on-one assault too close to home. He threw a sucker punch at Chico, dropping him, and leveled Donnie with a hard kick to the groin. A few more punches wrapped it up, and Eddie left his adversaries crumpled on the ground. Sherwood never got around to thanking his savior—a fact Cole recalled with obvious resentment thirty years later—but the incident made Cole a hero of sorts at Harry Ells, especially with the girls. They started calling him at home, anonymous gigglers, asking "Do you feel as good as you look?" Cole was surprised and flattered, taking the girlish interest to heart in those days when both sexes idolized Elvis Presley. Suddenly obsessed with "image," Eddie stood before his bathroom mirror by the hour, combing his hair until his arm got tired.

No cause for celebration when his time ran out at Harry Ells in June 1954. Uprooted again, he enrolled at El Cerrito High School that fall, his fan club scattered. Starting over. "A few years later," he remembered, "Harry Ells became a junior-senior high school. I can't help thinking of this as another turning point, wondering if things may have been different if it had turned junior-senior before my graduation. Maybe not."

At least he had the summer left, and that meant evenings at the Uptown Theater, on McDonald Avenue. In 1954, the Uptown's popularity had less to do with first-rate films than smuggled alcohol and "making out," defined by Cole as "very, very heavy petting" once the lights went down. Cole worked the passion pit with Valance Briggs at first, and later by himself, their separation hastened by an incident with Briggs's girlfriend. Cole had done his share of grappling with Rhonda Pearsall in the darkened theater, but Briggs regarded her as "his girl." When she moved out to Martinez, forty miles away, Cole joined his friend one night to hitchhike out and visit. Rhonda's parents drove them home, the back seat crowded, Rhonda smiling at her boyfriend while she clung to Eddie's hand. Cole blamed her "fickle" nature, but the guilt came home to roost as he described himself: "A saint by no means, at the best of times."

Another of his defects, Cole decided, was his face— specifically the left side, which he arbitrarily regarded as "deformed." Around the Uptown, Eddie made a point of staying on the left side of the theater, to hide his shame, and only ventured to the far side of the room if it was dark, or he could cover the offending profile with his hand.

An alternative hangout on warm summer nights was Point Richmond, a deserted stretch of beachfront, where police did their best to ignore bonfires and drunken teenagers cavorting in their underwear—or less—well after curfew. Cole remembered the beach parties as "pretty wild," but he remained virginal, despite the abundance of suds and skin. Hung up on fondling as the point of no return, he went home frustrated night after night, compelled to satisfy himself by hand.

Cole's first, best shot at "going all the way" was Ellie Roth, two years his senior, with dark hair, a killer body, and "the nicest set of cans you'd ever want." Ellie's parents were professional dancers, and their show business liberalism colored the girl's view of sex. She had a crush on Eddie, and he found her "very agreeable" to petting at the Uptown, moaning softly as he slipped a hand beneath her bra. The close encounters left him simmering, and Cole was ready to approach a new frontier the night that Ellie steered him to a park, close by her house.

They start out on the swings, Cole standing, Ellie seated, with her knee between his legs. She rubs against him, teasing, feeling his erection through the fabric of his Levi's jeans. They adjourn to some convenient bushes, but the grass is damp, and Cole suggests the back seat of an unlocked car, nearby. He fumbles Ellie's clothes off, awestruck by her beauty. Her breasts are pale, the nipples dark and stiff against his palms. He sucks them, trembling in his urgency, as Ellie spreads her legs. Warm moisture on his fingertips, and Ellie moaning as she grapples with his belt. He tried to penetrate her willing flesh …and suddenly his penis shrivels, failing Eddie when he needs it most.

Confused at first, frustration turning into anger, Ellie tries to wriggle out from under him. Cole pins her down, hands braced against her shoulders, inches from her fragile throat. He pictures Ellie on the cover of his favorite detective magazine, the kind he stares at while he masturbates at home. It would be easy, choking her. No trick at all.

No trick for the police to trace him, either, since her parents know they are together for the evening. Fear of jail stops Cole from acting out his fantasy, and thus saves Ellie's life. She sees the pent-up fury in his eyes and makes no move to stop him as he stumbles from the car, a running shadow, leaving her to dress and walk home on her own. Discretion is the better part of valor, and she makes her mind up to avoid the Uptown for a while.

A night came when LaVerne Cole felt the urge to play a father's role and teach his younger son about the facts of life. With supper cleared away, they took a walk around the house, for privacy. LaVerne worked through the bare mechanics—nothing new so far, though Eddie had not managed to experience the joy of sex himself—but they were treading thin ice when the old man veered into philosophy.

"No matter what," LaVerne advised, "don't ever let a woman dominate your life."

Stunned silence for a moment, Eddie gaping at the man beside him, lip curled in a sneer. He has to ask: "And how can *you* say that, for Christ's sake?"

Standing on his feet one instant, stretched out on his back the next, lips swelling from the impact of his father's fist. A taste of blood like bitter gall.

"I feel shame and sorrow now," Cole wrote in 1985, "but at the time I hated him. Not because he hit me, but because he let me down. To this day, I regret that night, because I think he really knew about my mother's infidelity."

Eddie's high school performance reflected the turmoil in his life. He pulled straight D's his first semester at El Cerrito, with conduct grades of U—for "unsatisfactory"—in English, boys' glee, and machine shop. The second semester, it was failing grades across the board, with Cole absent twenty-seven out of eighty-eight days.

Girls weren't the only thing contributing to Eddie's academic slump. He had a new friend in the neighborhood who had wheels. Together, they made a routine of burglarizing a local liquor store, forcing the lock and stealing one case of beer at a time, stashing the suds in the friend's trunk for consumption at school, on their lunch break. Afternoons became an alcoholic blur, and it was working like a charm until police belatedly mounted a stakeout, nabbing their suspects in the act.

It was the first arrest for both young men, and the friend's parents promptly bailed him out. Cole's mother overruled LaVerne's attempt to do the same, consigning Eddie to a two-week stint in "juvey" hall. He cried himself to sleep at night, but showed a stone face to the counselors and staff by day, resentment festering inside. His father's cowardice was worse, in Eddie's mind, than Vesta's cruel vindictiveness. He hated both of them by now, determined not to buckle and submit to any form of punishment. A man doesn't have to stand tall, but he has to stand up.

After Cole returned to Richmond there were more arrests, more trips to juvey, most of them for alcohol or curfew violations. Cole and another friend had joined the National Guard on a whim, lying about their ages and forging parental signatures on the applications, but the lie caught up with Eddie after half a dozen busts. The Guard released him without dishonor in June 1955, on account of his age, and a sympathetic judge suspended Eddie's latest sentence to the California Youth Authority, on the condition that he give the local cops a break and leave the state for ninety days.

It was decided that he ought to spend the summer with his brother Richard and Richard's wife, Edna, in Elko, Nevada. (El Cerrito got wind of the move and mailed Eddie's transcripts, perhaps in the hope he would never come back.) Instead of simply putting Eddie on the bus, his parents made the drive. Four hundred miles one-way, with Vesta berating her son nonstop as a disgrace to the family. LaVerne tried to intercede at one point, meekly backing down when Vesta told him to shut up.

In Elko, Richard was working as a bellhop at the Commercial Hotel, while Edna stayed home with the kids. Eddie's sister-in-law was about his own age, passably attractive, bored with motherhood and keeping house. A few days into Eddie's stay, he started feeling uncomfortable around Edna, and once accidentally caught a glimpse of her in her bra and slip. By that time, Cole knew trouble when he saw it coming, and he took a day job busing tables at a highway truck stop, to avoid temptation. Later, Richard and Edna separated. When Edna took the kids back to her mother's, Cole was stranded, seventeen years old and banned from going home.

He found a job at the Commercial Hotel, meager pay with a room on the side, and began collecting "some odd people" as friends. One of them, an older man, volunteered to relieve Cole of his unwelcome virginity. Together, they picked up a waitress at the competing Stockman's Hotel, all three piling into bed for a party, but the woman changed her mind once Eddie's friend had worn her out. Cole came up short again, and spent his next few weeks in Elko dodging the woman's irate fiancé.

One afternoon, off duty, he was hanging out in the Commercial's coffee shop with fellow workers when a bleary drunk reeled in and saw the young men crowded in a corner booth. It struck the booze-hound funny, and he called them "queers," an insult penetrating to the very heart of Eddie's secret doubts about himself. In something like a second and a half, he flashed on Vesta's dress-up games and masturbating in the bathroom with another boy, the brooding fear that he would never "get it up" with women. Eddie cursed the older man, was starting for him with a steak knife, when the hotel manager stepped in and told the drunk to leave.

Cole's friends dismissed the incident, but Eddie could not let it go. He trailed the drunk outside, around the corner to a service station rest room. Coming out, the stranger found Cole waiting for him, stooping down to grab a broken bottle from the ground. Cole found a bottle of his own and smashed it on the wall, prepared to spring when two employees from the station pulled him off and sent him on his way.

The incident cost Cole his job, but he was more concerned about the insult he had suffered. In his mind, the thoughtless slur was meant for him, and him alone. He asked an older friend for help, and managed to acquire a .22 revolver. With the gun to give him courage, Cole went looking for the drunk who had maligned him, but the man was nowhere to be found. In place of a specific target, then, he started to imagine choosing one at random, squeezing off a few rounds for the hell of it.

"I finally gave the gun away," Cole said, "because I started having thoughts of shooting someone—anyone —who crossed my path."

Back in Richmond for the start of another school year, Eddie found it difficult to concentrate on books. He missed thirty-three out of ninety-three days in the first semester, earning straight F's, and finally dropped out on his eighteenth birthday, to the relief of all concerned. It wasn't bad around the house, with Vesta working part-time in the kitchen at a nearby school, but Eddie needed money of his own. Over the next few months, he worked at a series of menial jobs, always quitting or getting himself fired in a matter of weeks. The pay was fair, but steady work held no appeal for Eddie Cole.

Between their jobs, Cole saw his mother less and less, but Vesta still had ways of getting under Eddie's skin. When he invested in a 1937 Mercury coupe, she stole the keys, watching with a smirk on her face while Eddie scoured the house, high and low. He finally broke into the car's steering column, bypassing the ignition switch and doing damage in the process. Ever after, turning corners was a crap-shoot, Eddie never certain when the wheel would lock and send him skidding into an adjacent lane.

Nor was Vesta the only problem at home. Cole had been dating a girl named Randy Godwin, a classmate of sister Linda's at Harry Ells. One night, he was waiting at Randy's apartment when Linda and Randy arrived in a car with two boys. Cole watched them necking for a while before he finally approached the vehicle and ordered Linda out. She stubbornly refused, and Eddie gave it up, his mind inflating her "betrayal" on the long walk home.

Ironically, Cole felt no major loss with Randy. She was just another slut in his mind, her infidelity predictable, but he had *trusted* Linda. Her duplicity—not only covering for Randy's fickle games, but acting like a tramp herself—was unforgivable, and Eddie took that anger to his grave. "More and more," he later wrote, "I'm starting to understand the workings of the female mind, hating them worse all the time."

Not that hatred was enough to make him swear off girls. Most nights found him cruising the strip in his Mercury or hitting the Uptown, usually drunk. Still a virgin at eighteen, despite boasts to the contrary, Cole never progressed beyond necking and "copping a feel." His *other* fantasies were getting in the way, distracting Eddie from the finer points of making time as he imagined killing every girl he met. "It seems my mind really dwelled on the subject," Cole said, "because I thought most girls were tramps."

Like Vesta.

Striving for a vestige of stability, Cole joined the naval reserve at Treasure Island and was packed off for two weeks of training in San Diego. He visited relatives there, on his time off, and they told him he was welcome ... as long as he didn't show up in uniform. Throughout San Diego, civilian resentment made itself felt in snubs and sneers, cropping up on signs that read: DOGS AND SAILORS KEEP OFF THE GRASS. Two weeks into his navy career, and Cole was confronted with one more rejection by strangers and family alike.

In Richmond, after boot camp, Eddie found a good job with the Rheem Manufacturing Company, but his tenure was brief—this time through no fault of his own. Appendicitis struck him down on the assembly line, and while his new employer covered all the bills, Cole spent his convalescence pondering the limitations of a nine-to-five career. He didn't know exactly what he wanted out of life, but punching time clocks like his father wasn't on the list.

Emerging from the hospital, he chucked the job at Rheem and signed for active duty with the navy. On February 18, 1957, Cole reported to the USS *Ingersoll,* moored in San Diego Bay. Two weeks later, he was steaming toward the West Pacific and—he hoped—a whole new world.

FIVE

WHATEVER EDDIE COLE EXPECTED FROM THE NAVY, he was in for a surprise. Instead of the adventure promised by recruiting posters, he encountered drudgery and discipline, close quarters, Spam and powdered eggs—the tedious routine of shipboard life. It was enough to make a rookie change his mind …but there was worse in store.

A few days out of port they neared the equator, a demarcation line in any salt's career. Those sailors with an equatorial crossing behind them were dubbed "shellbacks," and they made a point of looking down on virgin "polliwogs" with open scorn. A seaman's first-time crossing came complete with an initiation ceremony, not unlike a college hazing. Clipping off a lock of hair in front to designate their lowly status, polliwogs lined up to run the gauntlet, paddles slapping naked flesh, and swam a pool of rancid garbage to the point where good King Neptune sat upon his throne. A kiss on "Neptune's" navel was required before a polliwog could shed his fins and claim a shellback's rightful place among the crew.

For his part, Eddie viewed the childish ceremony as a personal affront, an insult to his pride. He made it known that he was not about to "swim in shit and kiss some asshole's belly button" for the pleasure of his shipmates. Anyone who tried to force him would be making a mistake.

"Of course, I spoiled their fun," he wrote, years later, "and I never won any popularity contest, but I didn't care. They weren't going to subject me to any humiliation. I'm bigger now, and I'm not letting anyone fuck me over."

The fleet's first stop was Melbourne, Australia, part of a goodwill mission in the wake of World War II. Cole regarded himself as "a hell of a person to participate in something like that," but he managed to enjoy himself despite a total lack of shipboard friends, spending some rare, happy days with Aussie families who took sailors into their homes. Three weeks went by too soon for Eddie's taste, and they were off to sea again.

If nothing else, the navy kept its promise of exotic ports. The tour included stops at Hong Kong and Formosa, with a side trip to Japan.

Cole learned to mix his beer with more exotic liquor, flirting with the Asian bar girls, always pulling back before the teasing went too far. "I still hadn't gotten laid," he recalled, "partly afraid of catching a disease, mainly concerned about my performance, not getting it up."

In lieu of one-night stands, he collected tattoos, marking his flesh with memories. On his right forearm, a heart with the legend "True Love"; above the elbow, a sailing ship and the caption "Hong Kong." His left forearm hosted a voluptuous woman and the initials "USA"; on his biceps, another heart and ribbon.

By the time the fleet turned homeward, Cole was drinking constantly, reporting to his duty shift on rubber legs. His captain noticed, and a transfer to the flagship placed him under close supervision. He remained a friendless loner, coming home with all the same old baggage he had carried out to sea. No matter where he went, most of the women qualified as tramps and whores. They crept into his dreams and fouled his waking thoughts, compelling him to masturbate at least four times a day, and he despised them all.

In San Diego, Eddie settled into the routine of life in port. More freedom than the weeks at sea, but it was still monotonous. Instead of hitting local bars when he was fortunate enough to get a two or three-day pass, Cole caught a navy flight from North Island to the Alameda Naval Air Station near Oakland, thumbing or taking a taxi from there to his old Richmond haunts. Girls at the Uptown were impressed by his uniform, and Eddie helped out by promoting himself from seaman apprentice to second-class petty officer with an extra, unauthorized hash mark on his sleeve. He also bought a flashy collection of service ribbons to dress up his act, pinning them on once he was safely away from the base.

Brother Richard was a serviceman himself, by that time, putting in his two years with the army, and they sometimes went barhopping together, in uniform. Eddie had a fake ID that added three years to his age and thereby made him "legal" in the clubs where women were attracted to a uniform like moths to flame. His brother scored from time to time, and Eddie often claimed success the morning after, but in fact, he never got beyond third base. Some of the women asked him what was wrong, and that was worst of all, his failure vocalized. He couldn't wait to drop them off and shut himself inside the bathroom, tugging at his useless cock while morbid fantasies ran through his mind.

One night in San Diego, running short of beer money, Cole doubled back to his ship, moored in a neat row with others at the naval supply depot. Half-drunk already, he was nothing that the sentries hadn't seen before. On board, instead of going to his quarters, Eddie had a sudden inspiration. Stumbling down a ladder to the mess deck, he was hoping to meet someone—anyone—with cash to spare, but then he passed the armory and had another thought.

The chain-link gate is fastened with a padlock, reminiscent of the liquor store he used to loot for beer in Richmond. Eddie hurries to the mess hall, hoping now to find himself alone, and comes back with a sturdy knife. It takes him several moments, bleary as he is, to snap the lock, but then he is inside. So many rifles, shotguns, submachine guns all around. He takes two automatic pistols, G.I. .45s, and checks to see that both are loaded. Tucking them into the waist of his bell-bottoms, covered by his uniform blouse, he shuts the gate and slips the broken padlock back in place.

It is the best that he can do.

Nerves overtake him as he starts to leave the ship. The sentries will remember him, his quick trip in and out. Their evidence could be enough to land him in the brig. Instead of leaving by the gangway, Eddie slips across the railing at the fantail, thirty feet above dark water, boarding the next ship in line. Pumped up with adrenaline, emboldened by alcohol, he repeats the stunt half a dozen times, creeping from ship to ship like a runty ninja, disembarking from the last one in line. No questions asked as Eddie leaves the base, all smiles.

A pedestrian bridge spans Harbor Drive, Eddie crossing over traffic, cars and semitrailers rushing past beneath his feet. He stands and watches for a moment, with an idea taking shape. Not here. He needs a better vantage point.

Across the bridge, he winds up in an empty field beside some naval housing. Windows mostly dark by now, the tenants safely tucked in bed or still out boozing, on the town. He watches headlights flashing past, the drivers perfectly anonymous, invisible. If any of them notice Eddie staring, they are too wrapped up in private thoughts to care. A sailor standing near the navy base is hardly news.

He draws one of the pistols, whips the slide back to put a live round in the chamber. The gun weighs three pounds on the nose, its metal warm from contact with his skin. He sights along the slide, the head-lights blurring slightly, making Eddie feel a trifle dizzy. Still not drunk enough to drown his graphic fantasies of death.

A good one coming up, some kind of family sedan. He tries to hold the pistol steady, tracking. Something in his memory about the need to lead a moving target, let your enemy do half the work and run to meet the slug that brings him down. His finger curls around the trigger, taking up the slack.

The muzzle flash is startling, the gunshot loud enough to sober him. Cole stands there, smelling cordite, watching as his target rolls away and passes out of sight.

A miss? No way to tell.

His nerves are strung out like piano wire, and Eddie gives up on the trick-shot competition. Easing down the pistol's hammer, he returns the weapon to his waistband, plodding toward the nearest bus stop for a ride downtown. On Broadway Eddie sells the pistols to a taxi driver and immediately spends the cash on beer.

By breakfast time next morning everyone on board was conscious of the theft. No one suspected Cole directly, and he told himself that he was in the clear. For all the shipboard sentries knew, he had returned last night and gone directly to his bunk, to sleep it off. They had not seen him leave the ship again, and he was careful when it came to leaving fingerprints, a lesson from his misspent adolescence. Even if he *was* suspected, it would be his word against official doubts, and he could not be forced to take a polygraph exam.

No sweat.

Until he caved in and confessed.

"Call it an act of remorse or stupidity," Cole wrote, years later. "Either way, I went to my division officer and told him what I'd done."

Perhaps a twinge of conscience, long suppressed, but penitence meant nothing to the U.S. Navy. Instead of leniency, they hit him with the kitchen sink, a special court-martial on charges of stealing govern-ment property. Conviction was a foregone conclusion, his punishment including forfeiture of pay and reduction in rank to seaman recruit, ninety days in the brig, and a bad-conduct discharge for dessert.

In Eddie's time, and for at least a decade afterward, the navy brig in

Silent Rage

San Diego was a little bit of hell on earth. The guards were all marines, a part of the navy on paper, well known for their hatred of "swabbies" in the flesh. Brig duty attracted the worst of the lot, as any prison draws its share of bullies, itching for a chance to throw their weight around. And while the Uniform Code of Military Justice calls for equitable, humane treatment of prisoners, reality is often light-years distant from the book.

For starters, "brig rats" were assigned to barren cells with cots and nothing else. Bathroom privileges were routinely denied for minor infractions, prisoners forced to relieve themselves in rusty cans that overflowed and fouled their cages. More serious problems —like speaking out of turn or showing disrespect to any of the guards—could mean a beating, fists and boots and billy clubs, until a prisoner was black and blue, his urine streaked with blood. Some prisoners were handcuffed to the chain-link ceilings of their cages, dangling there for hours while their arms went numb. Noisy inmates were frequently hog-tied, their heads swathed in tape like mummies, noses bared to let them breathe. Others were bound with straps in a painful crouching position, unable to sit, lie, or stand. Straitjackets were also popular with the guards, long straps drawn up between an inmate's legs to mash his testicles as he was dragged around the cell block. Some prisoners were chosen on a whim for calisthenic details, exercising till they dropped, subjected to a vicious beating when their muscles failed.

Emerging from his three months in the brig, Cole wrote that "All I felt was hatred." For the guards, the navy—even, one is tempted to imagine, for himself. Assigned to transit housing pending an appeal of his bad-conduct discharge, Eddie enjoyed more freedom of movement. Despite the punitive reduction in rank, he still had his "special" uniform, wearing the chevrons and ribbons whenever he slipped off base to drown his rage with alcohol. His luck had turned, though; in the first week of September 1958, he was detained by San Diego officers on suspicion of burglary and auto theft, ultimately released without charges in the absence of conclusive evidence.

Finally, sick of waiting and too proud to ask for clemency, Cole approached the warrant officer on October 1, demanding his discharge as ordered by the military court. Two days later he was a civilian, back in Richmond by October 4, moving in with his parents again.

"At this point," Eddie wrote, "you might ask why I kept going home to an impossible situation. My only answer is that I somehow hoped it would change, hanging on when I should have let go. Maybe I actually thought I should be punished, for some reason. Who knows?" The guilt he carried—for Duane, for all his violent fantasies, for helping to deceive his father through the years—was backing up on Cole, a painful abscess of the psyche that devoured self-respect and poisoned hope.

Vesta Cole was duly embarrassed by Eddie's bad-conduct discharge, but she did not turn him away. Perhaps it was too much to resist, another golden opportunity to punish her son, rubbing his nose in failure, reminding him that he had smeared the family name again.

A short week out of uniform, Cole found a job at Nopco Chemical in Richmond, working six days a week as a shipping clerk. Before long, he had enough money to strike off on his own, renting a small "efficiency" apartment. Acquaintances from high school and the local bars dropped by to visit at all hours of the day and night, most of them female. Seven months shy of his twenty-first birthday, Cole finally surrendered his virginity and proved himself "a man."

"It was my first experience with sex," he recalled, "actually getting down to the nitty-gritty." After waiting so long, the event was anticlimactic in more ways than one. Instead of relief or excitement, Eddie felt dismay at the ease with which young women—some of them virtual strangers—tumbled into his bed. He used them willingly, but viewed them with contempt. Satisfaction eluded him, and he continued his daily pattern of masturbation, as if from force of habit. Nothing seemed to fill the void inside, where angry voices called for blood.

By early spring Cole was fed up with the routine at Nopco Chemical. He quit his job and moved back to his parents' house, defeat personified. His afternoons and evenings were devoted to barhopping, while the money lasted. That April police in Placerville, east of Sacramento, nabbed him on two counts of driving without an operator's license, and he served two weeks in lieu of a hundred-dollar fine.

Vesta's nagging was intolerable, after that. Cole fled from Richmond to Lake Tahoe, moving in with sister Nancy and her husband, Ronald. Nancy had worked her way up as a dealer at Harrah's casino, in Stateline, bringing home good money in wages and tips, but things were often tense around the house. Eddie described Ronald as extremely possessive of Nancy, claiming that he thought all men were constantly lusting after her. The arguments rankled Eddie, torn between defensive feelings for his sister and his darker feelings toward women generally.

Driving in the car one night, with Eddie and some friends in back, the argument resumes. Insinuations for a start, with Ronald working up a head of steam. Nancy holds her own, dismissing him as paranoid, but Ronald has a prosecutor's zeal. Behind him, Eddie rears back in the seat and aims a kick at Ronald's skull. A moment's panic as the car veers wide, across two lanes. Horns bleating in the darkness, drivers swerving to avoid a head-on crash. The others hold him back as Eddie curses Ronald, telling him to stop the car and try a man for size. In time, they calm him down and bloodshed is averted, but the rift runs deep.

Eddie moved out the next day, living in his car and working the graveyard shift at a local gas station, "robbing them silly" and gambling his money away in Stateline or Reno. His boss could never really pin the thefts on Eddie, but he lost the job regardless, finally selling off his car to cover gambling debts before he caught the next bus westbound.

Back to Richmond.

Back to Vesta and LaVerne.

On the plus side, a friend Gary Nixon was fresh back from Denver with his new bride, Nancy, and they made a threesome, hanging out together several nights a week. Without a car, Eddie was stranded, and Nancy often came to pick him up while Gary caught a shave and shower at the house. No one but Vesta thought anything about it, seizing the chance to taunt Eddie with innuendo, as if her own track record left any room for throwing stones.

One night, an old girlfriend from the Uptown, Pat Morris, turned up at the Nixons', invited by Gary and Nancy without Eddie's knowledge. He was glad to see her, even so, impressed with the way Pat had filled out since high school. They soon began dating again, sometimes doubling with the Nixons or Eddie's sister Linda and her latest boyfriend, getting down to business at the local drive-in movie. Pat was still a virgin, and she meant to stay that way until her wedding night, but she was not averse to back-seat fondling, sweaty handjobs, sometimes stripping to the waist and letting Eddie rub his naked chest against her nipples. With a beer or two inside her, she would even kiss and lick his penis on occasion, always stopping short of climax, finishing the job by hand. Frustration gnawed at Eddie, and he wound up masturbating after every date, imagining his hands locked tight around Pat's neck, her body limp and lifeless as he entered her and found release.

Cole worked odd jobs to keep himself in pocket money, pulling shifts at Nopco Chemical from time to time, and bought himself another car. It was convenient for his dates with Pat, but trouble also came on wheels for Eddie Cole, and he began to log arrests. December 1959, police in Richmond caught him driving drunk, without a license; six weeks later he was jailed again, this time for petty theft. A local judge combined the counts in early February, packing Eddie off for thirty days at the county work farm. In May he was busted again, charged with buying alcohol for minors.

"It got so that Pat didn't know if I'd show up for dates," he recalled, "or just phone her from jail." For all that, she was loyal enough. In time, they spoke of marriage. Cole put money down on an engagement ring. A halting step in the direction of normality.

One afternoon, between jobs and jail terms, he stops at a bar on Cutting Boulevard, near his parents' home. The place is always dark, a nod toward "atmosphere," with emphasis on privacy. He scans the faces, dedicated daytime drinkers, stopping short when he sees Vesta at the bar. Beside her, leaning close enough to whisper in her ear, a man he doesn't recognize. La-Verne at work, of course; no one but Eddie to observe his mother's mating ritual.

Cole slips into a corner booth, unseen, and pays the barmaid for a beer. Across the room, he watches Vesta and the stranger laughing, snuggling, kissing. A proprietary hand slips down to cup his mother's buttocks. Bitter gall in Eddie's throat, the beer not helping. When they rise to leave at last, his mother turns to face him, meeting Eddie's gaze, contempt and self-assurance in her eyes. She has no fear of her accomplice, after all these years.

When they are gone, he flags the barmaid down and questions her about the couple, claiming that they look familiar but he can't recall their names. She tells him that the woman is a regular, inclined to leave with different men from time to time. As far as couples go, she seems to play the field.

He should not be surprised, but Eddie can't escape the pain. Fierce anger burning in his gut like acid as he leaves, drives aimlessly, winding up at another bar in Point Richmond. He drinks till closing time, reluctant to go home, the alcohol fueling his rage. At half past two o'clock, he waits outside and sees the female bartender leave on foot, walking home. He falls in step behind her, tracking her toward Alvarado Park, where he used to prowl in junior high school.

"I fully intended to waylay and strangle her," Cole recalled, "but we got to her house and some people were waiting for her, spoiling my chance."

Next evening, when he stopped in at the bar again, the woman looked at him suspiciously, Cole thought. Imagining that she had seen him stalking her and recognized his face, he lost his nerve and gave it up.

Frustration.

Fury.

Cole considered speaking out at last, a confrontation with LaVerne and never mind the cost, but he had wasted too much time. Three quarters of his life devoted to a secret that may not, in fact, be secret after all. If he is right in his suspicion, and LaVerne knew all about his mother's infidelity, then telling him would do no good in any case.

June 1, 1960. Eddie sets out cruising after dark, no destination clear in mind. The car is an extension of his brooding personality, another way to prowl for human targets. Passing Harry Ells, he makes a right between the school and Nichols Park, his headlights picking out a dark sedan with huddled shapes inside. Two couples working up a sweat and doing God knows what. The land of things his mother does with other men.

He drives across the railroad tracks and kills the engine, parking on familiar ground. Beneath the driver's seat, an old claw hammer for emergencies.

Tonight should qualify.

He creeps back through the darkness, keeping to the bushes where he can and circling around behind the car, to take them from their blind side. Retribution for surrendering to pleasures of the flesh. Up close, he hears them whispering and moaning in the heat of passion he has never felt without a darker side. For that, too, they must suffer.

Swinging overhand against the broad rear window of the car, he revels in the crash of glass. A scream, one of the girls moon-faced and staring at him, quickly covering herself. He rushes to the driver's side and aims his next blow through an open window, at the driver's face. A miss, and strong hands lock around the hammer, twisting it from Eddie's grasp.

He runs for cover, hearing angry shouts behind him, half expecting one of them to pitch the hammer at his head, or try to run him down. He crashes through the undergrowth, a wide loop working back in the direction of his car, to throw them off. He doesn't count on being recognized, one of the girls from Eddie's neighborhood, familiar with his face.

The cops showed up on Thursday morning, booking Cole for assault with a deadly weapon. Convicted on June 28, he was sentenced to thirty days on the county farm. Facilities did not allow for diagnosis of the inmates, much less any kind of therapy. The officers who dealt with Cole dismissed his violent outburst as a consequence of too much alcohol. They knew him as a low-life boozer, sometimes rowdy when he drank— and that was damn near all the time. The best thing he could do was serve his thirty days, dry out, and try to "get his shit together" when he hit the street.

In late July he came back home to Vesta's carping, silent disappointment from LaVerne. Cole blamed himself for much of what had happened, feeling that he should have spoken up when he was five or six—to save himself, if nothing else.

Too late.

He tried to drown his bitterness in beer and whiskey, stayed out late to keep away from Vesta's razor tongue. Cole managed to suppress his violent urges for a time, but he could not avoid collisions with the law. Arrested for outstanding traffic warrants in San Pablo, north of Richmond, Eddie pulled another thirty days. This time around, he lost his car for missing payments while he was in jail.

By January he could feel the pressure building up at home, and in himself. On foot, he flagged a Richmond squad car down and huddled with the officers, explaining his compulsive urge to rape and strangle women. At the station house he ran it down again for a lieutenant who was skeptical, at best. It wasn't every day that a potential killer walked in off the street and warned the bluesuits of his violent feelings in advance.

Cole waited while the officer made several phone calls, coming back with some advice he thought might do the trick. If Eddie *really* wanted help, he should consider psychotherapy. It didn't have to cost a bundle, if he checked into a state facility. In fact, if he was interested . . .

He was.

On February 2, 1961, Cole was admitted to Napa State Hospital, twenty miles north of Richmond, in the heart of California wine country. He gave the doctors ninety days to see what made him tick.

SIX

Seeking help was one thing; opening himself up to receive it was another. Eddie went to Napa with the knowledge that a mention of Duane could lead to murder charges. He would have to keep that secret to himself, no matter what the cost. And once he started lying to the doctors, it was difficult to stop.

Dr. R. C. Hitchen handled Cole's first interview at Napa, readily accepting Eddie's fabrication of "a happy childhood." Listing his religion as Catholic, "fairly active," Cole also described himself as a "temperate drinker" who had "only been drunk about two times in the past year." As Eddie now recalled the last two decades, he "got along very well at home" prior to his bad-conduct discharge from the navy. He could not explain his morbid urge to rape and murder women, which, he said, had only plagued him since the latter part of 1959.

No mention of a strangled puppy in the crawlspace, yo-yo contests, Ellie Roth, the darkened paths of Alvarado Park. So many secrets locked inside.

"The patient talks about both of his parents in rather glowing terms," Dr. Hitchen recorded, "stating that they were always affectionate; they did all they could for him, and that he has not always done as well as he could for them." The years of pent-up guilt and hatred muzzled Eddie, though he did concede both parents were "hard to talk to at times" and "they always stuck together against me." If Dr. Hitchen saw a conflict in the two descriptions, it is not recorded in his notes.

When it was Vesta's turn, she put on the performance of a lifetime. Eddie's constant shaming of the family was forgotten, as were Vesta's little dress-up games, the threats and beatings, her adultery. If Eddie told the doctor he had started school when he was six, instead of seven, who was she to argue? Overnight, the son she hated had become "the least trouble of any of my children. He was a good child, never cried too much or got into too much trouble until he went to high school." Listening to Vesta, you could almost catch a whiff of apple pie.

And Hitchen bought it, describing the Cole family as "a fairly closely knit unit but one quite undemonstrative." Eddie himself was "pleasant and alert," though largely self-centered, with "no insight." Dr.

Hitchen diagnosed Carroll "Edwin" Cole as suffering from a "schizophrenic reaction, chronic undifferentiated type."

New patients at Napa spend their first two weeks in a closed unit—segregation—so the staff can see how they behave, pick out their quirks and flash points. Four days after his admission, Eddie was examined by clinical psychologist Lee Ryan, who noted overt symptoms of depression and anxiety. Ryan found Cole "suspicious of the testing and somewhat evasive at times," but the Rorschach test and others helped him come to grips with Eddie's personality ...or so he thought. Although the patient's history is suggestive of a sociopathic character disorder (Bad Conduct Discharge from Navy, attempted rape, etc.), the tests indicate that his behavior is based on a neurotic condition; that is, he acts out his neurotic conflicts in antisocial behavior. Unlike a sociopath, he has an over-punitive superego and is constantly feeling the pressure of guilt. As a result of this heavy burden of guilt, he feels depressed and anxious most of the time. His frustration leads to angry feelings but does not allow him to act out these feelings in any planned manner (as would a sociopath); rather, he bottles up these feelings and when he reaches his frustration tolerance point along with the presence of an appropriate target for his hostility, he impulsively acts out his anger without much thought or judgment about his actions.

*****

His neurotic conflicts center about three main areas: (1) conflict with authority figures which appears to be a generalized response learned from his interaction with his father; (2) a masculinity conflict where he feels the need to constantly prove to himself and others that he is a "man." This conflict not only is revealed by the testing results, but is reflected in his need to display tattoos on his arms, and the Don Juan behavior with girls that never results in anything but infantile sexplay and flirting; (3) a dependency conflict where he is attempting to give the impression of being independent but wishing to maintain childlike dependency.

*****

His deepest anxiety is that he is unlovable, and he feels that people won't like him because he doesn't deserve it. As a result he tends to avoid close personal ties with others. If people got to know him well, he believes, they would discover the traits that make him so unlovable. Hence, he keeps everyone at the same distance; that is, his relationships with others are always superficial. He has lots of friends especially girl friends, but he does not develop a close relationship with any one person. Since he has been rejected in the past, he finds the safest road is to avoid close personal relationships in the future. This technique tends to reduce some of his anxiety but does not provide him with any satisfaction of his basic needs or solutions to his neurotic conflicts.

Because of his poorly controlled hostility, guilt and anxiety, his judgment is undependable, and his relationships to others is [sic] continuously fraught with fluctuating emotional attitudes.

In place of Dr. Hitchen's schizoid tag, Lee Ryan labeled Cole an "emotionally unstable personality."

With his two weeks of isolation behind him, Cole was moved to an open unit, granted access to the playing field, tennis courts, and the inmate canteen Dr Hitchen found him a job on the grounds, cleaning up and prescribed a course of treatment.

"They put me on no medication," Cole recalled, but I had to go to group therapy sessions once a day No one else had the same problems I had, and I was embarrassed to discuss my urges. There was nothing that said I had to tell the group anything about me, though I *did* speak privately to the psychiatrists."

At first.

Pat Morris came to visit Eddie several times, but he could tell that she was catching heat at home, her parents frightened at the prospect of their daughter spending time around a crazy man. In time, the visits stopped, and Eddie was alone, increasingly convinced that checking into Napa was a grave mistake. The last straw came when one of Eddie's doctors pegged him as a "textbook case," parading him before a class of student nurses and psychologists.

"He told them all about me, and I almost died from the humiliation," Eddie wrote. "From that day on, I really clammed up. Anytime I saw the doctors, I said nothing more."

It was an impasse, but the staff had seen enough of Eddie Cole. A conference on March 10 reviewed his diagnosis and the disposition of his case. As Dr. L. M. Jones described the meeting: "It was felt by some that he was a possible sexual psychopath, potentially dangerous to the community. Staff made a diagnosis of Anti-Social Sociopathic Personality Disturbance on March 21st and recommended that he be discharged, Not Suitable, Not Mentally Ill and recommended that he apply for outside psychiatric treatment or voluntary admission to Atascadero State Hospital because of his sadistic, abnormal sexual tendencies."

Sadistic.

Abnormal.

Potentially dangerous.

And free to walk on Saturday, the twenty-fifth of March.

Cole's doctors had delivered three conflicting diagnoses in the space of seven weeks, and they prescribed no medication. Pills were very much beside the point in Eddie's case.

He was not suitable ...but he was on the street.

*****

From Napa, Eddie ran back to his parents' home in Richmond, where the "close-knit" family showed increasing signs of strain. LaVerne was drinking more than usual around the house, and creeping menopause did nothing to improve Vesta's irascible temperament. She nagged Eddie nonstop about finding a job and "settling down," finally "making something" of himself. Cole responded by ducking out early each morning, hiding in the nearby park until his parents left for work, then going home to watch TV all day. A man of leisure in his prime.

Cole's chronic unemployment was a sore point with his fiancée, as well. Pat's parents hammered at her for associating with a mental case and jailbird who could never hold a job. Cole did not help his case by dropping in with whiskey on his breath, and it was finally too much when the collection agency came after Pat's engagement ring.

She cut him loose.

In Eddie's mind, it was another crass betrayal by a female he had trusted with his heart. Forget about the countless times that he had pictured strangling Pat and ravaging her corpse. She had been "something special," but it didn't last.

It never would.

Cole felt a sudden, pressing need for change. He started thumbing eastward, toward Nevada. Hoping for a job, new faces, anything. A change of scene. "Actually," he wrote from death row, "I think now it's just my way to get away from Richmond. Now I'm running."

All the way to Reno, where he found a hotel room and landed a job as apprentice bartender, at the Horseshoe Hotel and Casino. The job was brief, since Cole would rather drink than serve. His parents sent along a $250 check from the state, one benefit of being "mental," and Eddie quit his job the same day, blowing the money on liquor and dice. He became a fixture on Reno's skid row, drinking and gambling till exhaustion overtook him in the small hours, prowling for an unlocked car to sleep in when he didn't have the money for a room.

"It seemed I was withdrawing from society," he later wrote, "and living like a common derelict."

The trouble is, he almost never wins at craps, and drinking doesn't pay. The cash runs out, and Eddie knows from past experience that it is easier to steal than work. More satisfying, too. But who to rob? Who better than the miserable faggots he has feared and hated all his life?

Nevada's second largest city has its share of homosexuals, but they are not inclined to flaunt themselves in public. "Gay" is still a synonym for "happy" in the spring of 1961, and Eddie has to ask around among his drinking pals, discreetly, to discover where the "queers" hang out and mingle.

Nothing ventured, nothing gained.

He picks a club and stakes it out, observes his chosen prey. Disgust and anger churning in his gut like acid, forcing self-doubt to the surface, urging Cole to prove his masculinity. It takes a while, most of the faggots leaving two by two, but finally he picks a solitary mark, falls in behind him, shadows from the streetlights making giants out of two small men.

A block or two, and Eddie's target knows that he is being followed. Breaking for an alley, he attempts to flee, but Cole is faster, driven by a hunger that surpasses simple greed. The man who stands before him, cringing, is a traitor to his sex, a shame to all men everywhere. How can a youth like Eddie Cole expect to get it up and be a man, when faggots and the memories of "Mama's little girl" are never far from mind?

"What do you want?" the stranger asks.

No words for Eddie's craving, so he lashes out with fists and feet, excited by the sounds of impact and his victim's whimpering. He takes the faggot down and turns his pockets out, relieves him of a hundred-something dollars. Easy money, and a swift kick to the ribs in parting. Eddie feeling ten feet tall as he emerges from the alley.

Feeling like a man.

The stalk becomes a part of his routine from that time on, whenever Cole runs short of cash …and that means almost nightly. He enjoys the violence, punishing an underdog who won't fight back or run to the police. Gay-bashing in the days before it has a name. The money is a bonus, gravy on the side. It feels so good to kick a faggot's ass that Cole would gladly pay, if there was someplace he could do it by the hour.

Unlike Richmond, Eddie managed to avoid the police in Reno for the most part. His one arrest, for disorderly conduct on May 24, was settled with the payment of a ten-dollar fine, and Cole kept his nose clean, as far as the cop on the beat was concerned. Nobody caught him sleeping off a drunk in someone else's car, and there were no complaints to the authorities from homosexuals he victimized. Loose lips could sink careers, in those days. It was better to ignore a backstreet mugging than to open a potentially explosive can of worms

Cole's favorite bars produced a handful of acquaintances who passed for friends. The most intriguing was a California redhead, Carla, roughly Eddie's age, just marking time in Reno for the six-week special on divorce. Cole remembered her as a "good-looker" who could "really put away the booze," but she was running short of cash around the time they met. Unfit for strong-arm robbery, she toyed with the idea of turning pro and working on the street. Cole threw a screaming fit at that, and they were finished, leaving Eddie to console himself with Lydia, a blonde he picked up on the rebound. "She wasn't bad-looking," Cole said, "but she was a slob, on the rag from the first day I met her. I'd rather have been with Carla, but Lydia put up her sex."

And not for Cole alone, as he would later realize.

They made a threesome with an older guy named Rick, who had adopted Eddie as a kind of special project, showing him the ropes. One night in May, the three of them decided they were sick and tired of

Reno. Eddie rolled another queer to get them started, and they stole a car belonging to a friend the cops had jailed for public drunkenness. Before the sucker knew it, they were Sacramento bound. Three boozy musketeers in search of some adventure on the road.

They made an aimless loop of Sacramento County, spending their nights in cheap motels with bars nearby. Cole and Lydia in bed, while Rick slept on the floor, pretending not to hear them humping through the night. The lady may have been a slob, but she was energetic in the sack, with an imagination that could almost satisfy Cole's needs.

Almost.

Perhaps, if he could choke her for a while, before they fucked . . .

Driving through Woodland on June 5, en route to the country club managed by Cole's grandparents, they were stopped by the highway patrol. The car was plainly stolen, no point arguing the fact, but Pack and Eddie claimed responsibility, so Lydia could walk. Without a drunk or queer to rob, they couldn't make bail.

One afternoon in jail, awaiting trial for auto theft, Rick sidles up to Eddie with a pained look on his face. Confession time. Does Cole remember one time, back in Reno, when he left their shabby digs to buy another pint, and Lydia was waiting with a big kiss when he came back through the door? Well, as it happened, she had put her mouth to better use on Rick, while Cole was out. It has been preying on Rick's mind, in case Cole started thinking that she tasted funny, just that once.

He really *does* see red, a crimson blur before he grabs Rick by the throat and drags him to the floor. Handful of greasy hair for leverage, as he slams Rick's face against the concrete slab. Again. Content to play percussion all day long, if no one intervenes. Another solid lick before they pull him off, and even then he has a chance to kick his newest enemy a time or two as they are dragging him away.

On July 13 Cole pled guilty to auto theft and drew a six-month sentence on the county farm. With good time off, he could be free in sixteen weeks or so. He had a month behind him, pulling easy time, when it occurred to Cole that he should make another try at getting help.

That evening, when the guards are counting heads, he beckons one aside and spills the story of his urge to rape and murder women, even screw them after they are dead. The word gets back to a lieutenant in command of Eddie's unit, and the guards remove him to a barren cell without a bunk or mattress, where the roaches swarm at night. Three weeks in solitary, then a transfer to the county mental ward, where he will spend another month alone. By this time, Eddie has some doubts about the system's willingness to help.

He is about to chuck it and recant, when he is called before a board of county doctors. Will he volunteer for treatment at Atascadero, where the rules of maximum security apply?

He will.

Judge Raymond Coughlin signs the order of committal on October 6, and ten days later Cole is on his way.

Round two.

*****

Cole's entry examination at Atascadero was conducted by Dr. Karl Klokke, whose notes describe Eddie's "quiet, introvertive tendency." Despite some initial hostility, Cole demonstrated "considerable loosening up" as the interview progressed.

Unfortunately, "loose" is not a synonym for truthful. Cole was still intent on covering, despite his self-acknowledged need for help, and he was not above rewriting history to make himself look "normal." Dr. Klokke's first report includes a note that Eddie "denies ever being drunk," along with the false information that Cole began masturbating "at age 11, alone, not with other children." With each successive interview, another detail of his past was altered or erased, until his morbid urge to rape and kill was isolated as a total aberration, disconnected from Cole's history and therefore inexplicable.

Dr. Klokke noted a "very marked condition of vasomotor instability" in Eddie Cole—that is, a nervous condition that constricts or dilates blood vessels, including those in the brain. Klokke diagnosed Cole's problem as a "personality trait disturbance, passive-aggressive personality, with sexual and homicidal aggressive tendencies." In closing, the doctor dubbed Eddie "a definite menace to society," recommending further tests to pave the way for treatment.

Once again, no medication was prescribed, but Eddie found a source for smuggled Valium and dosed himself, to keep things cool. Group therapy had no more impact now than when he played the game at Napa, Eddie feeling isolated from the other inmates, too embarrassed to discuss the feelings he kept bottled up inside. Another motive for his reticence was fear, engendered by the visible effects of Thorazine, electroshock therapy, and lobotomies among his fellow inmates.

"I was deathly afraid of these treatments," he recalled, "and though other help was probably available, I wouldn't tell anyone anything. I acted as normal as I could, confiding in nobody, watching the zombies walk around the ward."

In April 1962 Cole sat for a new battery of psychological tests, including Rorschach, word association, sentence completion, and the classic Minnesota Multiphasic Personality Inventory. Clinical psychologist Irwin Hart found Eddie "somewhat tense," insisting that he was ready for discharge. The test results disagreed. As recorded by Hart:

The psychological data are very puzzling and contradictory. On the one hand, the projectives do not suggest psychotic processes. On the other hand, the MMPI does reveal psychotic features. At this point it should be noted that the validity scales of the MMPI overwhelmingly suggest some kind of faulty test-taking attitude on the part of the patient—perhaps he was intentionally attempting to falsify the results, perhaps he was unwittingly engaging in self-deceit, perhaps he was extremely careless in responding, or perhaps he misunderstood the questions. But if he was faking the MMPI situation, what would have been the objective? Clinically, he seemed intent on making a good impression and on demonstrating his mental health. If we are to accept the MMPI at face value, he is saying something like the following about himself: "I am crazy—crazy as a hoot owl, and it doesn't bother me." Maybe his admission of all kinds of florid schizophrenic ideation and reaction is the result of an over-active imagination. Nevertheless, one would suspect that behind the smoke there must be some fire, and his MMPI scores reflect some malignancy, although not as much as might appear at first blush. Thus, I think we could analyze the results as indicating that he is saying: "I am a mentally sick person, but it doesn't hurt." Or: "I have problems and complaints and difficulties, but I don't care."

What kind of person would attempt to present himself as above? I think his emphasis on psychotic-like reactions represents an appeal for help, and a cloak of intensely strong, underlying dependency longings. But his "I don't care" attitude suggests that he cannot accept his dependency longings, but instead assumes a pose of self-reliance, assertiveness, and independence. His MMPI record also indicates extreme impulsivity, over-reactivity, and under-control —which appear to stem more from dependency-independency conflict than from hostile impulses. He has his share of hostile feelings, but these seem to be no more than the average of our patients, and further revolve primarily around familial, as contrasted with authority, figures. Impulsivity, as a defense against dependency, is quite ironic for him, as the consequences leave him feeling irresponsible, inadequate, and ineffective.

The patient also demonstrates very strong feelings of difference, detachment, apartness, and unrelatedness. He also describes very strong feelings of inadequate ego controls and inhibitions concerning thoughts, feelings and behavior. Further, he indicates bizarre sensory perceptions compatible with a severe schizophrenic psychosis. While many of these declarations appear to be a function of an hysterical-type suggestibility and imaginativeness, it would seem tenuous reality contact must be involved. The feelings of dissociation and depersonalization which are reflected in the foregoing, strongly suggest a severe identity problem. In this connection, it may be noted that the Rorschach strongly suggests a confused sexual identification and underlying difficulty in accepting the masculine role. He appears to be attempting to handle these conflicts by denial and reaction formation. An example of his tendency to handle sexuality by denial and also literally reversing it, may be observed on the word association test, where his response to the stimulus word "breast" was "back."

The patient's medical history indicates that he has been preoccupied with an urge to kill and then rape. In his discussion with me, the patient indicated that he no longer had the urge, but was still bothered to some extent by the fantasy of it. One might speculate that the urge or fantasy stems from his sexual identity conflict and difficulty with acceptance of the male role, and consequent perception of females as threatening. One might presume that he reacts to this threat with hostility, and that the kill and rape imagery are expressions of his hostility. One notes that the sequence is not rape and then kill, but rather kill and then rape, suggesting that even under these conditions that sex with a living female would be too threatening.

The heart of this patient's problem appears to be severe conflicts centering around sexual identity and acceptance of dependency. He reacts to these tensions with impulsive acting-out of hostile ego inflationary impulses, and with feelings of depersonalization. His MMPI configuration indicates the presence of psychotic pressures; the projective data do not reflect such pressures. While evidence of dissembling and faulty test-taking attitude have made reconcilliation [sic] of disparate data more difficult than usual, my conclusion is that psychotic mechanisms are operating in this patient. I suggest that the patient be referred for retesting, after about two months, so that comparisons may be made with present data, in the hope of obtaining more definite conclusions.

Hart's recommendation was ignored by the Atascadero staff, and Cole took matters into his own hands that August, filing a writ of habeas corpus to secure his release. Judge Coughlin was inclined to grant the motion, based on Eddie's grasp of legalese, but the psychiatrists demurred. Dr. Hart got another crack at Cole on September 4, finding the patient "very downhearted" in confinement, hoping for a transfer that would mean more freedom. This time, as reported by Hart, the test results contained at least a glimmer of hope.

These data suggest that this is a very passive-dependent person with a facade of independence, and confusion concerning sexual identification. Although he perceives himself as quite masculine, he demonstrates underlying feelings of apprehension concerning the male role. However, the feeling of discomfort with the male sex role is considerably less pronounced than on the previous psychologicals. He does not demonstrate on either the current Rorschach or the MMPI, processes which suggest a psychotic reaction. Currently, the MMPI indicates extremely strong anti-authority attitudes, but not much readiness to carry them out. One of his Rorschach concepts suggested very strong hostile feelings. The total constellation suggests that he has managed to erect defenses against acting out of hostile impulses, and that the defenses are reasonably adequate at present.

The current psychologicals do not demonstrate the previously observed disparity between data obtained on a projective as compared with a structured basis. The previously observed psychotic features are not apparent now. He still demonstrates strong conflicts in the areas of passive-dependency and sex-role identification. He also revealed strong, underlying, hostile impulses and freely expresses anti-authority attitudes; but for the most part his defenses against the acting-out of these appear reasonably adequate.

With new results in hand, Cole was transferred to Stockton State Hospital, a minimum-security institution, on September 12. Dr. Maxwell Gage assigned him to a closed ward for observation, and while Eddie was initially cooperative, his temper had begun to show by mid-October. Chafing at confinement, he refused a kitchen work assignment unless he was granted ground privileges. The necrophilic urge had vanished, Eddie said, but Dr. Gage was skeptical, noting his opinion that "this patient may well be sociopathic rather than schizophrenia [sic]." Cole began to work part-time with the hospital's drama group, building sets, but it made little difference. On November 2 Gage reported that Eddie "continues to be making a sociopathic adjustment ...characterized by becoming angry if his request is not immediately fulfilled."

Eddie's case was reviewed by the staff on November 26, with Dr. I. I. Weiss presiding. The exercise included a fresh interview with Cole, in which Eddie continued the process of rewriting history. His theft of pistols in the navy now became a plot to kill an unnamed girl he thought had given him venereal disease. Of course, there was no girl, no dose of "clap" to be avenged, but any violent whim was preferable to an admission of virginity at age nineteen.

Cole came a little closer to the truth in a description of his dreams, here summarized by Dr. Weiss.

Significantly, in his dreams at night when he has unpleasant dreams, he sees clearly the figures and images of his parents, his sisters, and other relatives. Once he saw Dr. Gage, his ward physician. All of these dreams are bad and unpleasant because he is upbraided, bawled out, punished, criticized, etc., in all of them. There is no question in his mind, he sees the faces quite clearly and identifies very accurately each and every person in these dreams at night in his sleep, and he remembers them clearly in today's discussion. Obviously, this dream material is more than just "dreams"; they reflect very accurately his relationship with the people with whom he is in most intimate contact. Even his ward doctor is looked upon in the same vein as his father—both are hostile, critical, punishing, and threatening him.

His father, in his dreams, is not quite so bad as the mother. He seems to be willing to stop after awhile and to relent in his criticism and upbraiding, but the mother keeps urging him on. She is the one with whom he has his quarrel in every day life much more than his father. He says openly that he could learn to get along with his father if the mother wasn't around to continually push the father more and more in the direction of criticizing the son.

Dr. Weiss concurred with the Atascadero findings where Eddie's fear of women and confusion of sexual identity was concerned. The November report explains:

He seems to be afraid of the female figure and cannot have intercourse with her first but must kill her first before he can do it. This is shown not only in theory but in actual practice—he wanted to kill the woman whom he suspected of having given him a venereal disease in the Navy and stole the guns to do it. Of course, he changed his mind and never killed her, but that was his intent. Incidentally, he never did have V.D.; it was just a fear or an obsession at the time.

Such a fear effectively kept him away from completing the heterosexual act. He has reflected this in other heterosexual experiences. For example, until a few months before commitment, he had been in love with a girl; they loved each other dearly. They were going to be married; and in his sexual relations with her, she asked him not to ejaculate for fear he would impregnate her and they would have to marry earlier than planned. He was able to accomplish the act of intercourse with her, stopping short of ejaculation each time. Regardless of the rationalizations behind this, we must regard this as an intense effort to thwart the completion of a full heterosexual act. In this regard, he says that he often has had different varieties of impotence with his female partners; the last three are identified clearly, and he admits it happened many times. He wants to blame alcohol for the reason for impotence manifested so often, just as he blames alcoholism for the vague, confused episodes of his life.

Nor were Eddie's hangups limited to heterosexual encounters. As described by Dr. Weiss, his recent background also indicated a deep-seated homophobia.

The Atascadero records document the patient's upset at the numerous homosexual approaches on the wards there. This is common at that hospital, and a number of the patients undoubtedly have the same complaint, but rarely does it enter into the records of a patient. The fact it did here in this case shows that the homosexual threat was quite prominent. Obviously, the subject still has a great deal of difficulty in his sexual identification. He is threatened terribly by a homosexual approach, and he is incapable of assuming fully and completely the masculine role.

The female figure is very threatening to him, and he wants to kill it as he did the girl he thought had given him V.D. [sic] He is hostile toward his mother, the prototype of all female figures. He dare not rape the woman in his obsessions; he must kill her first.

In other words, his mother's calculated torture and sadistic dress-up games had done the trick.

Dr. Weiss diagnosed Cole's condition as a "schizophrenic reaction, chronic undifferentiated type," and recommended him for ground privileges, in line with Eddie's request to work in the carpentry shop. Released from confinement in early December, Cole wasted no time sniffing out a stash of bootleg liquor on the grounds, sedating himself in the absence of prescribed medication.

A little exercise and alcohol worked wonders, so it seemed. By February 7 Cole was doing well enough to rate a "town pass," freeing him to look for work in Stockton. He reported nailing down a job, and a notation in his file declares that "Social Service has investigated this and confirmed that he is working." In fact, Eddie spent most of his time in skid-row bars, drinking up the federal disability checks he received for being hospitalized.

In retrospect, the hospital's "investigation" was a joke. It failed to note Cole's March 4, 1963, arrest for disturbing the peace, which earned him a ninety-day jail term with three years suspended. Apparently unaware of his patient's incarceration, Dr. A.B.R. Smith signed release papers on April 19, granting Cole an "indefinite leave of absence to self."

He was free to go home …just as soon as he got out of jail.

Back in Richmond, holed up with his parents, Eddie took a new interest in current events. "In Boston," he wrote, "someone they called the Boston Strangler was creating havoc, which stimulated me beyond description." He collected clippings on the case, lapsing into familiar behavior, prowling Nichols Park after sundown "like a creature from last night's late, late show."

Dumb luck that no one fell into his hands. At home, you could have cut the tension with a knife.

"The family was solicitous, to some extent," he said, "but they were really wishing I was elsewhere." Brother Richard had a place in Dallas, with his new wife Mary, and the deal was struck in early May. LaVerne bought Eddie's one-way ticket on the Greyhound, headed south.

Another shot at independence, going nowhere fast.

SEVEN

DALLAS WAS A DIFFERENT STORY. Raw and violent, with a reputation for defiance. Politics that placed the average voter somewhere to the right of Genghis Khan. Big money lay in oil and cattle, but an enterprising man could find a hundred different ways to turn a dollar, if he knew the score. The cops shot first and got around to questions later; never mind the questions, if the dead were black or Mexican. A popular lieutenant on the force rode shotgun for the local oil tycoons and openly solicited donations for the Ku Klux Han.

It looked like Eddie's kind of town.

Mary met him at the depot, recognizing Cole from family photographs and smiling at him as he hobbled off the bus, legs stiff from sitting on his butt for hours straight. She was approximately Eddie's age, in line with Richard's thing for younger women, but without his first wife's roving eye. She made Dick's brother feel at home, but there was never any hint that he should count on more than room and board.

It was a short two miles between the Greyhound depot, on Lamar, and a small house on Throckmorton Street, in North Dallas. Richard had a day job, as a fry cook in a nearby restaurant, but he would soon be home.

A family reunion, and with any luck they could forget about the last time Eddie came to visit, up in Elko. Mary knew that Cole had spent some time in a hospital, lately, but she was vague on the reason, and Eddie planned on keeping it that way.

"They spent the next few weeks showing me Dallas through bar and tavern windows," Eddie wrote, "when Dick wasn't working." When he grew tired of hanging out around the house, Cole hit the bars alone, drinking up his government disability checks. Somehow, he never got around to looking for a job.

One night in June, he prowls the bars on Cedar Springs, a short walk from the house. Not drunk enough to stagger, but he feels no pain. It strikes him that he ought to drop by Richard's diner, but he never gets there. Passing the corner of Oak Lawn and Lemmon, he spots two women in a group of people, waiting for a bus. One tall and plain; the other short, well built, attractive. On a boozy whim, he lingers. When the bus arrives, he gets in line.

The bus takes Eddie north on Lemmon, toward Love Field. Another stop, before they reach the airport, and the two young women rise to disembark. Adrenaline pumping as he lurches to his feet and follows. Eddie has not come this far to let them get away.

No parting comments on the sidewalk, nothing to suggest the women even know each other. Blind coincidence. Plain Jane stays on the east side of the avenue, well lighted, but his first choice makes the crossing toward a dark expanse of open field. Cole follows, tingling with anticipation as they move along a plain dirt path, beside a ratty wooden fence with houses on the other side. Downrange, the woman's destination seems to be the looming bulk of an apartment complex on the far side of the field.

A tracker knows when it is time to make his move, and Cole has played this game before, in Richmond. This time, though, he means to see it through. He slips his belt off, fashioning a makeshift noose, prepared to spring.

A few more steps . . .

The woman hears him, stopping short and turning to confront the stranger. Something like defiance in her eyes, until she recognizes Eddie from the bus. Relaxing.

"Oh, it's you."

She turns away, dismissing him, and Eddie sees his chance. He drops the noose around her neck and pulls it tight, the woman lurching backward, suddenly off balance.

Something wrong. The belt too stiff to cut her wind off or provide control. She manages to turn and face him, kicking, fingers tangled in his hair and twisting painfully. A heartbeat later, they are on the ground, all fists and knees, and she begins to scream.

No matter how he twists the belt, Cole cannot shut her up. Beyond the fence, a porch light blazes on, a man's voice telling them to can the goddamn racket or he'll call the cops.

Cole panics, rolling clear and struggling to his feet. He leaves his belt around the woman's neck, a souvenir, no way to save it as he runs for cover. Putting her behind him, racing through the darkness till her cries for help are faint and far away.

Frustration will not let him leave the neighborhood just yet, however. Eddie waits to catch his breath *then* doubles back toward the apartment complex, rightly estimating that the woman is a tenant there. He lingers in the darkness, hoping for another chance, another victim, watching as the uniforms arrive in answer to reports of an assault. The officers assume their man is well away by now, and let it go without a search.

Dumb luck.

Fatigue replaces hunger, by and by. Cole makes the short walk back to Lemmon Avenue and sticks his thumb out, hitching home and holding up his jeans with one hand, all the way.

Next day, he scans the paper, picking out a tiny piece about the incident. The one who got away is named Priscilla Hoase, a ticket agent for a major airline at Love Field. He thinks of going after her again, but knows the risk involved and puts it out of mind.

That afternoon, another bar on Cedar Springs. As Eddie enters, waiting for his eyesight to accommodate the dark, a woman brushes past him, moving quickly toward the exit. Tracking her, he recognizes his intended victim from the night before. From the expression on her face, Cole knows that it is mutual.

He finds an empty bar stool, orders beer, and settles in to wait. It won't be long, he estimates, before Priscilla finds a pay phone on the street and the police arrive to haul him in. Disgust and resignation make the Lone Star taste like vinegar.

He waits, but the patrolmen never come.

To Eddie's dying day, he puzzled over why Priscilla Hoase allowed him to escape that afternoon. It was, perhaps, a would-be victim's best revenge.

The incident left Eddie shaken, drinking heavily to keep his morbid fantasies at bay. Depression stemmed from his apparent lack of self-control, and at the same time, Eddie was embarrassed by his failure as a murderer. It seemed he couldn't do a damn thing right, except for drinking to forget.

July 5, 1963. At 9:08 P.M., patrolmen dragged a limp, unshaven rag doll into the emergency receiving room of Parkland Memorial Hospital. Cole was nearly unconscious and reeking of liquor, barely coherent enough to explain that he had swallowed twenty caps of Mellaril—a "mood elevator" normally prescribed for manic depressives—in a bungled suicide attempt. The doctors pumped his stomach, shot him up with Emivan to counteract the Mellaril, and passed him to "6 East"—the mental ward—for observation on a diagnosis of "acute brain syndrome."

Eddie met with staff psychiatrists over the next three days, blaming the deliberate overdose on "money problems." Dr. Kenneth Timken filed a diagnosis of "emotionally unstable personality disorder," which was unimproved by Tuesday, July 9. Cole was released that morning with a referral to the State Adult Mental Health Clinic, which he promptly ignored.

Back on Throckmorton Street, Eddie threw himself into a series of short-term jobs, repeating his familiar employment pattern, putting a hundred dollars down on a 1950 Ford coupe (later repossessed for lack of payments). Dick and Mary celebrated his "recovery" with another tour of skid-row saloons, introducing Eddie to a barmaid. A bleach-blonde with "no build to speak of," the woman was captivated by Eddie's youthful appearance, refusing to believe that he was old enough to order beer. That morning, close to 3:00 A.M., she phoned the house and asked him over for a nightcap. They wound up in bed, and Cole never went home, moving his handful of things into her seedy hotel room.

At that, it was hardly a love match. Cole predictably regarded the woman as a slut, while she saw Eddie as a surplus bank account. A few weeks after their affair began, she told a girlfriend of her plan to skip with Cole's next paycheck, but the word got back to Eddie through the girlfriend's husband, a coworker on his latest dead-end job. Instead of going home on payday, Eddie found himself another cheap hotel and let it go at that.

Small loss.

Across the hall, a mismatched couple checked in on his second night at the hotel. Returning from a bar that evening, Eddie heard the woman vocalizing during sex, free entertainment for the neighbors. In the morning, heading out to work, he saw the woman sitting by herself, apparently despondent, with the door ajar. He knocked and introduced himself, stepped in when she invited him to join her, listened to her tawdry tale of woe.

Her name was Neville Whitworth, but she went by Billy. An attractive redhead with a decent body, resignation in her eyes and voice. Within an hour, Eddie knew her whole life story. Native of Melissa, Texas, fifty miles from Dallas. The oldest of three children born to respectable parents, pregnant in her early twenties by a man who fled from marriage like it was a terminal disease. She had a daughter named Lucinda, three years old, and an unquenchable thirst for alcohol. A diabetic, Billy had been warned by several doctors that her drinking was a form of suicide, but she ignored the risk—or, maybe, welcomed it. It put Cole off that she was working as a prostitute, but who was he to criticize? As Eddie sized her up, "She was neurotic and unstable, just like me."

Billy was waiting for Cole that night, when he came home from work. Undressing her for bed, he bent to kiss the surgical scar that ran between her pubic hair and breastbone like a zipper on a jumpsuit. In the sack, they seemed to fit together perfectly, all eagerness and liquid heat.

"If I had any doubts about my sexual performance," Eddie later wrote, "they quickly disappeared, because I seemed to satisfy her totally."

In one respect, at least.

Cole's second day with Billy set the pattern for their lives. Returning from his job, he found her stretched out on the couch, half-drunk, immersed in television while a small voice sobbed and pleaded from the closet. Opening the door, he found Lucinda wailing, seated in a pool of urine.

Eddie heard another child's voice in the screams. His mind went blank.

"I beat the hell out of Billy that night," he recalled, "but I came to find out that's what she wanted. Of course, like an idiot, I harbored thoughts of changing her, helping Lucinda and keeping Billy off the streets. Wrong in all respects. We were just two sick people, making each other miserable."

Their new, chaotic life resulted in a series of arrests: Billy for whoring and public intoxication; Eddie for vagrancy, drinking, and slapping Billy around. By that time, Cole had given up on work entirely, living on his disability and change from Billy's tricks, despising himself as her pimp. They moved from one cheap flophouse to another, frequently evicted for their raging late-night battles. Billy didn't cook, so they dined out at greasy spoons or fed themselves bologna sandwiches, potato chips, and pop. Cole opened bars at seven in the morning and remained until they shut the doors again, at 2:00 A.M. That left five hours free for tracking Billy down and brawling with the redhead or her tricks. Lucinda, for the most part, stayed with relatives or spent her time in state-run foster homes.

A part of Eddie's mind was clear enough to grasp the irony of his pathetic situation. He had found himself a woman who exaggerated every attribute he hated in his mother, from the crime of child abuse to drunken infidelity. He had become a caricature of his father, going back for more each time she rubbed his nose in filth, occasionally watching from a bar stool while his faithless woman trolled for johns. He dreamed of killing her, to finish it, but never found the nerve.

A major thorn in Eddie's side, where Billy was concerned, was one Jack Ruby, proprietor of the notorious Carousel Club, where visiting gangsters stopped in to say howdy and city cops drank on the house. Strippers at the Carousel "took care of" special customers on Ruby's order, and Billy had picked up some spare change from Jack in the past, for services rendered. Ruby also had a yen for Billy, on his own. As Cole described their strained relationship, "Jack just couldn't keep his hands off the woman. We went 'round and 'round about it, many times."

A typical encounter at the Carousel saw Ruby sneaking up behind them at the bar, nuzzling Billy's neck and groping her buttocks. Cole slapped the straying hand away, prepared to take it further if he had to, but Ruby backed down. "Jack was a real emotional guy," Eddie recalled. "He almost cried." But he did not give up.

A few weeks later Billy came home late as usual, drunk and giggling, showing Cole a naked snapshot of herself, legs splayed as she reclined on Ruby's desk. It cost her one hellacious beating, but she never seemed to mind. Jack Ruby, meanwhile, started playing hide-and-seek with Cole, evaporating from the Carousel whenever Eddie blew in off the street with payback on his mind.

The problem finally resolved itself in late November. John F. Kennedy was killed by sniper's bullets on the twenty-second, and Jack Ruby passed into history two days later, gunning down the alleged assassin on live TV. In custody, Ruby described his murder of Lee Oswald as a favor to the First Lady, but Cole remained skeptical. "There's no doubt in my mind," Eddie wrote, "that Ruby's involvement was more than what came out. He was a very dubious person, at best."

The city was still in turmoil when Cole and Billy tied the knot in a brief civil ceremony, moving into a small house on Sycamore Street, in East Dallas. Eddie found a job, and things seemed to improve for a while; the newlyweds even began attending the Carroll Avenue Baptist Church, a half block from their home. One weekend they took the bus to Melissa and dropped in on Billy's parents for the day. Cole's new mother-in-law took Billy aside, chiding her for marrying a younger man, and Billy had to explain that Cole only *looked* younger. They stayed for supper, seemed to get along all right—except for Billy's old man, acting so reserved—and caught the Greyhound back to Dallas shortly after dark

A few days later Eddie knew the honeymoon was over. Billy went back on the bottle, started hustling tricks again, and Cole's reaction was predictable. "I quit my job and stayed home, watching horror shows with women being strangled, and we stopped going to church." When neighborhood parishioners stopped by to see if anything was wrong, Cole told them off in no uncertain terms, booze heavy on his breath. The new leaf withered, crumbled, and was gone.

The house on Sycamore had little room to spare, but Billy's sister Jean began to drop by unannounced, a weekend visit here and there. Still in her teens, Jean had her sister's looks and then some. The tension started mounting after Cole walked in on Jean one evening, just emerging from the shower sleek and naked. Eddie tried his luck that night, with drunken neighbors stopping over for a party, but the crowd and too much alcohol got in his way.

"Billy never left us alone for a minute," Eddie wrote, "because she was jealous of other women around me. I never could understand why it was alright for her to fool around, but not for me."

Most nights, Cole lay awake and waited for his wife to stagger home, still smelling of her last trick's aftershave. "I went through a lot of alarm clocks, throwing them at her," he recalled. "I lost a lot of jobs, too, using the excuse that I was too tired for work, after staying up all night."

Without a clock to punch, he started killing time at the saloons on nearby Bryan Avenue, sometimes with Billy, often by himself. At home, his morbid fantasies edged closer to reality. When Billy's cat had kittens, Cole dispatched them one by one, wringing their necks over a period of weeks and claiming they had run away. He also got a kick from strangling Billy during sex, a stunt that often left her bruised, with bloodshot eyes.

Silent Rage

"Choking her became a habit and a necessary stimulant for sex," Cole said. "Many times, in years to come, women would complain about this practice, as it scared them. Of course, that only heightened my excitement."

As for Billy, if the roughhouse bothered her, she kept it to herself. An alcoholic masochist, she may have enjoyed the mistreatment to some extent, and there are many ways to register displeasure. Sometimes, coming home from a long night of play-for-pay, Billy would leave the bathroom door wide-open while she washed herself, forcing Eddie to watch while she douched in the sink. Other nights, she wet the bed, deliberately or in a drunken stupor, lying in her own urine while Eddie retreated to sleep in a chair.

A disintegrating life-style encouraged mobility, and the Coles began shuttling from place to place, residing in cheap hotels and run-down apartments. At one location, Cole took advantage of Billy's frequent absence to move on a nineteen-year-old "nymphomaniac" neighbor. The young woman boasted of selling off three children via baby brokers, living with a brother whose chronic voyeurism provided free entertainment. More than once, killing time with the bizarre couple, Eddie fondled or fucked the young woman while they watched her brother, peering through a makeshift peephole to a neighbor's bathroom. Billy would occasionally interrupt them, pounding on the door and calling Eddie home to start another round of drunken, pointless arguments about fidelity and trust.

Meanwhile. Cole cherished fantasies of murdering the woman who had willingly become his toy. "If the situation had been suitable," he wrote, "I would have strangled her, as surely as I'm sitting here. My urges were strong, even then, but I wasn't stupid."

Witnesses.

Too much at stake.

One night, in the summer of 1964, Billy decides to bring her work home. Eddie stumbles in a short time later, still not drunk enough to find the sweaty bedroom scene amusing. In the kitchen, spilling drawers of silverware, he grabs a foot-long meat fork. Mr. X blows past him, out the door, a naked Billy rushing to confront her husband, spitting scorn. Cole slashes her across the stomach, drawing blood, but she escapes before he has a chance to try again. Deprived of his intended target, Eddie turns upon Lucinda, slapping her and dragging her around the small apartment by her hair. In a crunch, any female will do.

Downstairs, patrolmen spot a naked, bleeding woman from their cruiser, stopping short and switching on the colored lights. They corner Eddie in the flat and easily disarm him, carting him away to jail on charges of assault. Next morning Billy borrows money from her folks to bail him out, refusing once again to prosecute the case.

A few days later Cole and Billy took Lucinda to stay with her grandparents, in McKinney County. Billy's parents gave Cole the fish-eye, trying to convince their daughter she should dump him in the name of self-defense. Cole blew it off, went riding in the old man's truck with sister Jean. The sexy eighteen-year-old showed him where to go and told him when to park it, led him through the trees until they found a shady When Cole and Billy returned home later, by bus, stone silence was the order of the day.

The Dallas cops knew Eddie Cole by now, and they were keeping track of him. Years later he would claim a pair of bluesuits picked him off the street one night and drove him to the desert, threatening to kill him if he didn't mend his ways. It may have been a drunken fantasy or a deliberate lie, but then again, it wouldn't be the first time that a redneck with a badge decided he should put the fear of God into a good-for-nothing sleaze.

On January 5, 1965, Cole logged another bust for public drunkenness, but this time he was feeling talkative. Remorse or something else caught up with Eddie, and he spilled the details of his 1963 assault upon Priscilla Hoase. A lineup was arranged, the victim fingered him without a moment's hesitation, and he filed a guilty plea. The penalty was ninety days and costs, with no provision for analysis or therapy. With time for good behavior in the lockup, Eddie hit the street on March 13.

By that time, Cole and Billy were ensconced at the Carlton Hotel, on Gaston Avenue, in East Dallas. As spring turned into summer, Eddie convinced himself that his wife was servicing most of the Carlton's male tenants—a suspicion that may easily have had some root in fact. Booze helped him put the lid on anger for a while, but he could only drink so much, and Eddie's doubts—his certainty—were always right there waiting for him, when the alcoholic haze began to lift.

The night of Tuesday, August 10, he let it go, unloading all his accusations in a jealous tirade, Billy cursing him and calling Eddie seven kinds of fool. He stormed out of the Carlton, thumbing his way across town to see Richard, hitting several bars along the way. Gained courage by the fluid ounce. Dick parted with his car keys easily, oblivious of Eddie's state of mind.

"If he knew anything about the shitty way I lived," Cole wrote, "he never said a word."

Outside, behind the wheel, he takes a moment to collect his thoughts. Revenge emerging from a jumble of emotions, uniformly negative. At last, he starts the car, drives eastward till he finds a service station. Buys a shiny gasoline can, fills it up, and pays the tab with cash.

At 1:00 A.M., he parks behind the Carlton, in a tiny lot reserved for tenants. Going in the back door with his can of high test dragging down one shoulder, reeking with explosive fumes. Outside the room he shares with Billy, he begins to leave a trail, retreating as the can grows lighter by the moment, spilling gasoline along the baseboard. Near the exit, Eddie strikes a match and drops it, startled by the flash of heat and light. His parting curse at Billy swallowed by the sound of hungry flames.

A short run to the borrowed car. He does not hear the fire alarm go off, preoccupied with self-congratulations for a job well done. Behind him, sirens wailing in the darkness. Eddie smiles, imagining the panic, Billy and her ragtag, low-life friends evacuating in their underwear. He doesn't give a damn if some of them go up in smoke.

Revenge is sweet.

The pay phone is a brainstorm. Fumbling a dime into the slot and dialing up the Carlton, grinning as the switchboard operator answers.

"How'd you like that fire?" he asks her, feeling ten feet tall.

A heartbeat's hesitation, but she seems to know a real man by his voice. "Hey, that was really something!"

"So, you liked it, huh?" Imagining the operator, young and not bad-looking. He has passed her by at least a hundred times before.

"You bet."

A ladies' man knows when to make his move. Cole asks her out, the operator happy to oblige. She is about to go off work, if he would care to drive around in back and pick her up.

Damn straight.

Policemen waiting for him as he pulls into the lot. A spotlight in his eyes, and handcuffs, bent across the fender of a squad car, feeling like a goddamn idiot. They book him for investigation of arson, newspapers dismissing Cole as "a glassy-eyed husband" who warns the booking officer, "I'm going back out there and burn that place for good, as soon as I get out of jail."

He never got the chance.

Detained in lieu of bail he couldn't raise, Cole was formally indicted for arson on August 19. Three weeks later psychiatrists at Parkland Memorial had another chance to pick his brain. One doctor noted Cole was "carrying magazine clippings and photos of men strangling women, and claims he gets sexual satisfaction with acts of this nature." Ho-hum. Diagnosed with a "schizophrenic reaction, chronic simple type," he was returned to jail pending trial. Convicted of arson in March 1966, Cole drew a two-year sentence for his trouble. Officially received by the Texas penal system on March 25, he entered the Wynne unit for psychiatric evaluation on April 7. Five weeks later, on May 10, he was transferred to the Eastham prison farm with a clean bill of health.

By the time Cole was born, Eastham had already earned its reputation as the Texas prison network's "Burning Hell." The farm processed men along with crops and livestock, pushing them beyond the limits of endurance as a conscious mode of management. The cons were underfed and sometimes dressed in tatters; brutal whippings in the fields were commonplace—by guards, by trusties, sometimes with the other inmates pitching in. Infractions meant a beating or a session with the "barrel cavalry," a rough-hewn pickle barrel mounted on sawhorses, where offenders were left to sit for hours in the blazing sun. Clyde Barrow cut his toes off with an ax to get away from Eastham, back in 1932, and little had changed for the better by 1965. Penal reform was a pipe dream in those days prior to the judicial recognition of prisoners' rights.

Cole had no visitors at Eastham and received no mail, but Billy took the time to call his jailers and complain that Eddie wasn't writing home. The word came down: Take pen in hand, or else. Cole shrugged it off, absorbed more beatings rather than submit to bullshit mind games.

"I was only there nine months," he wrote in 1985, "but it was the most fucked-up prison I ever saw. If you treat people that way with the idea of rehabilitation, you're making a big mistake. All it achieves is people coming out of prison meaner and more bitter than they went in, with only hatred in their hearts."

For all that, Eddie's prison file from 1966 reflects a "clean conduct record" at Eastham, and he passed the high-school general equivalency test while still inside. On January 5 they turned him out and put him on a bus to Dallas.

Back to Billy.

Status quo.

EIGHT

Cole's Dallas reunion with Billy was brief and bitter. Nothing had changed in the sixteen months he was jailed, and Cole foresaw trouble in store if he tried to resume their old life. Within a week of his release from Eastham, Eddie moved to Fort Worth, but a friend from Dallas spotted him there, and Billy showed up on his doorstep a few days later. Cole welcomed her grudgingly ...and caught a bus to Oklahoma City, the first chance he got.

It was the closest he would ever come again to starting fresh.

"In Oklahoma City, I was picking up any and every woman I could," Cole remembered, "having myself quite a time." There were male friends, as well, from the bars he hung out in, and one of them owned a decrepit hotel on skid row. Eddie didn't care much for the neighborhood—there were too many whores and black pimps for his taste—but ex-cons can't be too selective when they're unemployed and spending all their pocket change on alcohol.

The good news was that Eddie had himself a teenage girlfriend, young and fine enough to make his drinking cronies drool. Her name was Lisa, and she didn't seem to mind the fact that he had done some time. If anything, it was a turn-on, living on the edge and bedding down with danger every night. Cole did not burden her with talk about the mental wards and fantasies of raping corpses, one of them her own.

A man should have his secrets, after all.

One evening, near the end of February, Billy turned up in the neighborhood, inquiring after Cole and showing off his photograph. A black pimp put her up and came for Eddie, hoping it would finish off the strained relationship and give him one more bimbo on the street. Cole needed Billy like a dose of clap, but in the circumstances, he could think of no way out. Against his own best judgment, Eddie took her home and broke the news. No answer for the curses Lisa shouted at him, with a stinging slap across the face before she left.

"It was the same old shit in Oklahoma City," Cole recalled, years later. "Both of us were drinking day and night, with Billy's diabetes getting worse and worse. We moved from one sleazy hotel to another, Billy turning tricks when she was well enough, me soaking up the booze."

Work was out of the question, but at least he had a piece of Billy's earnings now, to supplement his disability checks. On April 8, 1967, Cole was jailed on a charge of "vagrancy by pimping," living off the income of a whore. He got off with a twenty-dollar fine, but money was beside the point. In Eddie's mind it was the final straw. A man could sink no lower and survive.

*****

A few days after his release from jail, he caught the morning bus to Tulsa. Leaving town, the Greyhound passed his cheap hotel, and Eddie caught a glimpse of Billy entering the bar downstairs.

"I guess she was looking for me," he said. "It's the last memory I have of her."

In Tulsa, Eddie found himself a dingy room and worked odd jobs for several days, the money spent to quench his thirst. One night, half-drunk and working on the other half, he met a young woman who walked with a pronounced limp. She seemed cheerful in spite of her handicap, warming a stool beside Cole's and regaling him with stories of a big inheritance she was expecting any day. With several drinks inside her, she began to think that Eddie might be just the man to help her spend it. She could promise him a life of ease, if he was man enough to earn his keep in bed.

It sounded like the kind of boozy fantasy you often hear in bars, near closing time, but Cole was not about to look a gift horse in the mouth. If nothing else, he had a chance to get his ashes hauled, and if she came through with the cash, so much the better.

Back at her place, Eddie trailed her to the bedroom, watched her strip for action, barely noticing the limp. What threw him was the porno magazine she took from underneath her bed, propped open to her favorite section as she lay there with her legs splayed, waiting for him.

"Well?"

Cole did his best, all things considered, trying not to focus on the magazine, the way her dark eyes never left its pages. When she started panting, working up to climax, Eddie closed his eyes and concentrated on some mental snapshots of his own. Hands clenched around the woman's throat and squeezing tight until her tongue protruded. Mottled color in her face. Her body limp and unresisting as a rag doll when he turned her over, thrusting from behind.

It was enough to get him there, and all that saved her life was Eddie's knowledge of the witnesses who saw them leave the bar together. Otherwise, it would have been so easy, turning fantasy to flesh.

Inheritance or not, the woman left him cold. Next morning, making lame excuses, Eddie struck off for the Greyhound depot and a ticket out of town. He picked St. Louis on a whim, regretting it as soon as he arrived. "It was the most depressing place I'd ever seen," he wrote. "A bunch of sleazy bars, flophouses, mostly niggers on the street." Cole stayed in town just long enough to earn himself some money for the road.

This time, he felt like heading west.

On Saturday, May 27, Eddie stood beside Interstate 44 and stuck out his thumb, no destination in mind. He did not plan on visiting his family—what for?—but if he made it to the Coast …well, things would take care of themselves, in time.

His ride that morning was a foursome, two young couples bound for Miller County, to let their hair down and party at Lake Ozark. They had lots of pills, and beer on ice to wash them down with, sharing freely with a stranger on the road. Eddie was feeling no pain by the time they reached their turnoff, and he gladly accepted the invitation to tag along.

Cole didn't know it yet, but it would be the longest detour of his life.

His three days in Lake Ozark were an alcoholic blur. All dancing, drinking, dropping pills with his new friends, barely missing them when they were separated, later on. Experience had taught him how to sniff out places where a man could sleep while the saloons were closed, and there was always someone who would buy a round, if he ran short of cash.

No sweat.

A few more days and he would have to find some work, but that was fine. By then, he just might feel like moving on.

The bars shut down at 2:00 A.M. on Tuesday, putting Eddie on the street. He needs a place to sleep it off, a few short hours till they open up again and he can start another day with some hair of the dog that bit him. Bleary, not quite staggering, he makes his way down Highway 54, the main drag through Lake Ozark. Shops all locked and dark on either side.

Passing Bartlett's Cafe, he notices a staircase on the side, leading upward into darkness. On a whim, he mounts the steps, unsteady legs encouraging a firm grip on the banister. With any luck, he just might find himself an open storeroom, maybe even something he can steal and pawn for drinking money, after sunrise.

At the top, a door.

A small town on a weeknight, call it fifty-fifty. Eddie tries the knob, relaxing as he feels it turn. All darkness as he slips across the threshold, shuts the door behind him, waiting for his eyesight to adjust.

No storeroom, this. Cole realizes he is standing in a small apartment, probably connected to the diner down below. His nostrils pick up cooking smells and something else.

Perfume.

In front of him, a bed. The place is smaller than he thought, if they are sleeping in the living room. He waits another moment, concentrating on the outline of a figure underneath the covers, dark hair fanned out on the pillow.

Female.

Sleeping?

Eddie blinks, imagining the woman's eyes wide-open. Watching him. A drowsy smile of welcome. Waiting for it.

Even in his drunken state, Cole knows enough to keep it quiet, going down on hands and knees. He takes his time, alert to creaking floorboards, covering the distance at a snail's pace. Hampered by the swell of his erection now.

When he is close enough to touch her, Eddie has a brainstorm.

"I find myself crawling under the bed," he recalls, "lying there for some reason, and I remember my thoughts as those of some prowling animal, seeking prey."

He doesn't mind the dust at all. It is enough to feel the woman pressing down on top of him, sheets rustling as she shifts her weight. In Eddie's mind, the stranger wants him, needs his help to realize a fantasy as urgent and compelling as his own. Postponement only heightens the anticipation. He can almost hear her whispering his name.

Need drives him out in time, a shadow hulking by the bed and bending down to lock his hands around her throat. She struggles, gurgling incoherently and thrashing at the sheets, but Eddie is determined, hanging on. Long moments pass without a sign of weakening on her part, heaving in his grip until the muscles in his hands and forearms start to cramp.

He lets her go for just a moment, flexing fingers that have let him down again. The woman takes advantage of his hesitation, shrieking with a power that belies her size, avoiding Eddie's grasp and tumbling out of bed.

Behind him, startled voices. For the first time, Cole discovers there are other people—children—sleeping in the room. He makes the door in three long strides, half stumbling down the darkened stairs, with sharp screams lancing at his brain. It sounds as if the woman is behind him, following him to the street.

Blank faces on the sidewalk as he races past late strollers, dodging, weaving. Hard right at the corner, scanning cars along the curb until he finds one open, ducking in and huddling beneath the dashboard.

Unbeknown to Cole, pedestrians have spotted him, and they direct a makeshift posse to his hiding place. Rough hands extracting him, arms twisted up between his shoulder blades as he is marched in quick-step toward the local jail.

Highway patrolman Herb Thomas got the call in Camdenton, at 3:00 A.M., but Cole had already spilled his guts before Thomas completed the twelve-mile drive to Lake Ozark. "At first, I denied any knowledge of the assault," Cole said, "but then the girl came in, bleeding from the nose and barely able to speak. She pointed me out as the one who attacked her, and I admitted it."

It was the victim's youth, as much as anything, that did the trick. The "woman"—one Virginia Rowden— was eleven years of age.

Patrolman Thomas drove Eddie to the Miller County jail, at Tuscumbia, and delivered him to the sheriff's custody. Held in lieu of $1,500 bond, on charges of felonious assault with intent to ravish, Cole first requested a preliminary hearing, then changed his mind on June 7 and waived it. Three weeks later he stood before Judge James Riley, defended by attorney LeRoy Snodgrass, and pled "not guilty by reason of mental defect." Judge Riley packed him off for ninety days observation at the Fulton State Hospital, where doctors found Cole sane and competent for trial.

It would be months yet, before his day in court, Eddie sitting in jail at Tuscumbia while local residents debated the merits of rough justice. "The public was so aroused," Cole wrote, "that in another time frame, I would doubtless have been taken out and lynched." At that, security around the jailhouse was sometimes surprisingly lax. One afternoon the cells were left unlocked by careless workmen, Eddie and two other inmates free to roam the building with no guards in sight. Cole considered escaping, but finally decided it wasn't worth the effort. Even so, he had a chuckle when the duty officer returned from lunch and gave the red-faced workmen hell.

Plea bargains are designed, ideally, with the spirit of justice in mind. In Eddie's case, conviction on the standing charge would mean a ten-year maximum, but Miller County's prosecutor had a deal in mind to spare the voters an expensive trial. If Cole pled guilty on a "lesser" charge of assault with intent to *kill,* he would be guaranteed a five-year maximum, without a sex-offender's tag. With time for good behavior in the joint, he could be out in two or three.

It was an offer he could not refuse.

On March 11 Eddie filed his guilty plea and took his five years like a man. Two days later he was transferred to the state's maximum-security prison at Jefferson City. If he recognized the irony of being locked up in Cole County, Eddie gave no sign. Five years can be a lifetime in the joint, and some men never see the other side.

*****

"When I first entered the prison," Cole remembered, "I could look down on a grassy yard and see guys making out on the lawn, in plain sight. I'm thinking, 'What the hell have I gotten myself into?' "

He didn't take long finding out.

Opened for business in 1836, "Jeff City" is the oldest prison west of the Mississippi—and, some say, the worst. Perched on a ragged bluff overlooking the Missouri River, its gray stone walls enclose forty-seven acres, widely known as "the Bloody 47" for the rate of inmate homicides. A convict newspaper, the *Jefftown Journal,* describes the prison with a note of perverse pride as "The Big—The Bad—The Ugly." Situated two blocks from the governor's mansion and seven blocks from Missouri's capitol building, Jeff City is an open sore. As Patrick Buchanan, future speech writer for President Nixon, told the world in 1964: "It is deplored by politicians, neglected by entrenched officials, damned by a persevering press, and run by its hapless inmates."

The state pen had worked hard to achieve its malignant reputation. As far back as 1854 it was described in editorials as a "school for rogues." An early warden, interviewed by legislators, boasted of flogging prisoners with a cat-o'-nine-tails "until blood filled their shoes"; "I guess," he proudly declared, "I have whipped more men than any man alive." In the 1930s a team of penologists dispatched by Franklin Roosevelt were shocked by Jeff City's A-Hall, where black inmates were segregated, seven or eight men crammed into cells built for three. They recommended demolition of the cell block, but A-Hall would outlast FDR, along with Presidents Truman, Eisenhower, and Kennedy. in 1954 a fifteen-hour riot left five inmates dead, with several other cons and guards among the wounded, seven of the prison buildings in ashes. An ex-Marine Corps colonel, named as warden to restore the status quo, was soon calling Jeff City "the roughest damned prison in the country." He urged abandonment of the whole facility, but no one was listening. In 1963 another major riot was suppressed with reinforcements from the highway patrol.

That same year, a state legislative committee reviewed Jeff City's history of violence, scanning prison hospital records since 1961. The published summary of mayhem reads like something from a combat zone:

Acts of Violence—All Types
1961-1963

Stab wounds: 145
6 died
14 required surgery
37 required hospitalization
88 sutured, bandaged
and treated as out patients

**Struck with some
object:**   134
1 died
12 required surgery

	(8 jaws wired, 2 eye removals)
	36 required hospitalizations
	85 sutured, bandaged and
	treated as out patients
Fist fights:	199
	12 required surgery (wired jaws)
	12 required hospitalization
	175 sutured, bandaged and
	treated as out patients
Burns	
(lye, acid, coffee, etc.):	11
	11 required hospitalization

Total acts of violence: 489

**Custodial officers
injured:** 1

1 struck in head; required 2 sutures

Well-run federal prisons, meanwhile, averaged one stabbing per year in the 1960s, suggesting the chaotic state of affairs at Jeff City. As for the prison hospital, where the wounded lined up for treatment, legislative investigators wrote that "It would need a Jonathan Swift to do it justice." They also noted that for some time during the 1960s, Jeff City's psychiatric ward was run by a man who used drugs and alcohol and who had been discharged from the military on grounds of emotional instability. Tin cans were planted under the legs of hospital beds and tables, to frustrate crawling vermin, but reports note that "thousands of bugs scampered before the committee's eyes during our visit." One emaciated convict, found with rubber tubes inserted in his nose and through his stomach wall, was diagnosed as suffering from an "upset stomach." On the side, prison authorities permitted a private physician to experiment on inmates, skewering their necks from front to back with long needles. Volunteers for the pointless torture were rewarded with a deduction of sixty days "good time" from their sentences.

On the flip side of the coin, investigators found one ward-sized hospital room converted to a private luxury suite for two inmates with no apparent medical complaints. As noted in the final report: "The sight of ten electric fans blowing on the two beds had a smack of indulgence not commensurate with the other surroundings."

In fact, indulgence was the name of the game at Jeff City. Within those walls, the inmates had effectively assumed control, forcing their keepers to buy "protection" with gifts and favors. Ranking cons collected payoffs from inmates seeking medical or dental treatment, and they also served as "switchmen," opening the cells at will for sex or the elimination of their enemies. Homosexual convicts could be "married" for a price, while underpaid guards were reduced to moonlighting as bellhops, cabdrivers, and clerks in the state capital. As for A-Hall, it remained strictly segregated until 1964, when experimental desegregation touched off another bloody riot. That December, a few days shy of Christmas, Warden E. V. Nash threw in the towel and shot himself to death at his desk.

Cole witnessed his first killing at Jeff City a few days after his arrival. "I was coming out of the mess hall with some other guys," he wrote, "when one of them let out a grunt and went down with a blade in his back. Another guy grabbed my arm and told me to keep walking like nothing happened, which I did."

It was the first of many homicides he saw within those walls, where a majority of inmates kept their "shanks"—homemade knives—close at hand for emergencies. Cole stayed out of trouble by hanging around with "some pretty heavy boys," avoiding hassles on the yard, and keeping the details of his crime to himself. Assault with intent to kill was a respectable rap at Jeff City, while strangling an adolescent girl with rape in mind would have marked him as "short eyes," a child molester, placing Eddie near the top of everybody's hit parade.

Even in the Bloody 47, Cole could not escape the past. Before year's end, he got the news of Billy's death in Oklahoma City, finished by a combination of pneumonia, diabetes, and rotgut. "I was depressed for days," he said. "Around the same time, a friend of mine in prison died of liver damage, caused by using a dirty needle to shoot up some smack."

Life and death.

It was the name of the game.

Cole distracted himself as best he could, enrolling in a vocational course for meat-cutters. The training took six months, with Eddie carving sides of beef and pork for prison cooks. It was supposed to help with rehabilitation, pointing Eddie toward a new career, but he would only use his new skills once outside the prison walls …and not the way that his instructors had in mind.

A few weeks after Eddie graduated from the training course, there was a riot at the prison. It began, this time, with casual brutality. An inmate bound for solitary, stripped and crawling naked toward "the hole" with guards for escorts, prodding him with their batons as if he were an animal. The cons went ape-shit, howling, throwing anything that wasn't bolted down, and setting fires. Tear gas and nightsticks won the day, but it had been exhilarating while it lasted, lashing out against The Man.

In the wake of the explosion, Cole and several other inmates were moved to a medium-security prison at Moberly, but they would find no peace. A short time after their arrival, a demented inmate went berserk, attacking guards, and others—Cole included—joined the fray. It was a brief rebellion, and they got another taste of gas, but there was nothing like a scrap to make a *man feel* like a man.

It was the best that he could hope for, living in a cage.

*****

Somehow, the riots failed to show on Eddie's prison record, and his keepers turned him out on May 1, 1970, with no apparent change of heart. "If anything," Cole reckoned, "I was worse."

Missouri's school for rogues was turning out another graduate.

Departing from the lockup, Cole received a shabby suit of clothes, fifty dollars "gate money," and a one-way bus ticket to Charlotte, North Carolina, to attend a school for heavy equipment operators certified by the state's vocational rehabilitation department. He stopped off in St. Louis long enough to tie one on and caught the Greyhound, heading south.

The rehab program offered Cole a weekly stipend while he went to school in Charlotte, learning to handle bulldozers, scrapers, and cranes. The course was uneventful, more routine, except the afternoon he lost it with a grader, rolling down a slope and narrowly avoiding impact with a school bus. "Nobody was hurt," said Eddie, "but it scared me bad enough, I had to take a break and change my shorts."

Most nights, he joined his classmates in the local topless bars. Ex-convicts for the most part, few of them believing that a three-week course could *really* make a difference in the free world. Everything in Charlotte seemed to grate on Eddie's nerves, from watered drinks and flat-chested dancers to the white girls he observed with blacks, along skid row. "They had no respect for themselves," Cole groused, "and certainly none for white males. If I had stayed in Charlotte, that shit would have changed, believe me."

Maybe so, but Cole had other things in mind as May wore on. His fuse was burning short by graduation day, May 25. That afternoon, diploma in hand, he stole a sheaf of traveler's checks from one of his classmates and hit the road. Heading west.

"I decided to go to El Paso," he wrote, "and get laid across the border." First, a stop in Dallas, forging checks to buy new clothes, but Cole was not about to linger. There were ugly, painful memories around that neighborhood, and he was thankful when the bus pulled out of town.

Arriving in El Paso, Eddie checked into the cheapest hotel he could find, walking across the border that night, into Ciudad Juarez. There was no shortage of hookers, and two girls attached themselves to Cole before he knew exactly what was happening. "I only wanted one," he said, "but they talked me into a threesome for forty dollars, and I paid them with the traveler's checks. I didn't get my money's worth, at that. No matter how they worked on me—and they tried *everything*—I couldn't get it up." At last, humiliated and disgusted with himself, he made his way back to El Paso, found a quiet bar, and drank himself to sleep.

The next few days Cole felt like moving on, but there was no place where he felt at home. The family was out, for all intents and purposes, uneasy with a hardcore jailbird in their midst. He drank *to* help himself unwind, to damp the anger down, but soon the stolen checks were gone, and he was running short of cash.

It was a no-win situation, all around.

One afternoon, a stranger introduced himself while Cole was soaking up a liquid lunch. His name was Roger, and he ordered ginger ale. An alcoholic on the wagon. Eddie looked familiar to him, not that they had ever met. A young man drinking in the middle of the day to drown old memories and keep his pain in check. It happened that the stranger knew the operators of a detox program on the Coast, near San Diego. How would Eddie like to hop aboard the next flight west and check it out?

It sounded fine, said Cole, except that he was currently a few bucks short of bus fare, much less the expense of traveling the friendly skies.

No problem, Roger told him. It was on the house.

Cole sized his benefactor up with bleary eyes. The stranger didn't come on like a faggot, and he couldn't do much damage on an airplane, anyway. If he tried something funny prior to takeoff, or in California, Eddie figured he could always punch the asshole out and talk a walk. But, on the other hand, if he was straight . . .

As Cole remembered it, "I figured what the hell, why not? I wasn't going anywhere, and I had nothing else to do."

They booked the flight, and Roger never made a move on Eddie, in the air or on the ground. From Lindbergh Field, in San Diego, Roger paid the taxi fare to Chula Vista, where his friends had organized their rehab center as the South Bay Pioneers. He introduced Cole to the management, arranged for clothing, room and board ...and then, he disappeared.

"Once I was settled in," Cole wrote, "he just left, and I never saw him again. I still don't understand what it was all about."

It was, perhaps, the one unselfish act in Cole's experience, too little and too late. The seeds would fall on barren ground.

In Chula Vista, Eddie took an honest shot at staying sober for a while. He went to A.A. meetings, did odd jobs around the house, but drawing monthly paychecks from the government was easier than working up a sweat. His disability had terminated with the latest prison stretch, but there was more where that came from. In lieu of Social Security, he signed up with the local welfare office as an indigent, receiving $120 per month, free and clear.

"California was very, very lax on welfare," Eddie noted, "and I made it a habit to let the state support me in years to come. It was a little game I liked to play, with nothing of my own at stake."

With easy cash in hand, the sober life began to pale. Cole worked a month or so with a local painting contractor, spending days off at the Del Mar racetrack, sleeping with a young woman from the rehab center, on the side. One morning, his boss called in sick, leaving Eddie to handle a job on his own. Instead of going to work, Cole returned his supplies to the store for a refund and drove to Del Mar, feeling lucky. A couple of winners put him ahead, and he dropped the company car in a downtown parking lot, hitting the saloons on foot.

When Eddie tumbled off the wagon, he hit hard. Patrolmen picked him up for being drunk in public, on July 21, and he skipped bail, running north. In Stockton, he tried to check in at the state hospital, but they turned him away, demanding a referral from authorities in San Diego.

Screw it.

Eddie hitched a ride to Reno, flying blind, looking for something he could not define. Familiar streets and bar stools, working part-time for a landscaper, drinking up his paychecks in advance. The morbid fantasies of violent death and necrophilia were back, full-bore, and alcohol was highly overrated as a sedative.

"On two occasions," Eddie wrote, "I tried to strangle women I had met in bars. One was up near Truckee, and the other was in Reno, in a parking lot just off the railroad tracks. They got away, both times."

It wasn't bad enough, this urge to kill a total stranger and defile her corpse. He couldn't even seem to get it right.

On September 19, 1970, Cole entered the Reno police station and surrendered to the desk sergeant, confessing his desire to rape and strangle virtually every female whom he met. He was booked on a charge of disorderly conduct, while the cops decided what to do with him. Four days later Officer W. R. Rigdon filed an application for examination with the district court in Reno, seeking Cole's commitment with a supporting diagnosis of "sociopathic personality" from Dr. Raymond Brown. Judge John Sexton signed the order on September 24, packing Eddie off to the state hospital at nearby Sparks, Nevada.

At Sparks, Dr. Felix Peebles recorded his initial impression of Cole as an "anti-social personality with alcoholism, with compulsion to strangle and rape pretty females." A question mark was penciled in behind the diagnosis, in Cole's file, but Dr. Peebles was unavailable for comment on the nature of his personal uncertainty.

Between the standard tests and interviews, Cole was assigned to work in the hospital laundry. He began a flirtatious relationship with a married hospital employee, now and then slipping away to meet her downtown, but the affair was never consummated. "I never went to bed with her," he wrote, "though she suggested it. I felt an urge to kill her for her infidelity, but I quit the laundry instead, before it went that far. She later sent word to the ward that she wanted to see me, but I ignored her."

On October 13 Cole was interviewed by psychiatric social worker Richard Watson. Watson noted that Eddie had "no particular plans for release at this time," recording his own diagnosis of Cole's fitness for treatment as follows:

> Our impression of Mr. Cole is that he is a highly manipulative young man who is utilizing his difficulties with the law in the past and his threats of violence upon others to find shelter when he is out of funds or ways to get what he wants. We also feel that because of this kind of insight, if it can be called that, he would not constitute a danger to himself or others because apparently he does seek assistance when he feels an urge to do harm. We also feel that he is not going to benefit substantially by any social work intervention.

Dr. Peebles agreed, and Cole was discharged ten days later as a hopeless malingerer. His release form reads:

Discharge Diagnosis:
Sociopathic personality disturbance, anti-social type, associated with alcoholism
Condition on Discharge:
The same as on admission
Prognosis:
Poor
Disposition:
He was discharged and placed on an Express Bus for Los Angeles where he was to change buses and go on to his home in San Diego, California. He was advised that should he feel the need for psychiatric follow-up to consult the mental health clinic in San Diego.

If Eddie was beyond their grasp, at least they could export the problem to another state. Within the next eight months the man who "does not constitute a danger to himself or others" claimed at least three lives.

One thing about the act of giving up: From that point on, you just don't give a damn.

NINE

Naming San Diego as his home was a strategic move on Eddie's part. He had developed a strange love-hate relationship with the city since his navy days, and at the moment it seemed perfect for his needs. "As a border town," he wrote, "it's wild and practically anything goes. Also, being in California, it's easy to get on welfare, and my record with the state hospitals qualified me for more disability." Playing the game.

On arrival, Cole briefly followed the advice of his doctors at Sparks, checking in with Traveler's Aid for the address of the community mental health clinic. Even so, he was covering his tracks. By the time Eddie spoke to psychiatric social worker Mary Pierce, on October 26, his assault on Virginia Rowden had become a case of "armed robbery with intent to kill," no mention whatsoever of his homicidal/necrophilic fantasies. Pierce's notes record that Cole showed up for crisis group sessions on October 27 and 28 before dropping out.

Along with his applications for welfare and state disability, Eddie also went shopping for a new vocational training program. Heavy equipment was fine, except that California's operating engineers had a two-year waiting list for new positions, making Cole unemployable. Without a job, his small room at the Palm Hotel costing a hundred dollars a month, he was suddenly hard-up for cash, unable to spend his usual twelve to eighteen hours a day in saloons.

Clearly, something had to give.

On a whim, Cole signed up for training as a nurse's aide. The six-month course featured practical experience in local convalescent homes, working with the elderly, and while Eddie breezed through the academics, he was repulsed by the way some nurses and orderlies treated their charges.

"Have you ever seen a patient eaten up with bed sores because someone didn't care enough to do their job?" he wrote. "And the verbal abuse was something else. I often thought of waylaying one of those nurses in the parking lot, killing her for the old folks, but unfortunately, our classes were in the daytime."

Eddie's chief instructor was a Mrs. Baker, kindly, the maternal type. She noted Cole's financial situation and persuaded him to ditch the Palm Hotel, moving into the large house she and her husband shared in a nearby housing area. Other students lived with the Bakers from time to time, but rent was a forbidden subject, even when the welfare checks arrived and Eddie offered to pay his own way.

At Christmas Mrs. Baker threw a party for her students with "booze galore," as Cole recalled it, a chance for the hardworking team to unwind. Everyone was fairly drunk by the time a half dozen of Eddie's classmates got together, approaching one of the new recruits and telling her that Eddie was her "Christmas present." With a few drinks under his belt, Cole got into the spirit of the game, and the young woman stayed behind when the others left for home or staggered off to bed. They wound up naked on the floor, with Eddie showing her his bedside manner, but the woman's conscience caught up with her in the small hours of the morning, and she tiptoed into Mrs. Baker's room, stark naked, asking for a ride before her parents or her fiancé got wise.

So much for mistletoe.

Administrators at the nursing school found out about the Christmas party, letting Mrs. Baker go on a charge of fraternizing with her students. Already chafing at the daily grind, Cole joined a number of his classmates in a walkout, but their protest failed and Mrs. Baker lost her bid for reinstatement in the courts. Meanwhile, Eddie's new career went down the tube, but if it worried him at all, he kept it to himself.

Around the same time, in mid-January, Cole's disability kicked in with back payments for the past eight weeks. Mrs. Baker still refused his offer of rent, and Eddie soon moved out of her house, driven by a mixture of embarrassment at his own "freeloading" and an increasing desire to be on his own, without so many prying eyes around.

"My urges were stronger than ever," he recalled, "but I wasn't concerned about it anymore. I just said to hell with it and waited to see what would happen."

From the Bakers', Eddie started sleeping in a different motel each night, sometimes staying over with the women he met in bars. For once, money was no problem. In addition to his disability, Cole worked a variation on his other favorite con, writing worthless checks to purchase painting supplies, returning them a day later for cash refunds. "Over a period of months," he said, "I pulled this scam on most of the paint stores in San Diego County. With my monthly checks and the paint trick, I supported myself and had plenty of drinking money on the side."

Cole still had his white nurse's uniform, and he soon promoted himself with a plastic name tag reading C. EDWARD COLE, R.N. SHARPE HOSPITAL. To amuse himself, he started dropping by various hospitals on the night shift, mingling with staff and patients alike. Few questions were asked, and if a head nurse pressed too hard, it was a simple thing to say that he was visiting a friend. Meanwhile, he had a brief sensation of acceptance and belonging ...plus a sly delight in putting one over on The System.

Drinking remained the focal point of Cole's life, and he sometimes wore his nurse's uniform to local bars, a guaranteed icebreaker for curious women. One of his favorite watering holes was a tavern on Market Street, where he became acquainted with a female bartender named ZeZe. ZeZe talked a lot about her Russian heritage, but she was living with a black man. Cole detested her for violating the taboo of race, but he would never let it show. Instead, he acted like a friend, and ZeZe often found him waiting for her when she came to open up the bar. An average day for Eddie, when he wasn't hustling paint, would find him planted on a bar stool, killing time with ZeZe, sipping beer.

One morning, early, Cole and ZeZe had the tavern to themselves, no customers in sight. The woman was complaining of a stiffness in her back and shoulders, Eddie offering to help. A nurse knows special tricks. With ZeZe seated at the bar, he stood behind her, starting with a slow subscapular massage, working his way up to the knotted trapezius muscles. Fingers encircling her neck from behind.

"The thing I remember most is her swallowing hard," Cole recalled. "I would have given anything to see her face."

Before his hands could tighten on her throat, the door flapped open, spilling daylight into gloom, and a foxy redhead friend of ZeZe's interrupted Eddie's plan. A glance exchanged between the women made Cole wonder whether he had blown the game.

"Even then," he wrote later, "some people knew what I was capable of, like that redhead, but they kept it to themselves."

A few nights later Cole was partying with ZeZe and a couple dozen others at a nearby house. The redhead was among them, looking fine and matching Eddie drink for drink. When the party broke up,

Eddie walked her home, the woman drunk enough to ask him in. They wound up on the bed, wet kisses, fumbling with buttons, but the redhead drifted off, and when his efforts to rouse her failed, Eddie caught some Zs himself.

He woke in darkness, no one on the bed beside him. Sudden apprehension as he searched the flat and found the redhead hiding in a closet, trembling as he dragged her out and back to bed. He had her blouse and bra off, working on her slacks, before she struggled free and ducked into the bathroom, locked the door behind her.

Flimsy doors and locks, a place like that, but Eddie let it go. Too many people saw them leave the party, and she had no solid grounds for a complaint to the police. Not yet. He let it go and walked back to his car, content to hunt another day.

"The funny thing about it," Eddie said, "is that I'm sure those girls discussed the incident and were afraid, to some extent, but nothing was ever said, and I still kept hanging around the bar."

In fact, his major trouble came when Eddie *left* the bars. On May 4, 1971, he was arrested for driving under the influence and spent the night in jail. Three days later he was stopped again, same charge, but this time he sobered up in time for an early evening release.

No sweat. The night was young.

He suited up and went to find out where the action was.

*****

Friday night, May 7. Eddie drives without direction through a drizzling rain. His visit to a Chula Vista hospital has left him restless, thirsty. Rolling east on El Cajon Boulevard, he spots a friendly-looking bar and stops, rain plastering his hair down as he makes his way inside.

The place is crowded, but he finds an empty stool at one end of the bar. His uniform invites the standard questions, and he spins a web of bullshit, making it up as he goes along. The tavern's owner is a slim brunette named Essie Buck, all friendly smiles as she engages Cole in conversation, makes him feel at home.

As luck would have it, he has walked into the middle of a birthday party. Essie's mother is the guest of honor, and the celebrants are just about to take it on the road. They have a list of other bars they want to hit before the mandatory closing time. Would Eddie care to tag along?

He would.

Still raining as they leave the tavern, bodies piling into cars. By this time, Cole and Essie Buck are "pretty thick," and she agrees to ride with him. Two hours, running into three, and pretty soon the bars all start to look alike. Cole laughs at jokes the third and fourth time they are told. Each time the boozy caravan moves on, it seems that Essie slides a little closer to him, in the car.

So far, so good.

Their third or fourth stop of the evening, Essie and her mother start to argue. Cole has no idea what it's about, nor does he give a damn. He doesn't bitch when Essie tells him that she wants to leave, find someplace they can be alone and get to know each other better.

Touchdown.

Driving aimlessly on rain-slick streets, with Essie dozing in the car. He finds a quiet place to park and kills the engine, waking her with kisses. She responds, a little groggy at the start, but warming up as Eddie fondles her, his busy hands at work.

And suddenly they close around her throat. No fight to speak of as he chokes her unconscious, pushing her back on the seat. Forget about the niceties of buttons, clasps, and zippers, Eddie tearing at her clothes, excited by the sound of ripping fabric. Recoiling, his erection wilting, when he finds that she has soiled herself.

"I ripped her clothes off more to humiliate her than anything else," he recalls from a distance of years. "I remember thinking that women like to go around exposing themselves, and she was damn sure going to be exposed. If there was any thought of rape, it was quickly forgotten because of the fecal matter."

Essie wakes up naked, gagging on the sharp pain in her throat. It takes a moment to regain the power of speech.

"Just let me up," she says, perhaps believing he has raped her. "I won't tell."

Cole smiles. "I know you won't."

No holding back this time as Eddie strangles her by hand. She struggles briefly, feeble blows against his ribs, but alcohol and oxygen starvation rob the woman of her strength. When Cole releases her the second time, he knows that she is dead.

Gone off to meet Duane in hell.

Removing Essie from the front seat to the trunk is not the cake walk he imagines, in his drunken state. Dead weight and flaccid muscles don't cooperate. He waltzes her around the car and dumps her in the trunk, headfirst, folding pale legs in behind her, staring for a moment, finally lowering the lid.

Her clothes make handy rags for cleaning up the mess and wiping fingerprints away. When he is finished, Eddie drops them in a roadside ditch, half-filled with muddy water. Essie's purse gives up a hundred dollars, and he leaves it in a Dumpster, in the shadow of an all-night market. Driving with the windows down, airing out her stench. He finds a cheap motel, checks in, and goes to sleep, her body curled up in the trunk.

Next morning Eddie has to verify his dream. A cautious look inside the trunk, his conquest waiting for him, deathly pale. He touches her, the flesh like wax. Reality hits home.

"How did I feel? The night before, I felt nothing— not elation, guilt, or any of the feelings thought to appease someone like me. Just cold nothing. In the morning, it was just the same, except for concern over what I should do with the body."

He spends the day drinking at a bar on Thirtieth Street, near Balboa Park, stepping out several times to visit Essie in the trunk. When the tavern closes at 2:00 A.M., he takes to the freeways, following 1-15 north to the cutoff for Poway, winding his way through foothills, past the Scripps Miramar Ranch. An open field near a school catches his eye, and he follows a narrow dirt road, bouncing over ruts and chuckholes until his headlights pick out a jumble of rocks on his left.

He parks, sitting in the darkness for a moment with the engine ticking as it cools. At last, almost reluctantly, he wrestles Essie from the trunk and drags her by the arms, her heels and buttocks scraping on the ground. He wedges her between two boulders, going back to fetch a six-pack from the car.

They sit together for a while, Cole sipping beer and breathing in the night.

He has reason to celebrate.

It is Sunday, May 9. His thirty-third birthday.

*****

Silent Rage

Midmorning Sunday, the corpse was spotted by a young boy cycling past the scene. He spent a moment staring, choked on something bitter in his throat, and pedaled off to summon help. A sheriff's deputy responded, saw enough to verify the boy's report, and placed the call to Homicide.

In May 1971 Robert Ring was the chief homicide investigator for the San Diego County sheriff's office. Driving out to Poway on a D.B. call was not his notion of a perfect Sunday morning, but it came with the job. Ring followed his directions, homed in on the waiting squad cars north of Garden Road, and took a walk.

The D.B. was a nude Caucasian female, lying on her side between two bulky stones. Ring had a crime photographer shoot snapshots of the body and the scene at large before he touched the corpse. Dark blotches of lividity were visible along the woman's left side, even though she now lay on her right. It was enough to tell Ring that she had died and lain elsewhere, resting long enough on her left side for the blood to settle and congeal. Abrasions on her buttocks seemed to match faint drag marks on the muddy ground, leading back to the adjacent road where tire tracks were found and photographed.

As far as ID went, Ring didn't have a clue. It was apparent that the woman had been moved, but there were no wounds visible, no clear signs of a struggle at the scene. Ring needed more, before he wrote it up as homicide.

Chief Deputy Coroner David Stark was no help, in that regard. His autopsy on the "Jane Doe" corpse revealed no signs of trauma, nothing to suggest a sexual assault, despite the missing clothes. The woman had been legally drunk when she died, but her blood alcohol reading of .13 was far from lethal. In short, the evidence was inconclusive, nothing you could build a case on.

Ring checked the recent missing persons reports and came up with a sheet on Essie Louise Buck, age thirty-nine. It was a lucky break in a county where many corpses remain forever nameless, and relatives identified Buck that afternoon. A background check revealed that Essie was last seen alive on the night of May 7, leaving a Santee tavern with a male nurse named C. Edward Cole, whose name tag linked him to Sharpe Memorial Hospital. Of course, no one at Sharpe had ever heard of Cole, nor was he listed in the various directories for

San Diego County.

Zip.

One thing a homicide detective quickly learns in southern California, dead-end cases don't monopolize your time. With jealous lovers, gang wars, trigger-happy stickup artists, cults, and crazies on the loose, you work the freshest leads available and let the rest chill out. If Ring's elusive suspect ever surfaced, fine. If not, he had himself a naked drunk, no evidence of homicidal violence that a medical examiner could find.

Priorities.

The beat goes on.

*****

Time slipped away, with Eddie half expecting the police to track him down. He clipped a small article on Essie Buck from the May 11 Saw *Diego Union,* noting that she left six children scattered in various foster homes. Good riddance. No suspects were named, and authorities said further tests were needed to determine cause of death. A trick, perhaps.

Or maybe not.

No follow-ups, and after two weeks Eddie let himself relax a little. Acting out his darkest fantasy did nothing to relieve the pressure that he felt inside; if anything, it served to whet his appetite. Without a conscious effort, he began to hunt again.

The Lady Luck, on Fourth Street, lived up to its name. His first night at the bar, he met a blonde named Wilma. No last name, a "West Pac widow." stranded while her navy husband spent a six-month tour at sea. "She wasn't exactly a beauty," Cole recalled, "but no guy would kick her out of bed, either." They hit it off right away, shooting some pool, Eddie playing big spender and buying the drinks. He listened to the woman talk about her loneliness and read between the whines.

Wilma lived in National City, midway between San Diego and Chula Vista, to the south. If Eddie had a car, she knew a little place much closer to her house. Nice atmosphere, good booze, and after that . . .

"Of course, I'd already decided to kill her," Cole said. "All I lacked was the place."

He follows her directions to the Western Club, in National City, Wilma sitting close beside him all the way, a warm hand on his thigh.

Silent Rage

The lot is dark and nearly empty when they get there, Eddie parking in the shadows, taking Wilma in his arms and kissing her. She squirms against him, stroking Eddie through his slacks and bringing him erect, stiff nipples poking through the fabric of her bra and blouse. Her eyes are misty as he strokes her face, then wide with shock as Eddie locks his hands around her neck.

Again, no struggle, Eddie wondering if drunken bitches really *want* to die. If so, she gets her wish, Cole hanging on and squeezing furiously even when his fingers start to cramp, relenting only when her bowels let go and fill the car with rancid gas. No heartbeat when he opens up her blouse and tugs her bra down, fondling her naked breasts.

It took a while for Eddie to unwind, rebuttoning her blouse and driving to an isolated spot across I-5. He left her clothes on, crammed her in the trunk, and drove until he reached a nearby residential area. Exhausted by his work, he parked against the curb, between two other cars, and sacked out on the seat.

Awake at dawn, with sunlight in his eyes, he killed time looking for an army-surplus store and waiting for the place to open up for business. Eddie bought himself a folding shovel, left it in the car, and spent the daylight hours in a Chula Vista tavern, sitting near a window so that he could watch his vehicle. The dead blonde wasn't going anywhere, but you can never be too cautious, as a rule.

At nightfall, Eddie bought two six-packs for the road and drove to San Ysidro, on the Mexican border, following a narrow dirt track into the foothills north of town. He found an isolated point where he could spot approaching headlights from a good half mile, and started digging. It was grunt work, scratching out a grave in rocky soil, but Cole kept at it, pausing now and then to kill a beer. When he was finished, Wilma safely planted in the ground, he finished off the second six-pack in a toast to his success. No loose ends for the cops to play with, this time.

Driving off, it struck him that he didn't even know the blonde's last name.

Tough shit.

*****

A week later Eddie was back at the Western Club, and this time he made it inside. Cruising for West Pac widows. The number of unescorted women confirmed Wilma's description of the bar as a favorite hangout for navy wives.

A happy-hour hunting ground.

When Eddie stopped to think about it, in his sober moments, it was clear what he was doing. Stalking drunken, faithless sluts who conjured images of Vesta in his mind. Or Billy, take your pick. The names and faces changed, but the duplicity of scheming, cheating females was a constant in the universe. It never failed.

That night he drank and danced with several women, picking out a young one who appealed to him, hanging back and watching her get soused with her friends. At length, the others rose to leave, but Eddie's mark refused to join them. As they left, Cole heard a parting reference to a man who would be mad as hell when he found out.

"I could only guess at what this meant," Cole said, "but I drew my own conclusion that she was playing around on her old man."

He made his move, all smiles, the young woman grateful for someone to talk to. Someone handsome and charming, at that. A few more drinks, and there was no resistance when he said that maybe they should slip away and find a quiet place to be alone.

Outside, a sudden flash of déjà vu. Same car, same parking lot. He doesn't know the woman's name and doesn't give a damn. She rubs against him, walking to his car, and Eddie feels the old familiar need take over. Never mind a drive. He guides her into the back seat, shuts the door behind him, anonymous lovers stripping in haste.

Her skin is flushed with alcohol and passion, slick with sweat. She moves beneath him, moaning, reaching for him, guiding Eddie home. He sucks her nipples, feeling secret muscles clench around his cock, a velvet vise that milks him dry. They come together— close enough, at any rate, in the confusion of the moment—and she clings to Eddie like a drowning woman afterward, until the sheer heat of their friction forces them to separate.

They smoke in silence, idle fingers teasing, Eddie's playmate thinking that a second helping wouldn't be so bad. He interrupts her train of thought.

"I guess you're married, huh?"

A boozy giggle. "Yeah, for what it's worth."

Case closed.

She starts to rise, but Eddie gets there first, strong hands on her shoulders, pushing her back on the seat. He strokes her firm, young breasts, feeling her nipples respond to his touch. The woman smiles, relaxing. Ready.

Cole leans into it, finding his grip on her throat and pinning her down with his weight as he starts to squeeze. Too late she understands, wide-eyed and gurgling underneath him, thrusting with her pelvis in a desperate parody of intercourse. Cole has the leverage on his side, and there is no way she can throw him off.

No way at all.

A long time later, finished with her, Eddie rolled her body to the floorboard, dressed himself, and drove across I-5 to the same spot he had parked with Wilma's body. Falling into a routine. The latest victim took her place in Eddie's trunk, her clothing tossed in almost as an afterthought.

In his motel room Eddie found it difficult to sleep. He played the latest killing over in his mind repeatedly, stroking himself to climax several times as he pictured the naked woman pinned beneath him, dying, going limp. "I wished I had the body with me," he recalled. A mental note.

Good times.

Next morning he retraced his steps from Wilma's murder. Drinking at the same bar in Chula Vista till sundown, with six-packs to go after dark. Back to San Ysidro, with his headlights boring through the night like dragon's eyes. Another sweaty night of digging, planting, covering his tracks.

At this rate, Eddie thought, the cops would need a fucking miracle to run him down.

*****

They almost got it on June 1, 1971. Cole was boozing on Broadway, letting the good times roll, when he met a young woman who called herself Kitten. A long night of barhopping ensued, before they wound up parked on the grass of a neighborhood baseball field. Kitten was passed out in the car, Eddie massaging her slender neck, considering the possibilities. On a whim, he let her live, firing up the engine and setting off in search of a motel.

An illegal turn on El Cajon Boulevard did the trick, Eddie too drunk to notice the black-and-white in his rearview mirror. Colored lights flashing as he pulled to the curb with a veteran drunk's exaggerated caution.

Busted.

It was his third DUI in a month, and Eddie didn't even have a driver's license. The deputies sent Kitten home in a taxi, and Cole never saw her again. If she reads this account, she will know how close she came to death that night.

As for Cole, it meant another trip to county jail. Outstanding warrants caught up with him this time, and he was sentenced to serve thirty days. Before his time was up, investigators made him for the paint scam, and he was formally charged with issuing fraudulent checks on June 30. It would take a couple of weeks to arrange for his trial, but Eddie wasn't going anywhere without bail money.

And in the meantime, word of his arrest got back to Robert Ring.

The homicide detective came to visit Eddie on July 14. Cole listened to the recitation of his civil rights and waived them voluntarily. Ring told him what they had: a woman, now deceased, last seen with Eddie when they left a bar together, on a Friday night in May.

Cole tried to shrug it off, ad-libbing. Sure, he'd spent some time with Essie Buck that night, but they had separated once they left the bar. She drove away with friends, and Eddie spent the night alone, in a motel.

Ring shook his head. No good. The friends in question disagreed with Cole, across the board. The punch line came when Ring produced a wrinkled clipping from the *Union,* found in Eddie's wallet when they booked him into jail, describing the discovery of Essie's corpse.

Cole slumped and dropped his gaze. "I just panicked," he said. "Okay, I'll tell you what happened."

In the new version Cole and Essie Buck reached the motel together, sharing a room for the night. They made love in the bed, fell asleep kissing-close. In the morning, when Eddie awoke, he found the woman dead beside him, cause unknown. Blind panic made him stuff her body in the trunk and drive around all day, until he finally dumped her after dark.

"It was farfetched," he wrote in 1985, "but Ring bought it. The only pointed thing he asked me, was I sure I didn't smother her with a pillow."

Cole denied it, and the homicide investigator left him. Eddie kept expecting Ring to show up with a murder warrant any day, but thirteen years would pass before they met again.

Conviction for check fraud was a foregone conclusion, and Eddie was sentenced to the maximum one-year term for a misdemeanor, transferred to the La Cima "honor farm" on July 23. He had sunshine and exercise, a chance to dry out, with occasional stints as a fire fighter that paid him thirty cents an hour.

Security at La Cima was almost nonexistent. "I could have escaped anytime, simply by walking away," he recalled, "but I figured what the hell, why bother?"

It was easy time, all things considered, but the wages sucked. Thirty cents an hour is chump change, and the county doesn't offer any gate money to parolees. When Cole was discharged, late in March, he hit the street with nearly empty pockets and a thirst that wouldn't quit.

No matter.

He was headed back to San Diego like a homing vulture.

Seeking prey.

TEN

SAN DIEGO ALMOST *FELT* LIKE HOME, by now. Returning with his pockets empty should have seen a shock, but Eddie wasn't worried. He had Mends in town, and he would soon be back on welfare, pending resumption of his state disability payments. On the side, he had a new idea, acquired from watching television ads for American Express traveler's checks. Two hundred dollars of government money made his first purchase, at a local bank, and he returned days later to report the checks lost, turning in his receipt for replacements of equal value.

"Over a short period," Cole wrote, "I did this to every company in San Diego that sold traveler's checks. I lived high on the hog for a long time, with several girls."

Like Josie, a slender redhead who "really liked to get it on."

Or Shelly the barmaid, who "couldn't get enough."

One of his favorites, Brandy, was a go-go dancer at a club on Broadway. They drank together frequently, and Cole slept over on occasion, when he had no place to stay. One evening, before a round of barhopping, they stopped by Brandy's apartment with a girlfriend who lived next door, the women splitting up to change clothes for a night on the town. Cole followed Brandy to her bedroom, watching as she stripped to bra and panties, seated at the vanity to fix her makeup.

"Coming up behind her, I began massaging her shoulders," Eddie recalled, "and she leaned her head back. In the mirror I could see her throat and larynx, with the veins on either side. It looked so soft and white, I found my hands encircling her neck. Her eyes were closed at first, and she was smiling, but then her eyes opened wide, her expression becoming one of fear."

And something clicked in Eddie's mind, the knowledge that he couldn't stop with Brandy, but would have to kill her girlfriend, too. How many others knew that he was with the girls that night?

Bad timing.

With a playful laugh, he mussed her hair, stepped back a pace. Brandy took a moment to relax, finally working up a smile.

"You kidder."

Essie Buck had taught him something, helping Cole absorb an urban predator's most crucial lesson: Leave no witnesses and break the chain of evidence by stalking strangers when you can.

It was a rule that he would violate on only one occasion, in the years to come.

*****

He needs a fix. The drive to San Ysidro gives him time to think it through. No special target, that would spoil the game, but he can visualize the kill. He wonders if the bitch will fight him, this time, or submit without a whimper like the others.

Eddie spots a Mexican restaurant and steps in from the darkness, waving the hostess off, making his way to the bar. A couple waiting for their table, sipping margaritas by candlelight. The bartender rinsing glasses, killing time. At the far end of the bar, two young women, Latinos, drinking wine and whispering to one another in Spanish. He pegs them as wetbacks, soaking up some courage for the road before they move on to the sweatshops in Los Angeles or the migrant camps, farther north.

The kind nobody is about to miss.

He takes a seat nearby and orders beer. Dos Equis, getting in the spirit of the game. He does not understand a word the two young women say, but Eddie only needs a moment to decide that they are drunk, or getting there. He bides his time before intruding on the conversation, making sure his smile is firmly fixed in place.

Does either one of them speak English?

Si. A little.

Nature takes its course, from there. Cole introduces himself, lets their names go in one ear and out the other. Useless information. Barroom small talk leading anywhere three healthy, consenting adults want it to go. He doesn't mind their broken English, since he isn't really listening. The biggest part of picking out a victim is the way she *feels,* vibrations telling Eddie everything he has to know about a woman's character, her hopes and dreams. He rates these two as zeros on the scale of human worth.

He buys the next round, and the next, collecting points for generosity. The two young women don't mind drinking up a stranger's money, if he treats them right. There may be other ways to tap his bankroll, if they use their charms to good effect.

The casual conversation turns flirtatious. Eddie doesn't mind. He knows what they are looking for, the same thing women always want, but they are in for a surprise. He is prepared when one of them inquires about a ride.

"They wanted me to take them somewhere," Eddie tells a prosecutor, twelve years later, "so I took them to their deaths."

His passengers are hazy on geography, but Eddie has a quiet place in mind. The foothills north of San Ysidro have become his private cemetery, no complaints so far. He has an army-surplus folding shovel in the trunk and time to kill. The hills and gullies all resemble one another in the glare of headlights, but precision doesn't matter when you have the whole wide world to choose from.

Take it as it comes.

He parks just off the shoulder of a narrow, unpaved road and steps out into darkness with the women following. A desert evening, starlight you can read by. Eddie takes a six-pack from the car and cracks a cold one, passing it around.

One of the women whispers something to her friend, embarrassed, moving off into the shadows to relieve herself. Cole recognizes opportunity and does not leave it standing on the threshold. Reaching back inside the car, he finds his trusty hammer underneath the driver's seat.

"You have a good view of the city lights from here," he tells her, pointing north.

"I see."

She has her back turned. Perfect. Stepping up behind her with his arm cocked, making sure to use the hammer's claw for maximum effect. Cole puts his weight behind it, startled at how easily the hooked steel penetrates her skull and drives the woman to her knees. A muffled grunt. She drops the beer can, pale suds hissing into foam on contact with the earth.

He jerks the hammer free and lets the woman topple forward on her face, prepared to strike again if necessary. Tremors ripple through her body, fingers clenching into helpless fists. The dark stain spreading on her slacks tells Eddie everything he has to know.

One down.

Another moment, and he hears her girlfriend coming back. Cole drops the hammer, stepping out to meet her on the roadway, empty-handed. She is smiling as she greets him, moving past him toward the car. The woman has perhaps a heartbeat left to wonder where her friend has gone, the body still concealed, before Cole's fingers lock around her windpipe from behind.

She struggles, this one, but the alcohol helps Eddie take her down. She tries to reach him, clawing with her fingernails, but Eddie plants a knee between her shoulder blades and pins her, choking off her wind, maintaining pressure even when his hands begin to cramp and she lies silent, still.

A double-header.

Twice the work, when it is time to dig the graves, but Eddie takes his time. He has all night, with beer to keep him going when fatigue sets in. He does not strip the bodies or molest them, this time, having gotten what he needs. The excavation takes him hours, sweating in the dusty dark, but Eddie finally gets it done.

"I was exhausted by the time I finished," he recalls, from prison. "I decided it was too much work, and I would never bury girls again."

A hunter needs his strength.

*****

Near the end of May, Cole was picked up on another drunk-driving charge, sentenced to thirty days in jail. He served his time as a trusty, supervising the drunk tank, making friends with an inmate named Russell. Eddie still had a few days to serve when the time came for Russell's release, but he took a chance and asked if they could be discharged together. His keepers agreed, and the two men were released on Friday afternoon, June 23.

Russell's wife was waiting for him with a car, and Eddie accepted his new friend's offer of a place to spend the night. One thing led to another, with beer and wine blurring the details, and Cole wound up staying the weekend in Russell's apartment, sleeping on the couch. Of course, he meant to find himself a place, but there was always time. A man would be a fool to piss away free room and board.

Late Sunday night, once Russell and his wife had gone to bed, Cole sat up drinking by himself. He felt a restless need to *move,* go somewhere, anywhere. Instead of calming Eddie down, the cheap wine seemed to fuel a pent-up anger, burning in his gut.

"I just went wild, like an animal," he remembered, "jumping down from the second-floor balcony, wandering in and out of different people's apartments. I don't recall exactly what I did, it's really a fog, but I must have scared someone and the police were called, with a crowd turning out to watch my arrest in front of the complex."

In custody, Cole's disorderly conduct charges were upgraded to criminal contempt on the old warrant for fraudulent checks, and he was sentenced to six months at the Viejas "honor farm." Before his transfer, Eddie charmed redheaded Josie into collecting his disability payments while he was gone, letting her believe the money was earmarked for their future wedding.

One more chance to teach a scheming female how it feels.

After two months at Viejas Eddie was cleared for transfer to the county's work furlough center in downtown San Diego. "The next day," he recalled, "I went out on the pretext of seeking a job, but work was the furthest thing from my mind."

Instead, he made connections with a friend and got a ride to El Cajon, where Josie worked as a live-in nurse. She was surprised to see him, swapping his checks for a kiss and a promise that he would call her as soon as he got settled in somewhere.

"Poor Josie," Cole would write from prison. "I never saw her again, and she never knew just how lucky she was."

Another one who got away.

*****

Eddie moved into a cheap skid-row apartment, next door to a drinking buddy who knew he was on the lam. An escape warrant was issued, but police weren't breaking their necks to track down a chronic drunk driver and penny-ante con man. The disability checks kept coming, but nobody made the connection, and Cole fell back into his normal routine, holding out enough money for rent and fast food, blowing the rest on liquor.

One boozy night he came home reeling, passed out on the bed without extinguishing his cigarette, and set the sheets on fire. The heat and smoke roused Eddie in the nick of time, but he was shaky on his feet, disoriented, gagging. Somebody had played a rotten trick on him and moved the door. He couldn't breathe, goddammit, even crawling on his hands and knees the way they show you on TV. The room was spinning, blacking out.

His next-door neighbor smelled the smoke and kicked the door in, dragging Eddie out into the hall, then going back to fight the smoky blaze. He put it out, somehow, and no one else on Eddie's floor was swift enough to call the fire department, so he didn't have to deal with any uniforms that night.

Back in his room, Cole rummaged through the dresser where he kept his bankroll, checking twice before he satisfied himself the cash was gone. He had the suspects narrowed down to one, his next-door savior, but an angry scene would only piss the neighbor off. If he got mad enough, the greedy little shit might drop a dime, put Eddie back inside.

No choice, then. With the damage to his flat, the landlord on his case, and nothing but the money in his pocket, Eddie hit the bricks. He spent his last few dollars at a bar and wound up at the City Rescue Mission, sleeping with the bums. Each evening, residents and walk-in candidates for supper had to line up on the sidewalk, wait their turns at serving time, and Eddie kept his face averted as the black-and-whites rolled by.

The mission was a dreary place, all things considered, and it didn't take Cole long to tire of snoring winos in the common room they shared at night. He started shopping for alternatives and hit on the Salvation Army, which was hiring helpers for the pickup routes. The job paid minimum wage, plus room and board, sometimes an off-the-record kickback from his driver if they made a decent haul. Hush money, when the driver had a little something going on the side, like stealing items off the truck and selling them himself. Cole proved himself an able worker, silent as the Sphinx where indiscretions were concerned, and he was soon promoted to a driver's slot. He lacked only one thing, and with his supervisor prodding him, Cole finally registered for his first driver's license, at age thirty-four.

The Salvation Army preaches abstinence from alcohol, but Eddie never got the message. Most days, after work, he hung out with his helper and some other drivers at the Copper Room, a bar close by their lodgings. There, he met a blond barmaid named Diana Pashal, her face familiar from the nights he used to watch her pass the rescue mission, on her way to work. They got acquainted, friendly shifting into touchy-feely over time, and one night Diana invited him back to the small apartment she shared with her mother, Joyce. Cole was drunk enough to forget most of what happened in bed, their first time, but he woke up feeling halfway decent, to the smell of coffee on the stove. Joyce was annoyed at having a strange man at the breakfast table, but Cole later smoothed things over with a round of boilermakers at the Copper Room, and Joyce became a friend of sorts.

Eddie and Diana began "going together officially" that day, and he soon moved into her apartment, but the arrangement never cramped Cole's style. Throughout his first month with Diana, he was simultaneously bedding yet another waitress, hoping the two women would not run into each other. He never knew which one of them passed on the virus, but a horn-shaped growth appeared on Eddie's penis, growing larger by the day. Doctors at San Diego Community Hospital called it a "devil's horn," and they were interested enough to snap some photos for posterity before they wheeled the laser out and trimmed Cole back to normal size.

Unfortunately, most of Eddie's problems could not be so easily erased.

On January 15, 1973, Cole was headed for work when he passed a police car, the officers noting his effort to cover his face. They pulled him over on suspicion, ran a check, and found the open warrant charging Eddie with escape from custody. This time, his term was six months in the county jail, where Eddie worked with the chaplain and performed odd jobs, like passing out glasses to nearsighted inmates.

Diana came to visit Eddie several times, but she was always drunk. By this time, Cole had her pegged for an alcoholic, her mother working through a string of husbands and near-miss fiancés. He felt a certain pity for Diana, sympathizing with the life that she had led, but ugly memories of Billy Whitworth and his mother colored all of Eddie's feelings with contempt.

The latter part of April Eddie wrote a letter to his trial judge, asking for a discharge on his birthday, and the judge agreed. Diana had a new apartment, one flight up from a saloon on Market Street, but she was not expecting Eddie for another month. He found her drinking, lapsing into tears as he embraced her. Eddie didn't need a crystal ball to know they were not tears of joy.

It took a while to pry the story out of her, another glass of wine, but finally he had it all. Diana told him that a sailor by the name of Charlie had assaulted her. They had been drinking, naturally, and when he made his move, Diana did not have the strength to fight him off. Cole had to understand that it was really rape, and not her fault at all.

Cole spread the word at all his usual hangouts: Charlie had a lesson coming, if he dared to face a man. A few nights later word came up from the saloon downstairs. Cole's man was at the bar, prepared to talk or fight, whichever was required.

Talk, first.

As Charlie ran it down, the feelings had been mutual, no force involved. Diana showed up late, shamefaced, admitting she had lied about the rape, and Eddie bought another round of drinks to wash away the taste of bitter gall.

"This bothered me for years, as you may well imagine," Eddie wrote in 1985. "It finally resulted in Diana's death."

Whatever lay ahead, Cole's anger did not stop him from proposing marriage in July. A quiet civil ceremony tied the knot, and the newlyweds moved into a four-plex on Twenty-first Street, with Joyce and her latest husband living a few blocks away. In addition to his driver's salary, Cole started swiping furniture, TVs, and choice appliances from items he collected on his route, buying his helper's silence with giveaways and cash. Some of the stolen items furnished his new apartment and Joyce's home, the rest going into a rented garage, bound for weekend swap meets in Chula Vista or National City.

Marriage changed little, in terms of Cole's life-style. After rent and basic bills, the spare money still went for liquor, with Diana drinking up more than her share. Most days, Eddie came home from work to find his wife drunk or well on the way, feeling the early pinch of domestic claustrophobia. When alcohol alone fell short of calming Eddie's nerves, he started looking for a little action on the side.

One object of desire was almost close enough to touch, a neighbor in the four-plex who was young, attractive, and a trifle careless with her window shades. The first time Eddie saw her naked, passing by outside her bathroom window, he was moved to stop and stare, but simple voyeurism didn't do the trick. A few nights later, when he knew that she was in the shower, Eddie crept around, removed a bedroom window screen, and crawled inside. He lurked beside the open bathroom door and watched her preening for the mirror, almost playing with herself, the swell of his erection taking up the slack in Eddie's jeans. When she emerged, still naked, heading for the kitchen, Eddie watched her go and took the opportunity to exit by the same route he had come.

"Of course, I had an urge to grab her from behind and strangle her," he said, years later. "I'm not sure what stopped me, possibly the close proximity of our apartments and the likelihood of something coming out in the police investigation. I was drinking, but I wasn't stupid. Anyway, I often fantasized about that night, but with a different outcome."

His second choice was Jean, a cocktail waitress at a bar where Eddie often left a portion of weekly pay. They soon got chummy, their relationship progressing from flirtation and raunchy jokes to hasty grappling on the sly. Cole's home life was degenerating through that winter, running into spring, Diana drinking more and Joyce discarding her new husband, spending too much time around the place for Eddie's taste. Jean seemed to understand, but she had standards, and she would not drop her panties for a married man ... at least not while he was living with his wife.

In July 1974, with his first anniversary coming up, Eddie made his decision. He would run away with Jean and try to find the good life in Nevada. If he missed the brass ring, what the hell. At least it would be different, something new.

His boss at the Salvation Army tried to talk him out of it, but Cole was adamant. He took his final check, went by for Jean in his convertible—a '64 Impala— and they hit the road. A stop for beer in San Bernardino, then off across the desert toward Bishop, drinking all the way. Outside of Bishop, Eddie found a cheap motel and signed in for a room.

The sex was fair, anticipation sharpening Cole's senses, but the aftermath was disappointing, waking in a sweaty snarl of sheets. "The next day, I had no further use for Jean," he recalled, "and a plan developed in my mind to kill her."

Waste not, want not.

Eddie started searching for the perfect place, drove by a wooded picnic area, and pulled into the parking lot. They took a stroll, six-packs in hand, and wound up in the shade beneath some trees, no other cars in sight. The timing seemed ideal, but Eddie hesitated, reconsidering.

"For one thing," he explained, "I had no shovel to bury her with, and if the body was ever found, it would lead right back to me. Another thing, I couldn't tell when someone else would happen by and catch me in the act." So much for serendipity.

In Washoe County Cole and Jean found living quarters at a trailer park on Highway 80, between Reno and Sparks. Jean got a job in the cafeteria at Reno's Federal Building, but the neighborhood held too many bad memories for Cole, and he was swiftly growing tired of Jean. "She was a domineering, bossy kind of woman," he recalled, "and I knew if I hung around something would happen to her, landing me in trouble."

August 23, with Jean at work, Cole robbed her jewelry box and split. Instead of leaving town directly, though, he started hitting bars in Reno, drinking up his pocket change. The officer who pulled him over smelled the liquor on his breath and filed a charge of DUI. Cole gave the stolen jewelry to a bondsman for collateral, retrieved his car keys, and was back across the California line before Jean noticed he was gone.

He took the fast route back to San Diego, 1-5 through the heart of Sacramento, Stockton, rolling south. Near Coalinga, he was stopped for driving ninety miles an hour, but he never got around to paying off the fine. It was the least of Eddie's worries, thinking of the mess that waited for him at his journey's end.

Diana met him at their favorite tavern, drunk and tearful. Everybody seemed to understand, except for Joyce, and mothers didn't count. It was a bittersweet reunion, but a few short weeks had changed some things in Eddie's world. His friends at the Salvation Army had moved on, one of them skipping town with several thousand dollars of the church's money, and a new job meant he would have had to start from scratch. Instead, he took a driver's spot with another charitable organization ...and ran into another hitch.

It turned out that his supervisor had the hots for Eddie's wife and didn't care who knew it, talking up his plans for getting her between the sheets. Cole took it for a while, but there is only so much pride a man can swallow. It was coming down to quit or kill, and Eddie finally told his boss where he could stick the job.

That night, at home, Diana readily agreed that they could use a change of scene. Las Vegas sounded good, the kind of place where you can really let your hair down, drink around the clock if you are so inclined.

Why not?

Four years in San Diego, Cole was ready for his luck to change.

He should have figured it would only go from bad to worse.

ELEVEN

COLE'S FIRST STOP IN LAS VEGAS, after renting a Cleveland Avenue apartment, was the state employment office. He registered as an ex-convict, on the theory that felons receive preferential treatment in job-hunting, to keep them from getting itchy on the street. True or false, it seemed to work, and he was sent to meet a woman named Marie, who ran the slot machine concessions out of Mr. Sy's Casino, on The Strip.

Marie was looking for a janitor, but Eddie's job had less to do with sweeping up and taking out the trash than helping her police the slots. When he was not behind a broom, Cole emptied out the one-armed bandits, trundled heavy loads back to the counting room, and dumped the coins into machines that sorted, bagged, and weighed the take. Some days, he also drove Marie out to McCarran International, where Mr. Sy's had banks of slot machines installed to catch incoming suckers first thing off the plane. On those trips Eddie was assigned to pilot an electric cart from one point to another, picking up as much as $30,000 on a busy day, escorting Marie to the airport's branch bank for deposits.

The sight of so much easy cash gave Cole ideas, but he was smart enough to bide his time and plot things out before he made a move. No rush. The slots would always be there, and new suckers were arriving every day.

Most evenings, after work, he stopped in at the Silver Slipper to drink and play keno, limiting his bets to fifteen or twenty dollars per day. Cole rarely marked a winning card, but he let Mr. Sy cover his losses, palming a roll of quarters at work on the days when he planned to go gambling. "You have to understand," he wrote, years later, "I had nothing but a drunken wife at home, so I was in no hurry to get there."

One night at the Slipper, Cole met an attractive young woman who seemed totally out of her element, no transportation and nowhere to go. Las Vegas regulars can spot the type at fifty yards: they wear a vaguely dazed expression, almost glassy-eyed, and hang around the carpet joints as if they're waiting for a long-lost friend. Unlike the stone habituals who show up wearing leather work gloves to protect their hands, refusing to be separated from a "lucky" slot machine at any cost, if it means urinating where they stand, the space cadets drift aimlessly and drop a nickel here, a quarter or a dollar there. Free liquor keeps them lubricated, snack bars keep them fed while money lasts, and they can hang around for days on end without encountering a clock.

Cole sized the new arrival up at once. Dark hair to match her sweater, slacks just tight enough to emphasize lean thighs and sculpted buttocks.

Nice.

They drank together for a while, made small talk, Eddie finally asking her if she could use a lift. Perhaps downtown? The woman shrugged, agreeable to anything, and Eddie walked her to his car. Instead of pulling into traffic, though, he drove around behind the Silver Slipper, to a parking lot in back. The woman offered no resistance as he parked, slid closer, took her in his arms. No one around as Cole began to kiss her, fondling her breasts beneath the sweater. Her response was tepid, but she did not try to fight him off.

Cole thought of strangling her, but there was something in the woman's manner that dissuaded him. Instead, he backed off, gave her twenty dollars and a ride downtown, to the Nevada Club. Another pit stop on the road to nowhere.

"To this day," Cole said, "I don't know why I didn't kill her. The time and place were right. At one point, kissing her, I even had my left hand on her throat. Maybe it was something akin to compassion."

At home that night, as most nights, Diana was passed out when Eddie came in. Her drinking continued to grate on Cole's nerves, despite his own addiction to alcohol, offering daily reminders of Vesta and Billy, rubbing his nose in habitual failure as a husband and a man. When she was conscious, bitter arguments ensued, Diana lashing out at Cole with kitchen knives on more than one occasion, Eddie grappling to disarm her and administer a pointless beating. In a rare moment of peace, Cole bought a pup to keep Diana company—a husky-German shepherd mix named King— despite the fact that they were living in a no-pets building. As it was, King simply wound up bearing witness to the skirmishes in their domestic war.

They had no social life to speak of, nothing in the way of friends, but Eddie liked to venture off on weekend fishing trips from time to time, driving as far as Yuma, Arizona, in his search for catfish and trout. He always tried to leave Diana in Las Vegas when he hit the road, but she insisted on tagging along, more often drunk than sober. Cole remembered one occasion, fishing on the Colorado River north of Yuma, when the desert sun was bright and hot, Diana begging for a chance to cool off in the water. Eddie tried to put her off, explaining all about the river's deadly undertow, but over time her nagging wore him down. When she had stripped down to her bathing suit, Cole tied a rope around her waist, played out the line, Diana splashing in the current like a giddy child.

"I was pissed off at her for screwing up my fishing," Eddie wrote, "and I thought how easy it would be to let go of the rope, just drown her 'accidentally.' "

He managed to restrain himself, but it was only a reprieve.

One morning, after yet another screaming free-for-all, Cole decided enough was enough. He left the apartment with no intention of returning, took King with him, not trusting Diana to care for a three-month-old pup on her own. He would need cash for the road, but that was no problem for Eddie.

It was airport day.

As usual, he drove Marie out to McCarran International, on Paradise. Inside the terminal he dropped her at a bank of slots close by the baggage carousels and drove his cart along the concourse, hitting several other pickup points. Instead of going back to join Marie and drive her to the bank, however, Eddie motored past the ticket counters, toward an exit facing on the airport parking lot.

Ahead of him, he spotted a policeman sauntering along the concourse, killing time. Cole parked his cart, unlocked the cash box, and began to stuff his pockets full of folding green. He left the heavy trays of silver dollars, too conspicuous for any kind of rapid getaway.

Outside, he kept expecting someone to pursue him, but he made it to his car without a challenge. Driving north on Paradise, he traveled half a mile before his thirst won over caution, and he found himself a quiet bar on Hacienda Avenue. Before he went inside, Cole counted out his loot, a little over seven hundred dollars. Chicken feed, but it had seemed like more with a patrolman breathing down his neck. Still, it was better than nothing. A traveling stake.

He hung around the bar till sundown, calculating that police would stop by his apartment first, then start to check the major highways out of town. Avoiding busy 1-15, he drove through Henderson and Boulder City, catching Highway 95 and winding up in Needles, California, where he checked into a small motel. The Colorado River lay a short walk from his room, and Eddie spent the next three days fishing, lying low, donating his daily catch to the motel managers. Looking back, he recalled, "They thought I was grand."

Moving on, slowly making his way back to San Diego, Cole was passing through a small town in Riverside County when he was stopped for a defective taillight. Eddie got off with a warning, but a sudden rush of paranoia hit him as the squad car pulled away. He drove another mile or so and found himself a narrow side road, pulling off the highway, switching off his lights and engine. Moments later the patrol car passed him in a rush, its beacon flashing crimson in the darkness.

Eddie watched it go, convinced that the patrolman had decided he should double-check Cole's license, turning up a warrant from Nevada. He completed the southbound journey on back roads, keeping an eye on his rearview mirror, worried that the $700 theft in Vegas had produced a manhunt out of all proportion to the crime. Worse yet, he knew the classic tales of Mafia involvement in Nevada, how the syndicate reserved a special punishment for independent thieves.

In San Ysidro, Cole was stopped again, another warning on the taillight. The coincidence unnerved him, and he spent the next few hours in a public parking lot, overlooking the nearby border checkpoint. Eddie spied another black-and-white, its driver watching motorists as they prepared to cross the border, his imagination kicking in with visions of an ambush waiting just for him.

He needed something for his nerves, and Eddie drove back to his favorite bar in Chula Vista, picking out a seat where he could watch his car the same way he had done on other nights, with Wilma and a nameless West Pac widow folded in the trunk. This time, he kept an eye on King and stayed alert for any uniforms that might show interest in his license plates.

The theft from Mr. Sy's had caused him more anxiety than any of his homicides, so far, and Eddie needed somewhere to relax. He phoned the four-plex, where Diana's brother Jeff had moved in with his wife the day Cole left. Jeff knew about the airport heist, and he had gone to fetch Diana from Las Vegas when the cops were finished grilling her.

Cole listened, feeling cornered as Diana took the phone and asked him to come home.

"Of course, I went," he said. "But first, I drove across the border to Tijuana and got laid."

Cole moved back into the apartment with Diana and his in-laws, Jeff and Laura staking out the master bedroom, while Eddie and Diana shared a Hide-A-Bed in the living room. Diana's health was on the skids by now, incipient cirrhosis overlooked through apathy and ignorance. Cole looked for work and came up empty in a labor market flush with college students, immigrants, and green-card workers up from Mexico. The idle hours, coupled with a bleak domestic scene, began to grate on Eddie's nerves.

He started looking for another way to kill some time.

*****

South of Chula Vista, Highway 75 takes him into Imperial Beach, no wife along to nag him as he cruises the main drag, searching for a likely place to start the hunt. The darkness is an old, familiar friend.

He picks a bar at random, parks the car, and makes his way inside. The place is crowded, but he finds an empty stool and orders beer. Cole takes his time examining the prospects, picking out a young brunette who has a smile for every man she sees. The slutty type, but she is perfect for his needs.

A casual remark leads into conversation, and she settles on the stool beside him, Eddie springing for another round. She flirts with the bartender in passing, leaning forward in her low-necked sweater, showing off her ample cleavage. Eddie feels the old, familiar fury building up inside him, but his face is bland, relaxed. A hunter's camouflage.

He tries to keep the lady entertained, but she reminds him of a butterfly, uncomfortable sitting still for any length of time. She borrows change to feed the jukebox, weaving through the crowd and brushing up against the more attractive men deliberately, exchanging smiles and comments Eddie can imagine, even with the woman out of earshot. How the little bitch enjoys her game.

She makes it back in time to find Cole on his feet, about to leave. A new expression on her face, some kind of pout designed to melt his heart, but she is well out of her league this time. The rules have changed.

She is about to gamble with her life.

"You're leaving?"

Eddie, stone-faced. "Yeah. I've had enough of this."

"I don't suppose you'd take me home?"

He makes a show of pondering the question, making up his mind. "Okay, let's go."

She can't resist a last wink at the barman, even as she leaves on Eddie's arm. He guides her to the car, gets in behind the wheel, and she directs him to a nearby trailer park.

"Have you got anything to drink at home?" he asks.

"Oh, sure. The thing is …well … my husband's there, you know?"

The click in Eddie's mind is loud enough that he suspects the woman must have heard it, nestled close against him as she is.

"I don't want any trouble," he informs her. "Maybe we should try and find a coffee shop or something?"

"Okay, if you want."

He gets the feeling *anything* would be okay with this one, an impression reinforced as she lies down across the seat, head resting in his lap. Cole's right hand settles on her hip, moves up to cup a firm, round breast. She purrs and nuzzles his erection through the fabric of his slacks.

So far, so good.

He drives beneath 1-5, away from all the downtown lights. The woman either doesn't notice or she doesn't give a damn. Cole finds a side street, nice and dark, braking the car as his hand leaves her breast, settling on the soft curve of her neck.

Some kind of sixth sense saves the woman's life. She bolts up in the seat before Cole has a chance to kill the lights or engine, reaching for the door and safety. Eddie lunges after her, both hands around her neck. The door pops open, and they tumble from the car together, tangled arms and legs. Somehow, he manages to keep his grip.

The woman does not struggle, now that they are stretched out on the shoulder of the road. She seems resigned to death, perhaps in shock, and Eddie's racing mind has time to register the details, filing them away for future reference. The smell of asphalt and exhaust. Her throat, so soft and white. The brittle spray net on her hair.

He shifts his weight for better leverage, prepared to finish it, when headlights blaze across the scene. A red light flashing over all, and Eddie rises to confront the sheriff's deputies, already thinking of a lie to save himself.

He tells them that he found the woman thumbing rides along the highway, with a male companion, and the couple tried to rob him. Her accomplice has escaped on foot, but Cole describes him, making up the details as he goes along. Dark hair, mid-twenties, average size. It could be anyone. Cole cannot hear the woman's version of events, but she is obviously less convincing. The patrolmen walk her to their car, leave Eddie with a warning not to put his trust in strangers.

Close, but no cigar. Dawn breaking as he parks outside the four-plex.

He will hunt again another day.

*****

Two friends of his, Tom and Sara, had an open marriage of sorts, meaning that both played around and each pretended the other didn't know. Tom's biggest score that winter was a threesome—Ann, Jane, and Susan—who operated from a flat near San Diego. Ann and Susan were the roomies, a divorcee and a single girl, respectively; Jane had a husband and two kids at home, but she liked to spend time with her girlfriends and whatever men they could find. All three of them were hot to trot, and Tom knew he had stumbled into something good the first night he dropped over with a friend called Swede. There seemed to be no end to liquor, sex, or weed around the party pad, and Tom began to calculate how he could make a good thing better, down the line.

One afternoon, while he was nagging Eddie for a loan, Tom let it slip that he could make it worth Cole's trouble. There were these three girls, see…

That night, Cole took a ride with Tom and Swede to check it out. They partied into the wee hours, Tom finally leading Ann into one bedroom, Swede and Susan taking the other. Cole and Jane wound up on the living-room floor, sans clothing, Eddie concentrating on the family she was betraying as he thrust into her eager flesh. The anger helped him function, in a way he never fully understood, and it was all the same to Jane, as long as he kept pumping till she came.

When Tom and Swede bailed out next morning, Eddie stayed behind. The women made him feel at home, and while he wished them dead with every waking moment, there was also something in their free-and-easy life-style that attracted him. Perhaps they helped confirm his jaundiced view of womankind, or simply offered sanctuary from the nightmare that his marriage had become. Cole hated them, but could not tear himself away. He had his dog, some spending money, all the sex that he could handle as he made the rounds from Jane to Ann, on to Susan, and back again.

What more could any unemployed ex-con desire?

Around the fourth or fifth night, Tom suggested that Eddie should at least phone home and tell Diana he was still alive, but Eddie put him off. He was beginning to develop a rapport with Ann, passing on the other girls until it started feeling like a steady thing. Sometimes he listened to her talk about the child now living in her husband's custody, and Eddie fantasized his hands around her throat, the final tremors when she lost control and soiled herself …but it was not the proper time or place.

Their money started running low, as winter crept toward spring, and Eddie hit upon the scheme of working as apartment managers, with Ann keeping books and handling the business end while he took care of maintenance. They wasted two weeks on a string of fruitless interviews before he saw an ad for house parents wanted in a community north of Escondido. The administrators hired them on sight to manage a home for wayward boys, removed from their families under court order, and they settled in with a group of ten youths, aged nine to twelve.

"Those kids weren't a bad bunch," Eddie recalled, "just confused, rejected, with the kind of problems only love could fix. But I'm afraid those ten didn't get the understanding and kindness they needed to put them on the right track. Not from Ann, and, sadly, not from me."

Cole was drinking heavily, though he made a stab at staying sober through the daylight hours. The job included riding herd on their unruly charges, driving them to and from a school run by the same organization that owned the "home." Cole soon discovered that his bosses drew a monthly stipend from the state, plus payments from assorted charities and all the families involved. "In other words," he said, "they were getting rich off the kids' misery. It was a hell of an operation."

Cole saw something of himself in the boys, hating Ann for the way she treated them when she was drunk, lacking the courage or will-power to stop her. Finally, in late March, one of the boys complained to a teacher, and word got back to the foundation's central office. After a perfunctory hearing, Cole and Ann were discharged with two weeks severance pay.

Back in San Diego, Eddie was arrested for drunk driving on April Fool's Day, 1975, and spent the night in jail. The incident revived his paranoia, visions of a jail cell in Nevada or another interview with Robert Ring, about the death of Essie Buck. Coincidentally, the grapevine told him there were jobs available for anyone who cared to work on oil rigs in the neighborhood of Laramie, Wyoming.

Out of sight and out of mind.

"I should have dumped Ann right there," Eddie said, "but I ended up taking her with me." They rented a U-Haul trailer, telling the dealer it was a local move, breezing through with a flat fifteen-dollar deposit. Eddie packed the trailer with their worldly goods and then some, ripping off a rented color television set from their apartment. Ann drove her own car, bringing up the rear while Eddie set the course across Nevada, Utah, rolling toward a new life in the Equality State.

Dream on.

The trip was uneventful, but Laramie was an immediate letdown, Eddie arriving too late for the oil boom in Albany County. He backtracked to a smaller town on Interstate 80 where jobs were plentiful, but there was no place to live unless you had a mobile home. At last, disheartened, they drove north to Casper, sleeping in the cars for two nights before they found a small apartment in suburban Evansville. Most of the neighborhood had been condemned, dilapidated structures waiting for the wrecking ball. Aside from the elderly managers and a young threesome next door, Cole and Ann had the complex to themselves.

Employment was still a problem in Casper, but Eddie found work at the Benton Clay Company, in nearby Mills. It was filthy work, described by Cole as "a job no one wanted, where they had trouble keeping employees." The bentonite dust fouled everything, from Eddie's clothing to his brown-bag lunches, and he tracked it into the apartment every night, eliciting complaints from Ann, not that she took any prizes in the cleanliness department.

Eddie still liked fishing on the weekends, often driving up to Soda Lake, due north of town, where he had dumped the U-Haul trailer shortly after they arrived. One Saturday a local officer happened by, noting the California license plates on Eddie's car, and Cole received a citation for fishing without a license. Adding insult to injury, the officer turned up on his doorstep next morning, to verify the address Cole had given him.

"He was a fucking Mexican and a real smart-ass," Eddie wrote. "I've always hated Mexicans and niggers."

Eddie had the officer's name by now, as well, and he decided it was payback time. With Ann sitting by to egg him on, he phoned the officer's wife at home, introducing himself as her husband's gay lover, demanding that she "give him up" and let the two of them find happiness together.

"I continued my attack for a week or so," said Cole, "and she would always slam the phone down, crying. Several weeks later, I saw the officer downtown, drunk and looking like a bum. I heard he'd had a fight with his wife, so I figured we were even."

Eddie's job at the clay factory paid less than $300 a month, but he maximized his take-home salary by claiming nonexistent dependents on his withholding form, a scam repeated on his April tax returns to give himself a tidy refund from the IRS. With his windfall in hand, he called in sick at the plant one day and went fishing at Soda Lake. As luck would have it, he was spotted by a neighbor whose girlfriend worked with the wife of Cole's foreman at a local restaurant, and word got back to the plant. When the foreman chided him about it later, Eddie flew into a rage and stormed out of the plant, threatening his neighbor's life for good measure. Even though he wasn't fired, Cole never went back to the factory. "Too fucking stubborn, I guess," he would later write from death row.

No work meant no income, but a barroom acquaintance tipped Eddie off to a hiring rush in the oil fields around Thermopolis, 120 miles northwest of Casper, in Hot Springs County. Cole and Ann made the drive in Ann's car, checked into a motel, and Eddie filed his application with the hiring office. He had no experience with oil rigs, but they hired him as a "worm," performing all manner of menial tasks on the drilling platforms. It was backbreaking, dangerous work, with many of the veterans missing fingers, but the risks never stopped Eddie or his cohorts from drinking on the job. By night, they made the rounds of local bars and whorehouses, drinking more in the mornings to counter fresh hangovers. If Ann had any complaints, she kept them to herself, hanging out at the motel.

Cole didn't need a shrink to see that he was in a rut. Three months, and his relationship with Ann had become a grim reprise of life with Billy and Diana. He was somehow drawn to women who epitomized the very things he hated most about their sex, and each new failure emphasized the fact that he was still his father's son, unable to control the women in his life.

Except for those he killed.

It was time for a change.

One night after work, with a week on the job, Eddie stopped at his favorite bar to relax. He spotted the blonde from the doorway. Shoulder-length hair, a model's profile, and a killer body in her skimpy nothing of a dress. He shouldered through the crowd, sat down beside her, focused on her wedding ring. The man immediately on her right could have been her husband or a one-night stand, but Eddie wasn't taking any chances. He had time to nurse a beer, stay cool until the blonde glanced to her left. A cautious smile, no reason for her date to take offense. They passed the time of day, as strangers will, expanding on the small talk when the other man displayed no overt signs of jealousy.

Her name was Terry Something, Eddie no more interested in surnames than he was in quantum physics or the Dow Jones average. He could feel the woman's need for some excitement, something new and different. Not unlike his own.

Another slut, but what can you expect to pick up in a bar?

The beer was working on her date, and in a few more minutes he excused himself to use the toilet. Terry watched him go, then turned and leaned in close to Eddie, one breast rubbing up against his arm. Her tone was urgent as she asked him for the name of his motel, the number of his room. He felt his pulse begin to quicken as he answered.

"Maybe I'll stop by tonight and tuck you in," she said.

"Your old man doesn't mind?"

"He's working graveyard on the rigs," said Terry. "What he doesn't know won't hurt him."

Eddie's frown was an unconscious reflex, but it almost put her off.

"I mean, unless you'd rather not . . ."

The smile came back, full force. "I wouldn't miss it."

Eddie waited for her husband to return before he finished off his beer and said good night. A wink from Terry as he turned away and started for the door. Outside, the night smelled fresh, alive with possibilities.

But Eddie still had work to do at the motel, before his rendezvous.

"First thing," he said, "I picked a fight with Ann over some bullshit and ran her off. We were up there in her car, so she packed her things and went back to Casper."

Eddie took a shower, straightened up the place a bit, and settled in to wait. It took another hour, but he finally heard a car pull into the motel. Brief apprehension, thinking Ann might have doubled back and he would have to ditch her in a hurry, but the knock on Eddie's door was muted, furtive. Terry on the sidewalk, looking fine.

"I didn't mean to take so long," she said. "My old man's slow, sometimes."

He stood aside to let her in. "Let's see if it was worth the wait."

It was.

They spent three hours in the motel bed, before they wore each other out. Cole would remember Terry as a knockout, but he hated her as much as he had ever hated any woman in his life. It was peculiar, how the brooding hatred gave him more endurance in the sack. Instead of making love with Terry, he was *screwing* her and every other slut who broke her wedding vows. The perfect climax would have found his hands around her throat, but Cole restrained himself. Too many risks involved, from lack of transportation to the fear that someone—even Terry's husband—might remember Eddie from the bar.

A freebie, then. When it was time for her to go, Cole felt relieved.

That weekend Eddie hitched a ride to Casper, thinking through his options on the drive. It was the kind of situation that could still go either way—a pointless reconciliation or another walkout, maybe his this time—and he resolved to play the scene by instinct, picking up on Ann's mood.

He never got the chance.

Arriving at the Evansville apartment complex, Eddie found his '64 Impala with a tire slashed in the parking lot. It went downhill from there, the small flat stripped of furniture, appliances, and clothing. Even

King was gone, a little company for Ann's beagle bitch. The only relic of their brief, depressing life together was a lamp that Ann had forgotten in the bedroom, standing in a corner by itself. Cole put it in the car, changed tires, and drove back to Thermopolis.

A free man starting over, one more time.

*****

Eddie works his way up—literally—to the job of derrick hand, scrambling around on a platform fifty feet in the air, stacking the various pipes and bits that emerge from the shaft. He thinks the operator is acting recklessly, but Eddie takes his chances for the extra money, till the third time he is almost toppled from his high perch in a single afternoon.

He calls a halt to drilling, scrambles down the narrow ladder, raging by the time he hits the platform. Coming at the operator like a madman, decking him. A length of greasy chain nearby, and Eddie grabs it, whipping it around the operator's neck. A perfect noose. The other crewmen drag him off and save him from a murder charge.

Cole's foreman takes the hard line, covering his butt. Opening a can of worms won't do the company a bit of good. New derrick hands are readily available at every bar in town.

Cole gets his walking papers, driving back to Casper and the central office to collect his severance pay. With five imaginary children on the books, he clears $950 and decides to celebrate.

Barhopping, Eddie winds up in an unfamiliar tavern out in Mills. The place is dead when he arrives, perhaps a dozen patrons all together, and he has no trouble picking out a stool with lots of elbow room. Away to Eddie's right, four spaces down the bar, he spots two women drinking by themselves. The nearest of the two has long, dark hair and dusky skin. Not Mexican, and yet . . .

By Eddie's second beer, they have a conversation going, Eddie moving closer so he doesn't have to yell. Her name is Myrlene Hamer, but her friends all call her "Tepee." Eddie realizes he is talking to an Indian. A married one, at that, if he believes the diamond and the slender band of gold around her left ring finger.

Click.

Her friend can smell a pickup coming, checking out to leave the two of them alone. Another drink, near closing time, and Eddie mentions that he just might know an after-hours club nearby. They make the trip in Eddie's rag-top, Tepee sitting close beside him, singing with the country-western music on the radio.

The after-hours club is crowded, but they manage, squeezing up against the bar. Cole is surprised to find that Tepee knows the lady barkeep, greeting her as if they are the best of friends.

Another goddamn lush.

The crowded bar is getting on his nerves, so loud that conversation is reduced to shouting, even from a foot away. Cole finally suggests they take a drive, and Tepee doesn't argue, holding Eddie's hand as he escorts her to the car.

The night is warm, and Eddie leaves the top down, driving with a destination fixed in mind. A narrow access road leads to the bentonite refinery, dark and silent now, as Eddie kills the lights and engine. Tepee lounges back against her door, reclining on the seat.

"You didn't have to bring me all the way out here," she says. "I would have fucked you anywhere."

Cole reaches for her, watching Tepee's eyes close in anticipation of a kiss. Instead, his fingers lock around her throat, a look of dumb surprise appearing on the woman's face as Eddie strangles her unconscious. Weak resistance, fading into tremors as her brain shuts down from lack of oxygen.

He has a sudden inspiration, reaching in the back seat for the lamp that Ann left behind. The cord is nearly three feet long, and Eddie has no trouble looping it around her neck. A simple job to finish her from there, the lamp wedged in between them, resting in her lap.

When she is dead, Cole drags her from the car and rips her clothes off, finishing the ritual. He takes her shredded blouse and wipes between her legs, where she has soiled herself in death. Whatever urge he might have felt to rape her body vanishes with the aroma of her bowels.

He scoops her up and slides her into the Impala's trunk, drives on until the plant is well behind him, motoring through sparsely wooded hills. He picks a spot at random, parks on grass, retrieves her body from the trunk, and dumps her on the hillside. She is pale and naked in the moonlight, simple caution telling him that she must be concealed. No shovel in the car, but Eddie has an old red sleeping bag. He drags it out and covers her.

Behind the wheel again, fatigue and alcohol gang up on Eddie, lulling him to sleep. He wakes at dawn, with sunlight in his face, bewildered for a moment as he watches traffic rolling past on Highway 20, close enough for damn near anyone to see him if they glance his way. Beside him, on the ground, a lumpy shape beneath the sleeping bag reminds him it is time to go, before a nosy jogger or a squad car comes along.

There is a lesson to be learned from carelessness, but it cannot erase the feeling of a job well done.

*****

Myrlene Hamer's body was found on Saturday, the ninth of August. Investigator Art Terry took the call for the Natrona County sheriff's office, supervising lab technicians at the scene. Before the corpse was moved, he noted livid marks of strangulation on the neck, his judgment verified when a pathologist confirmed the cause of death. A diamond ring worth $1,500 on the victim's finger ruled out robbery as a motive, and from the condition of the body, Terry reckoned that he had a sex crime on his hands.

The victim was identified by her husband, summoned to the morgue on the basis of a missing persons report, and Art Terry began the process of tracing Tepee Hamer's movements in the final hours of her life. A bartender remembered Myrlene's last visit to the after-hours club, coaching a police artist who produced composite sketches of the dead woman's date. It was better than nothing, but not by much. The sketches could have represented several hundred men around Natrona County, and the witness had no luck at all where mug shots were concerned.

Dead end.

Without a break, Art Terry had a hunch that the investigation wasn't going anywhere. He had no way of knowing it would take five years to find his man.

*****

The morning after Myrlene Harrier's corpse was found, she made the news, a story in the *Star-Tribune,* complete with photos of detectives scouring the scene. Apparent homicide, no leads, no suspects. The investigation was continuing. And it was time to leave.

Cole did not save the clipping this time, having learned from his mistake with Essie Buck. He didn't need a souvenir to keep his latest victim fresh in mind.

The same day Tepee made the papers, Eddie gassed up his Impala, bought a six-pack for the road, and said good-bye to Casper.

Heading west.

TWELVE

From Casper, Cole drove to Shoshoni and purchased supplies, including canned food and a case of beer. He spent the next three days camped out at Boysen Reservoir, on the eastern border of the Wind River Indian Reservation, fishing by day and sleeping in his car at night. When roughing it began to get on Eddie's nerves, he drove up to Thermopolis, killing time in familiar saloons and cathouses. There was work to be had on the oil rigs, even with Eddie's violent reputation, but his paranoia kept him from accepting any of the offers he received. At any moment he expected the police to brace him, haul him back to Casper for a murder trial.

Time to go.

Diana's brother Jeff hailed from Boise, Idaho, and Cole had heard so much about the city he decided it was time to have a look. No hurry, with a six-pack on the seat beside him. He could take his own sweet time and stop whenever he was moved to look around a town and check the taverns out. He had no schedule, no one waiting for him anywhere, and wandering the back roads made it harder for the law to track him down, if anyone was looking.

Driving through the Rockies, Eddie felt a sudden urge to lose himself among the densely wooded peaks, live off the land, a modern Jeremiah Johnson. Nobody would ever have to know, and if they found his car abandoned, weeks or months from now, the local sheriff would assume that he had kept on going, traveling by thumb.

The moment passed, a flight of fantasy, and Eddie kept on driving. West of Jackson, in the foothills of the Teton Range, he stopped in Wilson. One last bar to try, before he kissed Wyoming off forever.

As it was, the lady barkeep caught his eye, attractive, quick to smile. He wound up drinking through the afternoon and evening, hanging in till closing time, already planning how he could repay her show of friendship with the kiss of death.

Last call, and Eddie made his way outside to wait. He watched the last-ditch patrons straggle out, one of them hanging back and walking Eddie's target to her car. His anger had a sour taste, but there was time. If she was driving, he could always tag along and catch her at the other end. It might be better that way, off the street. Less chance of witnesses.

He waited, watched the lady barkeep say good night, her one-man fan club going on about his business. Eddie let her have a decent lead, her taillights leading him along dark streets, a left turn, then a right. In tiny Wilson, no one has to travel very far.

A wood frame house, perhaps two bedrooms. More than he would need, at any rate. Cole watched his prey turn in and killed his headlights, idling along. His mind was calculating angles of attack when someone switched the porch light on. He saw the screen door opening, a tall man stepping out to greet the woman with a kiss.

So much for best-laid plans.

Cole drove on in the general direction of Boise, choosing highways at random, scorning a map and the most direct route. He had cash in his pocket and nothing but time on his hands.

"I had thoughts of picking up a female hitchhiker and having some fun," Eddie wrote, "strangling her to break the monotony, but I never saw one. Funny. Even so, I asked myself why I hadn't started doing this before, instead of wasting time looking for help that was nonexistent."

Two days out of Wilson, he stopped at a market in Soda Springs, Idaho, east of Pocatello. Stocking up on beer and cold cuts for the road, he also found a new detective magazine, its cover featuring a pretty young woman in distress, her blouse torn open, a grinning strangler's black-gloved hands around her throat. A few miles farther west on Highway 30, Eddie pulled off to the side and masturbated in the Chevy, sitting with the top down and his magazine propped up between the windshield and the dash.

It wasn't half the fun of strangling a woman on his own, but it would have to do.

Cole arrived in Boise with several hundred dollars left, and he decided to save his money by signing into an Alcoholics Anonymous rehab house, trading a worthless pledge of sobriety for free room and board. As it happened, drying out was the furthest thing from Eddie's mind, and he still spent his evenings in neighborhood bars, dropping Jeff's name here and there in a search for new connections. He was startled when the bartender at one saloon informed him Jeff was back in town from San Diego, with his wife.

A phone call did the trick, Jeff sounding glad to hear from Eddie, no recriminations for his hasty exit from the married life. In forty minutes they were on the road, Cole picking up his handful of belongings from the A.A. house and trailing Jeff back to his place on Pine Street. Laura met them with a brand-new baby in her arms.

Aside from the geography, there seemed to be no change of any consequence in Jeff and Laura's marriage. The baby might keep Laura home at night, but Jeff still liked to go to bars with his buddies at night. A carpenter by trade, he found a paying spot for Eddie as his helper, but their jobs were interrupted sometimes by side trips to saloons. "Actually," Cole said, "Jeff and I were a lot alike—something I hated him for, because he reminded me of myself."

The tense situation came to a head one night, when Eddie was making the rounds with Jeff and Laura's brother. They met some women, but Jeff made something of an ass of himself, driving the women off and leaving Cole fuming as they walked back to the car.

A sucker punch dropped Jeff to the asphalt, Eddie moving in to finish it when the brother-in-law stepped between them. It was a long ride home, all three wedged into the front seat, with Jeff at the wheel, Eddie leaning around Laura's brother every mile or so to lash out with a stinging backhand. At the house on Pine Street, Eddie stuffed the remnants of his life into a duffel bag and said good-bye to Laura. Glares and stony silence in the morning, stopping by Jeff's office for $150 he had coming from their latest job.

Since the arson rap in Dallas, Eddie had become adept at burning bridges.

Fresh out of destinations, Cole drove sixty miles north, to Cascade, proceeding to have himself "a high old time" in various saloons. One night, a friendly barmaid introduced him to a tearful younger woman who was grieving over separation from her boyfriend. Eddie asked her out to dinner at a nearby restaurant and listened to her story: careless infidelity on her part, soon discovered by the lumberjack she lived with, climaxed by a screaming argument and her ejection from the house. Cole made a show of sympathy, already planning how to kill the cheap, two-timing bitch without incriminating himself. When they had cleaned their plates and paid the check, they took a drive northwest of town, along the river feeding Cascade Reservoir.

"It was my intention to park beside the white-water stream and strangle her," Eddie wrote from death row, "leaving her body to be found in the water." The barmaid who had put the two of them together knew him casually, but they were never on a last-name basis, she had never seen his car ... no problem if she wound up talking to police.

They found a spot to park and went into a clinch, all hands and hungry mouths, Cole taking full advantage of the woman's hurt and craving for affection. Hell, if he could score a piece of ass before he strangled her— or afterward—so much the better. It was all a game, and Eddie's mind was racing toward the touchdown when a glaring spotlight trashed his concentration, shriveled the erection in his shorts.

The highway patrolman was duly solicitous. Were they having engine trouble? Anything at all that he could do to help? Cole told him they were fine, just checking out the moonlight, and the officer departed, chalking one more up to love in bloom.

The mood was broken. Much too risky now, for any kind of major entertainment, knowing that the cop had seen his face and license number. If the woman turned up dead around Cascade, it would not take a crystal ball to solve the case. Cole made excuses, drove the woman back to the saloon where she had left her car, and started thinking where he ought to try his luck the next time out.

Five hours on the road brought Eddie to familiar territory. Elko, Nevada, had changed in the twenty-years since Eddie spent a summer on probation there, with brother Dick. Still small, by any but Nevada standards, with its major claim to fame the nearby juvenile facility for young offenders. The town's 8,000 inhabitants were roughly divided between agriculture and service occupations—meaning restaurants, bars, and casinos—that constitute the lifeblood of the Silver State.

New bars for Eddie to explore, as if the same old liquor might be different with a fresh song on the jukebox and a different neon sign outside. With any luck at all, he just might find a special lady who could help him to unwind.

In fact, he wound up with a street-wise hooker on his second night in Elko, rutting in a cheap motel. No thought of killing her, because she made no bones about her trade. Another service-oriented occupation in the land of easy come and easy go.

Next morning Eddie woke up with a hangover to keep him company. The whore was gone, along with all the money from his wallet, leaving Cole some fifteen dollars in a pocket of his jeans that she had overlooked. He cursed himself for trusting any woman, let alone a working hooker. Eddie knew the rules of play, and looking for the bitch in an attempt to get his money back would be a waste of time.

Move on.

The fifteen dollars got him to Los Angeles, but only just. The Impala was running on fumes, and it was still another 125 miles to San Diego, where he felt a twisted semblance of belonging. At a self-serve station, Eddie filled his tank and drove away while the attendant's back was turned, expecting red lights in his rearview mirror as he motored south.

The Chevy's engine burned up ten miles north of San Diego proper, near the site where Essie Buck was found. It was pushing 4:00 A.M. when Eddie stood beside the highway with his thumb out, but he caught a ride to Broadway, the neighborhood looking drab and lifeless with its taverns and massage parlors closed for the night. He found a pay phone, the directory in tatters, but it had the page he needed. Diana sounded groggy on the line, no screaming fit or curses. Eddie thought that she was weeping as she asked him to come home.

Diana's situation had gone from bad to worse since March. She was drinking nonstop, the cash drain since Eddie's departure requiring a move to a small "efficiency" apartment, one flight up above a bar on Market Street. A few weeks earlier Diana had been boozing on the sun deck when she fell asleep and wound up hospitalized, with second-degree sunburn over forty percent of her body. Most of her hair fell out, and she was still required to soak in special baths each day, drinking concoctions of liquid potassium. On the side, doctors had also diagnosed her cirrhosis, wasting their breath on strict warnings against further drinking.

Standing on the welcome mat with dawn's gray light behind him, Eddie thought she looked like "death warmed over," but his heart went out to her in spite of everything. A kind of fatalism as he stepped across the threshold, voluntarily reentering the trap.

Within his limits, Eddie tried to make a change. He went back to work as a pickup driver for the Salvation Army, refusing Diana the liquor she craved, but it made no difference in the end. If Eddie wouldn't buy the booze, Diana would get it somehow. In her cups, Diana soon fell prey to doubts and jealousy, phoning Eddie's job several times a day to make sure he was out on the truck, instead of pumping some slut on the side.

"After two weeks," Cole said, "I got tired of the bullshit and left Di again, also quitting my job." He lived on the street for a while, then checked in with Project Jove, a rehab program run by ex-cons, for ex-cons. The office referred him to Green Oak Ranch, near Vista, in northern San Diego County, and he went to check it out.

The operation was a working camp for wayward boys and girls, run in conjunction with the L.A. rescue mission. Families paid the tab for adolescent residents, while the kids dried out and got a taste of country air, working with a wide variety of barnyard animals, trying to forget about their problems for a while. The maintenance staff was composed of skid-row habitués, one step from falling off the wagon, and Eddie seemed to fit right in. Hired as a laborer on December 16, 1975, he worked hard through the week and spent the weekends drinking up his pay in nearby Escondido. After three months on the job, he got another bogus refund check from Uncle Sam and put the farm behind him.

"Like a magnet, San Diego draws me," Eddie wrote in 1985. "I've heard it said that 'Dago' sits at the bottom of the state in such a way to catch all the shit as the world tilts. Maybe so. In my case, who could say it wasn't true?"

In San Diego Eddie soon drank up his windfall from the IRS and found himself without resources. Six victims in five years had only sharpened his appetite for more, but there were also latent feelings of a need to change his life. Despite his resolution on the long drive west, Cole felt the old, persistent urge to look for psychiatric help.

On Friday, March 19, the San Diego Community Mental Health Center received a call from a local detox house. Counselor Alice Moran was on the line, reporting a new arrival whose threatening demeanor sent up warning flags. Moran couldn't be sure if the man was more dangerous to himself or others, but in her opinion, the need for examination and treatment was urgent.

The patient's name was Carroll Edward Cole.

Eddie checked into the mental health center on Saturday morning, sitting for a twenty-minute interview with a staff psychiatrist. Careful to avoid all mention of his victims, Cole requested therapy, in the doctor's words, "for his explosive, aggressive, and violent acting out behavior." Eddie reported himself as suffering from skin cancer, but his chief complaint was listed as emotional: "I feel like giving up." The examining physician took it as a self-destructive threat and noted in the file that Cole's "behavior now and in the past may be more reflective of passive suicide by provoking others to homicide than merely violent aggression."

It was different, anyway, this notion that he really meant to kill himself, instead of someone else. In fairness to the staff psychiatrists, their diagnosis was predominately based on what they heard from Eddie Cole and what they read between the lines, without a hint that he had murdered seven times before he came to them for help. As noted in his summary of treatment, Cole "revealed little of himself."

In his two weeks at the center, Cole participated in group therapy and other activities, but he always played his cards close to the vest, rewriting history when it suited his purpose. Interviewed by a psychiatric social worker on March 22, for example, Eddie denied any problem with alcohol and trimmed his bulky arrest record back to a mere three busts for public intoxication. He was discharged on April 2 with a diagnosis of "adult situational reaction with depression and suicidal ideation. Personality disorder, mixed type." It was a catch-all verdict based on slender evidence, Dr. Robert Cummings adding a note that Cole's overall condition had "improved as depression and suicidal ideation are no longer prominent symptoms."

Eddie spent the next ten days at Pathfinders, a halfway house for alcoholics. On April 12 he returned to the mental health center for another brief interview, and was referred to a psychiatrist in private practice. The social worker's final note explained that Cole was "walking over" to the doctor's office.

Eddie never made it.

Wandering the streets with pocket change and no desire to face his wife, Cole wound up at a peculiar religious shelter. The place was run by Sister Rachel, an evangelist of sorts whose ordination emanated from a mail-order diploma mill. As Cole described the operation, "Rachel played it for all it was worth, soliciting money from every religious organization and business she could think of." The alleged beneficiaries were fifteen derelicts who occupied an upstairs dormitory, sleeping on crude wooden cots without bedding, scrounging in supermarket Dumpsters for their next meal. When donations were slack, Rachel sent her charges out to peddle candy or wash cars without pay, returning gross proceeds to the "church." On the side, there were mandatory services where Rachel showed off her alleged healing powers.

"You never saw such hypocrisy in your life," Eddie wrote, "people getting up in front of Sister Rachel and fainting at her touch."

Cole could appreciate a good scam, but he was quickly put off by Rachel's amorous advances. Stalling her as best he could without risking eviction, Eddie wangled a promotion to chauffeur and later to "second in charge" of the shelter, a post that gave him access to Rachel's attractive daughter-in-law. He was not above lusting after the young woman, sustaining his erection with fantasies of murder, but his thoughts were always drifting. He was ready for a change of scene, and that meant he would need some ready cash.

One of the shelter residents, Fred Warren, put the touch on Cole for loans from time to time, but never got around to paying off his debt. As soon as he had cash in hand, it went for something else, leaving Eddie high and dry. The trend was pissing Eddie off, and he was mulling over ways to get his money back—or take a pound of flesh instead—when Rachel sent him out to fetch the mail on Friday afternoon, May 7. There, among the standard bills and junk mail, was a check addressed to Warren from the federal government.

The inspiration came to Eddie all at once. He looked around, made sure no one was watching as he slipped the envelope into his pocket, out of sight.

At first, he simply planned to hold the check for ransom, trade it for the twenty dollars Warren owed him, but it only made good sense to peek inside the envelope and see what he was holding. In fact, the check was made out for $1,556, and Eddie adjusted his plan in a heartbeat, seizing the chance to clear an 8000-percent profit on his original investment. Never mind the twenty dollars; he would find a way to cash the check himself, with Warren none the wiser to his loss.

Cole's mind went into overdrive, applying lessons he had picked up living on the street. His first stop was the Department of Motor Vehicles, where he falsified an application for a California state ID card, signing Warren's name and jotting down the address of a favorite bar on

Third Street. There was nothing more to do from there, but settle back and wait, imagining the things that he could do with $1,500 free and clear.

Before the ID card arrived, however, Eddie saw an advertisement in the *San Diego Union,* seeking a maintenance man for a hunting lodge at Jackson Hole, Wyoming. Perfect. The proprietor had an office in National City, and Eddie phoned ahead for an appointment. As he recalled the scene, years later, "I told him all kinds of bullshit to get the job, and he hired me on the spot. I already had it in mind to take Rachel's car, so when the guy asked what I needed, we settled on a credit card for gas and a hundred dollars for expenses on the road."

Eddie rolled out of San Diego on Wednesday, May 26, first stopping by a taxidermist's shop to retrieve a mounted goat's head his employer meant to display at the lodge. North of San Bernardino, he picked up Highway 395 northbound, reversing his path from the previous autumn, working on a six-pack for the road. Fred Warren's check was in the trunk with other papers and the goat's head, Eddie figuring that he could always find some way to cash it at his journey's end.

It was well past midnight when a blowout stopped him north of Independence, in Inyo County, near Kings Canyon National Park. Cole decided to sleep in the car and change the tire when he woke, explaining as much to the sheriff's deputy who stopped by with an offer of assistance in the early-morning darkness. Officer D. C. Dorsey ran a check on Eddie's license plates as a matter of course, and word came back of a stolen vehicle report from San Diego County. Moments later Cole was wearing handcuffs, riding back to Independence and the Inyo County jail.

In custody, he quickly folded and confessed the mail theft. Later, from death row, Cole wrote, "I figured what the hell, I'd rather have the check torn up than see it go to Fred, and they were bound to find it anyway." Returned to San Diego on May 28, he sat in jail for six days before the U.S. Postal Service sent Special Investigator L. E. Lyman around for an interview. Once again Cole admitted stealing the check, and auto theft charges were dropped when police delivered him to the United States Marshal on June 3, for transfer to the federal Metropolitan Correctional Center, on Union Street.

On Friday, June 4, Cole stood before U.S. Magistrate Edward Infante, and a formal arrest warrant was issued on charges of mail theft. He was remanded to the MCC in lieu of $500 bond, hanging tough until Monday morning before he let a forgiving Sister Rachel bail him out. There would be no return to the shelter for Eddie, however. Instead, he claimed his pocket money at the booking desk and went on a two-day binge to celebrate his release, culminating in another DUI arrest in the small hours of June 9. Freed that afternoon, Cole sniffed the wind and knew that it was time to leave. That evening, he turned up at Green Oak Ranch and got his old job back, in maintenance.

Around the same time Eddie Cole was getting out of jail and making up his mind to travel north, a federal grand jury was returning indictments against him on two counts of intercepting mail. A preliminary hearing was scheduled for Friday, June 11, but Cole didn't show, and a new warrant was issued for his arrest. The problem being, no one seemed to know where he had gone.

Two weeks of boozing every night around the Green Oak Ranch convinced Cole's supervisors that he was not fit to work with children in his present state. They packed him off to L.A.'s rescue mission, hoping the experience would dry him out, but Cole was thinking well ahead. He worked odd jobs around skid row for drinking money, kept himself well lubricated day and night, alert for any opportunity to claim another victim.

One who almost qualified was Macy, picked up in a smoky bar on Wilshire Boulevard. She took Cole home to spend the night, and he laid plans to kill her after sex, but in the course of idle conversation Macy dropped the name of a mutual friend in San Diego. Paranoia kicking in, Cole jumped to the irrational conclusion that a common link more than 120 miles away would somehow tie him to the crime. He scrubbed the plan, let Macy live, decided he was tired of living on the run.

At 2:00 A.M. on Saturday, June 26, Cole phoned the all-night number for the U.S. Post Office security force in Los Angeles, speaking with Officer Allen Young. He identified himself as a fugitive from mail theft and bail-jumping charges in San Diego County, expressing a desire to surrender. Young advised him to see Sgt. Glen Tinsley, at the L.A. Post Office terminal annex, but alcohol garbled the message ... or maybe Cole just had a different plan in mind.

At 3:25 A.M., Officer Young got another call, this one from the watch commander at the federal courthouse on North Spring Street. Cole had surrendered himself to security officers there, and Sgt. Tinsley was sent to fetch him, driving him back to the post office terminal annex. By 3:45, Postal Inspector W. J. Gillespie had been routed from bed to take charge of the case. A predawn conversation with his counterparts in San Diego confirmed Cole's story, and Gillespie dropped his prisoner off for safekeeping at the L.A. County jail.

On Monday morning Cole appeared before U.S. Magistrate Harvey Schneider, waiving his right to a removal hearing and requesting immediate extradition to San Diego. With their man jailed in lieu of $2,000 bond, the postal inspectors felt no need to rush, and it was Friday, July 9, before Eddie returned to his familiar cell in the Metropolitan Correctional Center.

Attorney Frank Gregorcich was appointed to defend Cole, but the case was a lost cause with Eddie's several confessions on file. An ill-conceived not-guilty plea on the bail-jumping charge didn't help, and Cole was convicted across the board on February 2, 1977. Five days later he was sentenced to a year and a day in prison on the mail theft charge, with five years subsequent probation for skipping bond. Ironically, with credit for the seven months he served before his trial and more time off for good behavior in the joint, he would be eligible for release in less than two months time.

The clock began running on Friday, February 11, when Eddie was booked into the MCC as a regular inmate. A physical exam turned up eight missing teeth and four others in need of filling, along with Cole's self-diagnosis as an "admitted alcoholic," but the prison medics pronounced him an "essentially [sic] healthy male," fit for regular work.

It should have been an easy stretch for Cole, compared to Eastham and Jeff City, but he was already chafing at confinement, actively looking for grievances. On March 31, with his release already in the works, Eddie fired off an angry letter to the director of the Federal Bureau of Prisons. It read:

Dear Sir,

On Monday, the 4th of April, I will be released from MCC at San Diego.

This letter is to protest the discrimination I incurred while at MCC.

Both against myself and others of the white race but the blacks as well.

Full details I will tell to the press next Monday. If your not mexican in MCC, you will be past over in every way. Just lied to and put off all the time.

A lot of my charges but the serious ones will be laughed over as I know you will. We'll see what the public say.

However, I'm here to tell you that when MCC tampers with and opens my incoming legal mail without my presents your in trouble.

Also, to blatantly exclude me from any and all programs and services offerred to other federal prisoner and benefits that will help me better myself in society were not allowed me.

To these charges the Bureau of Prisons will answer to as I fully intend filing charges. Both public and formal.

Sincerely,

C. Edward Cole #9398

For all its faulty grammar, the note signaled a new phase in Eddie's life: C. Edward Cole as jailhouse lawyer. On Sunday, April 3, he filed a formal "request for administrative remedy" harking back to June 1976, when some of his personal clothing was lost at the L.A. County jail. Released the next day, before anyone had a chance to respond, Eddie hit the streets fuming with righteous anger, determined to ignore the terms of his parole. As he wrote from prison, nine years later, "No half-assed federal probation officer was going to tell me what to do."

Within a week, he was back in Las Vegas, living the high life with a twist.

This time, he was a federal fugitive.

THIRTEEN

EDDIE TOOK THE BUS TO VEGAS, arriving with a hundred dollars in his pocket and nowhere to stay. At once, he fell into his usual pattern of drinking and gambling around the clock, catching a few hours sleep when and where he could. He was doing all right…until his money ran out.

St. Vincent de Paul is the leading Catholic charity organization in Las Vegas, operating a combination rescue mission, thrift store, and repair shop on North Las Vegas Boulevard, near Woodlawn Cemetery. Cole applied for admission to the transient dormitory and was granted a bed in return for volunteer work in the dining hall. He spent a few days there, dispensing soup and doughnuts to the homeless, but he wasn't getting anywhere, in terms of ready cash.

On Monday, April 25, Cole went to work full-time for Western Linen Supply, washing sheets and towels for various casinos and hotels. His supervisors were impressed enough to give him a raise after one week on the job, but Eddie left his new position on the fourth of May. Too many Mexicans around the laundry for his taste.

And in his spare time, Eddie drank.

One of his favorite bars was Dan & Ray's on Garces Avenue, between Main Street and Second—alias Casino Center. Three blocks north, on Lewis Avenue, the Casbah Hotel also catered to serious drinkers, and if Eddie sought a change of pace, there was always the salt-and-pepper hooker hangout one block south of the Federal Building on Las Vegas Boulevard. By early May, Cole's universe had shrunken to a seedy half mile in diameter.

But there were women, yes indeed. Not flashy tourists or the showgirl types who decorate the bars at carpet joints along The Strip, exactly. Some of them were hustlers, some were burn-outs. Many were a little bit of both. From time to time, you met one like Tanya, a housewife who preferred Jack Daniel's to the working stiff she married, pegged by Eddie as "a tramp who liked to go braless and raise her sweater or blouse to show off her breasts."

And then, there was Kathlyn Jo Blum. Late twenties, plump, dark hair and glasses. Eddie met her on the afternoon he split from Western

Linen, hanging out at a bar on Las Vegas Boulevard. He introduced himself as "Pepper," picking the name out of thin air, making up a non-existent job and teenage daughter to complete the picture. Killing time with beer and conversation, Eddie learned that she was living with the bartender, a black man known as "Shotgun," whoring on the side to make ends meet. At one point, Eddie watched her leave with an inebriated stranger, coming back three quarters of an hour later on her own.

It takes all kinds to keep a town like Vegas on the move.

For Eddie Cole, the all-night city had begun to look like one big, happy hunting ground.

The night of Friday, May 13, Cole wanders into Dan & Ray's. His cash is running low again, but there is still enough for one last binge before he has to find another job. He moves directly toward the men's room, spotting Kathlyn Blum at one end of the bar. It registers that she is straying off her normal range. Eye contact and a flutter of her hand as Eddie passes by.

The rest room smells like it could use an enema, but Cole is not concerned about the atmosphere. Emerging moments later, with his bladder empty and his thirst intact, he walks back to the bar and takes the empty stool on Kathlyn's left. It doesn't take a shrink to read the sadness in her puffy eyes and pouting lips.

Bad news.

The only kind that really counts.

She tells him all about her latest spat with Shotgun, walking out with nothing but the western outfit on her back. They're finished this time, swear to God. This breaking up is thirsty business, and the liquor makes her sleepy. Anyway, can Pepper take her in, for just a night or two? He won't be sorry. Satisfaction guaranteed.

Cole frowns and makes excuses, falling back on his imaginary child to make it stick. In fact, he *has* no place to stay, since splitting from the rescue mission, but he can't say that to Kathlyn Jo. A lie, once told, takes on an independent life of sorts, demanding sustenance.

She starts to nag him, playfully at first, by turns provocative and peevish. Eddie recognizes desperation when he sees it, but the role of Good Samaritan belongs to someone else. He stalls for time, strikes up a conversation with the barkeep, visibly relieved when Kathlyn mutters something to herself and wobbles off her bar stool, disappearing through the exit.

Peace at last.

For all of twenty minutes.

Eddie smells her perfume first, before she brushes up against him, resting one hand on his arm.

"What's keeping you?"

Well, shit.

He drains his beer and leaves some money on the bar, his bankroll looking perilously slim. Outside, the night is warm and neon-bright. They follow Garces past an all-night Laundromat with slot machines lined up beside the washers, pausing at a bus stop, settling on the bench to rest. Cole's mind is racing, Kathlyn pressing him to take her home and never mind his daughter.

"All that I could think of," Eddie says, "is that I met her at a bar where dirty nigger pimps hung out with their white whores. How many niggers had she spread her legs for? Any woman who would do that is insulting the men of her race."

Case closed. The sentence: death.

He spots a taxi passing on Casino Center, flags it down, directs the driver south to Cleveland Avenue. Familiar landmarks as they stop in the 200 block, where Eddie and Diana once kept house. Cole pays the driver off and comes away with nothing left but pocket change.

A paved walk leads them off the street, into the heart of the apartment complex, Eddie telling Kathlyn Jo to wait while he goes on ahead to check things out. She grumbles a complaint but does as she is told.

He climbs familiar stairs and stands outside the small apartment where he used to live, before the theft from Mr. Sy's. No point in knocking, even though the lights are on, somebody watching television in the living room. Nostalgia has no place in Eddie's world. He smokes a cigarette to pass the time, imaginary conversations with a nonexistent daughter playing through his mind. A few more minutes. Let her wait.

When time enough has passed, he goes downstairs and finds her waiting in the shadows.

"Well?"

"We can't go up right now," he says. "My daughter has her boyfriend over."

"So? How long?"

An easy shrug. "Let's take a walk."

"I'm tired."

"I want to show you something," Eddie tells her.

"Jesus."

Fewer lights behind the complex, facing on a narrow alleyway in back. The tiny parking lot is dead this time of night. No witnesses to interrupt.

"I have to pee."

He watches Kathlyn tug her jeans and panties down, crouching in the shadows to relieve herself. A sound of urine trickling on the ground, contempt and sudden fury tasting bitter in his mouth.

He steps in close behind her as she rises, pulling up her pants, and Eddie's fingers lock around her throat. He shakes her like a rag doll, drops her when her legs fold, straddling her prostrate body on the ground.

"You want to show off what you've got, I'll help you, bitch!"

He rips her blouse, the buttons popping, Eddie's fingers catching in her bra and tugging it away.

"No, Pepper! Stop!"

She might as well be speaking Japanese as Eddie wraps the bra around her neck and pulls it tight, elastic digging into Kathlyn's flesh. His strength is such that after several moments use as a garrote, the garment comes apart in Eddie's hands.

He rocks back on his haunches, winded, glancing left and right to see if anyone has heard the woman's cries. No sign of help arriving as she sits up, rubbing at her throat, a dazed expression on her face.

"For Christ's sake, Pepper!"

Time to finish it.

He grabs her by the neck again, the muscles in his tattooed forearms knotting as he puts his weight behind it, forcing Kathlyn backward to the ground. A car rolls past them in the alley, headlights blinding Eddie for an instant as he lies on top of Kathlyn Jo, their faces close enough that he can smell the liquor on her breath.

And finally, there *is* no breath. Her eyes wide open, sightless, staring at the sky where city lights have washed out all the stars.

Cole rests beside her for a moment, waiting for his pulse to stabilize. When he can move without a painful surge of blood between his ears, he lurches to his feet, grips Kathlyn underneath her arms, and starts to drag her down the alley, boot heels scraping gravel all the way. It is a calculated risk, a hundred yards of open ground before he finds the perfect spot. An unfenced yard, behind a small house facing Fairfield Avenue, all dark and silent now.

He drops her body near some shrubbery and strips her clothes off, ready for the sight and smell of feces smeared between her legs. No problem. Scooping up her tattered blouse, he walks back to the alley, soaks the ruined garment in a puddle, and returns to bathe the corpse. When Kathlyn Jo is clean enough to pass inspection, Eddie mounts her, thrusting deep into her unresisting flesh. Still warm, but he takes no real satisfaction from the coupling, even when he spurts inside her. It is all a part of shaming her, the only fitting treatment for a worthless, nigger-loving slut.

When he is finished, Eddie lingers with the body, smoking several cigarettes before he feels the restless need to move. A few blocks north, on East Sahara, the Jackpot Casino is open all night. Eddie spends his pocket change on beer, stops by the men's room for a wad of paper towels, and wanders back to Kathlyn Jo.

Another hump, for old times' sake, if he can clean her up enough.

Confronted with the corpse a second time, Cole loses interest, scattering the paper towels around her body, picking up her garments. Dawn's pale light is breaking as he moves along the alley, dropping off her clothes in different Dumpsters on the way. He saves her purse for last, extracting six or seven dollars and a photo that the woman carries of herself.

A wallet-sized forget-me-not.

*****

Homicide Detective Joe McGuckin was an eight-year veteran of Nevada law enforcement when he caught the latest squeal on May 14, 1977. He had joined the Clark County Sheriff's Department in November 1968 and stayed on when it merged with the city force to create the Las Vegas Metropolitan Police in July 1973. His posting to homicide followed a year later, and he had been cleaning up the city's dirty laundry ever since.

You never know about a murder in Las Vegas. With the tourists, teenage gangs, and transients, wiseguys dropping in from all points east and west, there is a high potential for explosive violence. Drugs are part of it, especially since the Cubans and Vietnamese began to filter in, but they have always played a role in life and sudden death. Some killers try to keep it private, like the homosexual who diced his lover up and dropped the pieces at the sewage treatment plant. Others—like the GI on his honeymoon who killed himself, his bride, and half a dozen strangers with a homemade bomb, inside the Orbit Inn—prefer an audience.

And some don't seem to fit the mold at all.

The uniforms were waiting when McGuckin parked his unmarked cruiser in the alley back of Fairfield Avenue, making his way on foot to the scruffy yard behind number 2210. They had the strips of yellow tape in place, its warning stenciled endlessly in stark black letters: CRIME SCENE—DO NOT CROSS. McGuckin ducked beneath it, careful where he put his feet from that point on.

The woman was completely nude except for socks, the kind you wear with tennis shoes or maybe boots, to keep from rubbing blisters on your heels. She was brunette, Caucasian, drab the way they always are in death. There are no sexy corpses outside pulp detective fiction or the daydreams of a necrophile.

McGuckin noted obvious abrasions on the woman's throat and smears of feces on her inner thighs. More fecal matter on a number of the paper towels that had been scattered carelessly around her body, someone making an attempt to clean her up, perhaps for sex. The strangulation and behavior afterward told Joe McGuckin they were looking for a man, and one who smoked, unless the several butts were mere coincidence. Between saliva and the possibility of semen from the corpse, they just might type the bastard's blood.

A bonus, right, if they could ever track him down.

McGuckin supervised the crime scene photographs and search for evidence. No personal effects remaining to assist him when it came to an ID. The tenants of the Fairfield home had noticed nothing strange the night before, but they were used to drunks and losers shambling down the alley, looking for a safe place to relieve themselves or hole up for the night.

In any given year, Las Vegas has its share of unsolved homicides.

The toughest ones to crack are those where the police can't even name the victim, thereby losing out on precious links to family, friends, potential enemies. The "John" and "Jane Doe" corpses come in every race and age—abandoned infants, teenage runaways who never made it to Los Angeles, unlucky senior citizens whose golden years have turned to tarnished brass. The worst, in terms of tracking down ID, are prostitutes. Besides the endless string of pseudonyms they offer every time the vice squad picks them up on misdemeanor charges, many hookers work a circuit from Las Vegas to L.A., and north from there through San Francisco, to the SeaTac Strip in Washington. The weather and accumulated charges keep them moving, two months here, six there, a few weeks down the road. And every time they move, the working girls shed their identities like reptiles sloughing off dead skin.

In this case, Joe McGuckin caught a break. A canvass of the bars downtown turned up no fewer than half a dozen regulars who recognized the victim's photograph. One of them—Shotgun, who was tending bar —had known her very well, indeed. Her name was Kathlyn Blum, and while he had not seen her on the night she died, the last time Shotgun saw her leave the bar, he thought she might have been accompanied by a Mexican.

Terrific.

Joe McGuckin was a conscientious cop, but only fictional detectives clear their desks and strike off on crusades while all else goes to hell around them. Sherlock Holmes has no surviving counterparts in modern life, and Dirty Harry wouldn't last five minutes on the street. When Shotgun failed to pan out as a suspect, Joe McGuckin found himself confronted with a blank stone wall. He could pursue the nameless Mexican, for what it might be worth, but even with a vague description they were looking at a full day prior to Kathlyn's death.

No good.

In Vegas murder just keeps rolling, like the dice. McGuckin would remember Kathlyn Blum, but in the meantime he had other work to do.

*****

The afternoon of May 14 Cole found himself adrift. The meager take from Kathlyn's purse had gone for alcohol, and he was still without a place to stay. He thought about the rescue mission, someplace he could lie low for a day or two …and suddenly he had a bright idea.

A few days back, lined up for grub at the Salvation Army, he had fallen into conversation with a fellow drifter. If he ever needed work, the man had said, there was a woman on the East Side who had trouble keeping help. Her name was Carrie Chadwick, and she ran some kind of private animal home. The drifter had her number memorized, and Eddie wrote it down, another scrap of paper in his wallet. Just in case.

That afternoon, he dug it out and made the call from Glitter Gulch, a pay phone on the sidewalk, winos rubbing shoulders with the tourists in their polyester leisure suits. Three rings before a woman's voice came on the line.

"Can I talk to Carrie Chadwick?"

"Speaking."

Eddie introduced himself, deleting the Salvation Army bread line from his recitation, telling her he needed work. A rundown on his skills, from carpentry to pushing broom.

"I *do* need someone," Carrie told him, "but you understand I can't afford a salary? The job pays room and board, that's all."

"No problem," Eddie said. "I'm tapped out as it is. I need someplace to stay."

New interest in her voice. "How old are you?"

The questions got more personal from there. It was the first time since his high school days that anyone had tried to size him up by telephone, but Eddie didn't mind. He played the game, almost enjoying it. His answers seemed to satisfy, and Carrie told him she would come by for him in half an hour. He should watch out for a blue Toyota pickup truck.

Prepared for anything from the Sea Hag to Mama Cass, Cole was pleasantly surprised to meet an average-looking woman in her early forties, long brown hair, whose taste in clothing ran to jeans and flannel shirts. Years later, on death row, he would recall Carrie Chadwick as "a pretty good looker, b somewhat horse-faced." The two of them got "pretty chummy" on the long drive to Carrie's home and compound.

The first thing Eddie saw, upon arrival, were exotic creatures. Some sat or paced in cages, sizing Eddie up as an annoyance or potential food. "Inside the house," Cole wrote, "we met another group of animals, in this case human beings." Carrie introduced him to her housekeepers, the Larsons, and a relic named Old George who seemed to have no function. (Later, Eddie learned that Old George used his monthly pension checks to pay Carrie for room and board.) While Carrie went to freshen up, the Larsons took him on a walking tour of the grounds—a spacious layout that included horse corrals, a barn, an aviary teeming with hundreds of parakeets, a kennel for dogs, more cages and pens filled with cats, rabbits, monkeys, raccoons, guinea pigs and pigeons, even a pair of peacocks. Paying visitors were welcome, and the smaller, less exotic animals were all for sale, if anybody cared to take them home.

It got on Eddie's nerves, so many wild things trapped in cages, but his mind was fixed on looking out for Number One. With any luck at all, he thought that he had found the perfect place to hide out for a while.

Carrie turned in early that night, after supper, and Eddie hung out in the kitchen, jawing with the Larsons until he heard her calling him from her bedroom, at the rear of the house. The older couple passed a knowing glance between themselves as Eddie left the table, but he shrugged it off. Whatever Carrie had in mind, he meant to play the cards as they were dealt.

She lay in bed, the covers up around her collarbone, bare shoulders hinting that she might be naked underneath. A chair was waiting for him at her bedside, and he did not hesitate. The scene had possibilities, Eddie thought.

It started with a rundown on the details of his job. In essence, Eddie would be doing anything and everything the Larsons didn't handle, from repair work to conducting guided tours, cleaning out the cages, feeding the assorted animals, and running errands. In return, there was a trailer out in back where he could sleep, and all his meals were on the house.

The conversation took a different turn from that point on, becoming personal. Cole learned that Carrie was divorced, with two grown children. Her son Todd was friends with a local motorcycle gang, the Gents, and he had given her the nickel-plated .38 revolver Carrie kept beside her bed. Her daughter Mary went with a biker, but she also helped around the place from time to time, when she had nothing else to do.

A model family.

They wound up holding hands as Eddie spun a censored version of his past, side-stepping murder, the asylums, big-league prison time.

What Carrie didn't know would not come back to haunt him, down the road.

"I think we'll get along," she told him, giving Eddie's hand a squeeze. Then suddenly the sheet slipped down just enough to let him glimpse her naked breast. "You'd better get some sleep. Long day tomorrow."

"Right."

Before he left the house, the Larsons tried to warn him off. "They cautioned me against becoming involved with Carrie," he recalled, "but of course I paid no attention."

On Sunday morning the Las Vegas *Sun* ran an article on Kathlyn Blum's murder, but Cole wasn't worried. Experience had taught him life was cheap, and dead whores were forgotten overnight. Unless he blew it with some kind of bonehead move, he had it made.

The next two months Cole went to bed with Carrie Chadwick many times, but it was nothing you could call a love affair. He also had his eyes on Mary, who dropped by Eddie's trailer on occasion. Cole focused on the younger woman as a target for his brooding rage.

"One afternoon," he said, "while Mary was sifting some feed in the barn, I came up behind her with the intent of killing her. We were there by ourselves, and I could have strangled her easily—then Carrie, when she got home—but I decided against it at the last minute. It was just too chancy, with all the people who knew me around the neighborhood."

Including his probation officer.

A fugitive since early April, Cole had dropped in at the Federal Building shortly after signing on with Carrie Chadwick. It was a gamble, like everything else in Las Vegas, but the feds decided not to jail him for evacuating San Diego, shifting his probation to Nevada under the supervision of one Helen Smith. Smith, for her part, was less than overjoyed at Eddie's latest choice of jobs, but she let it go. She made sporadic visits to the grounds, no warning in advance, but Cole could live with that.

At least he wasn't running anymore.

Except inside.

One afternoon, a teenage girl stopped by while he was working, asking if he needed help. "I told her she should come back in an hour,"

Cole recalled, "and park around in back. We would be closed by then and all alone, but I assured her Carrie would be home. A lie, of course. I meant to get her in the barn and kill her while I had the chance."

The girl came back as promised, Eddie showing her around the place for starters, working up a head of steam. They were proceeding toward the barn and destiny, when Carrie pulled into the driveway, leaning on her horn and calling Eddie to unload the pickup truck.

"At that time," Eddie said, "I would have taken my frustration out on anybody. As it was, the girl didn't hit it off with Carrie, and I never saw her again."

In mid-July, his new probation notwithstanding, Eddie knew that it was time to leave. Two months without a dime in salary, and he decided Carrie owed him one. She kept her bedroom locked, but Eddie found a crowbar in the barn and snapped the latch, taking her snub-nosed .38 and all the money he could find.

Downtown, he started hitting all his favorite taverns. Shotgun was behind the bar at Toots, and Eddie felt a sudden urge to blow the black man's brains out, but he managed to control himself. A few blocks over, dropping in at Dan & Ray's, he found Tanya the braless wonder, sitting with an older woman, soaking up the sauce. Cole joined them, chipping in when it was his turn, laughing at the same jokes he had heard a hundred times before.

Well after dark, Tanya came up with the idea of visiting some friends she knew in Parker, Arizona. Her companion, Kathy, had acquired a bosom pal by that time, and the four of them decided that a road trip sounded like a gas. Kathy's car was parked outside, but she was well past driving, and she gave the keys to Cole. He made a pit stop at a liquor store, for reinforcements, rolling south on Boulder Highway, through the heart of scenic Henderson. The rearview mirror was an education in itself, with Kathy and her companion grappling in the back seat, clothes in sweaty disarray. A few miles farther on, they reached the Railroad Pass Casino, and their thirst kicked in. Cole parked the car and led the way inside, Tanya sticking as close as a Siamese twin.

It had to be the liquor talking, Eddie later calculated, but he somehow let it slip that he was carrying a gun. Some kind of macho bullshit for the ladies, but it frightened Kathy so badly that she started sounding off, demanding that he give her car keys back. Cole pictured being stranded, miles from anywhere, and calmed her down enough that he could slip off for a moment, with Tanya. Outside, they made a beeline for the car and drove away. Another mile or so to Boulder Dam, and once across it, they were safe in Arizona.

Kathy could screw herself.

Five miles across the border, Eddie pulled into a picnic area on Highway 93. The alcohol was buzzing in his brain, and all that he could think of was Tanya, her husband sitting out another lonely night in Vegas, waiting for his wife to straggle home at dawn. He set the brake, got out, and walked around to hold Tanya's door. She smiled, already warming up for some gymnastics underneath the stars, amazed when Eddie cursed her as a lousy fucking whore and grabbed her by the throat.

Blind panic gave her strength enough to break his grip, high-stepping through the sagebrush as she sprinted down a hillside, disappearing in the shadows. Eddie drew his pistol, cocked it, waiting on the ridge for her to make a move and give herself away.

Instead, her voice reached out to Eddie from the desert night. "Don't kill me! Please!"

Relenting, startled by his own reaction, Eddie tucked the .38 back in his belt. "Okay. Where are you?"

"Here."

He tracked her voice, moved down the slope to meet her, found her stripping by the time he got there.

"Jesus, Eddie." Fear and a perverse excitement mingled in her voice.

It was a different kind of power trip, if not exactly what he had in mind, but Cole was flexible.

When they were finished, Eddie and Tanya drove south through Kingman, Yucca, Lake Havasu City. Parker, Arizona, stands beside the Colorado River, facing tiny Earp across the California border. Eddie had no fishing gear, this trip, but there were several quiet taverns where a man could lose himself. When cash ran short, he sold the nickel-plated snub-nose, ditched Tanya, and headed north.

By Tuesday the nineteenth he was back in North Las Vegas, killing time. That afternoon a traffic officer stopped Eddie for a moving violation, ran his plates, and hit the jackpot when they came back stolen.

Cole was on his way to jail, for grand theft auto.

Tanya and Kathy showed up at his preliminary hearing, on July 29. Forgiving to a fault, Tanya told Eddie not to worry, she was working on her friend to drop the charges; everything would be all right. In fact, Cole barely gave the stolen car a second thought, since Kathy had voluntarily supplied him with the keys, but Kathlyn Blum was something else. No rumbles yet, but if the cops connected him with *that* he would be facing heavy prison time, at least.

Without cash or collateral for bond, Cole was remanded to the Clark County jail pending his scheduled trial in September. Tanya kept promising to get him out, but talk was cheap, and Carrie Chadwick's single visit to the lockup had a different thrust. Todd and the Gents wanted the .38 back …There was little Cole could say. He told her where to find the pistol, if the bikers felt like searching Parker, Arizona, door to door and bar to bar, then Eddie settled back to wait and see what happened. He was working on the kitchen detail when his probation officer had a word with the judge and got Cole released on his own recognizance, with a promise to keep his nose clean.

"Why she did this," Eddie later wrote, "God only knows."

Tanya was waiting for him when he hit the street, and they "moved in" together, sleeping in abandoned houses slated for the wrecking ball, not far from Dan & Ray's, downtown. They shared the space with roaches, rats, and other homeless indigents, including several Indians. For cash, Cole scrounged the neighborhood, stealing money and other items from parked cars, spending the loot on cases of beer—described by Eddie as "our only form of nourishment."

One afternoon Tanya's husband showed up at the crash pad, calling Eddie out. Cole let him have the first swing—with a piece of pipe, no less—but his opponent couldn't fight for shit. A swift kick in the balls and he was down, Cole piling into him with everything he had, restrained at last by knowledge that a crowd had gathered, and he did not care to kill before an audience. Tanya turned up in time to jeer her battered husband as he staggered from the field of combat, Eddie more enraged by her behavior than the man's.

"If we'd been somewhere else," he later wrote, "without the witnesses, that bitch would probably be dead today."

On Wednesday, September 14, Eddie missed his court date in North Las Vegas, blowing off the charge of auto theft. Three days later

Metro patrolmen picked him up for possession of stolen property and giving false information to an officer, in the form of a bogus address. No charges were filed in that case, and in the absence of outstanding warrants, he was freed. It would be mid-December by the time police in North Las Vegas got around to issuing a criminal complaint on Eddie's failure to appear in court.

Too late.

And it was time to split, before the cops got any better organized.

For several days running Eddie had noted a white Nash Rambler station wagon sitting on a vacant lot downtown, where city architects would later plant the modern county jail. One afternoon he stopped to check the unlocked car for valuables, surprised to find ignition keys among the contents of the glove compartment.

Bingo.

On a whim, Cole decided to head for Oklahoma City. Bad memories there—his final glimpse of Billy, the arrest for pimping—but at least he knew his way around, and it was far enough from southern California that the feds would start their manhunt somewhere else, when he skipped out on his probation one more time. Tanya was anxious to accompany him, and Eddie could not find the words to put her off. With fifteen bucks between them, they began to drive southeast, through Arizona, hitting every church and rescue mission on the way for handouts. Food. A little cash. A tank of gas.

Praise Jesus.

In New Mexico their stolen Nash gave up the ghost. They hitch-hiked to the nearest town and sold the junker for $150, Eddie forging the owner's signature on the pink slip. They spent one night in a motel and caught the morning Greyhound into Oklahoma City, finishing the trip in something less than style.

A short walk from the Greyhound depot, Eddie found a cheap hotel above a skid-row tavern, where the desk clerk doubled as a bootlegger, keeping the drunks happy after hours. It would be their home for the next three weeks, Cole working odd jobs and selling his blood to the Red Cross for twenty-five dollars a week, moonlighting with the occasional liquor store burglary. Tanya, for her part, thought that money grew on trees and was designed to keep distilleries in business. On any given day, she drank throughout the afternoon and well into the evening, none too careful of the company she kept. One morning in particular, when she came stumbling in near daybreak, hours after closing time and smelling of another man's cologne, Cole beat her up and tried to throw her out a third-floor window. She escaped his clutches, crashing through their cheap door in the process, and they were evicted by the management.

Just like the good old days.

Traveler's Aid came to the rescue, with directions to a cut-rate boardinghouse and the personnel office at a nearby construction site. Eddie got a temporary job with the grounds crew, making friends with his boss, and he seemed to have a fair shot at a permanent position ... until the afternoon Tanya showed up, drunk as a lord, cursing the foreman and anyone else within earshot. Cole wasn't fired, but his employer made it clear that men with rowdy wives who dropped in on the job to raise a little hell were going nowhere fast.

In Eddie's mind, it was another golden opportunity shot down in flames.

The goddamned woman's fault.

Again.

*****

Thanksgiving Eve, November 23. Cole plans a good, old-fashioned dinner for the two of them, but Tanya is the fly in the ointment, as usual. "Like a lazy, worthless bitch, she wouldn't help me cook the turkey," Eddie says, "so in a rage, I ran her off."

He stuffs the turkey by himself and puts it in the oven, with the heat turned down to let it roast a good long time. He bastes the bird at intervals, no slouch at cooking when he has to, but his mind keeps coming back to anger, and from there to alcohol. He drinks the day away, and it is close to ten o'clock when he decides the turkey will be fine if he goes out for just a little while.

He finds a bar that advertises "Live Nude Girls" and squeezes past the slab of meat they call a bouncer, at the door. A willowy redhead with rose-tipped breasts is caressing herself on the stage, surrounded three deep by her fans. With all the heavy breathing, Eddie figures she can catch herself a buzz just taking in the alky fumes.

An empty bar stool beckons, Eddie sitting down beside a slender blonde. They start to talk, as strangers will, and Eddie gets the feeling she is interested, which suits his mood just fine. She lets it slip that she has done some topless dancing of her own, from time to time, and Eddie can believe it, checking out her ample cleavage in the low-cut dress.

Not bad.

They leave the bar together, driving back to Cole's apartment in the woman's car. "Nothing was ever said," he recalls. "It was just settled."

In the kitchen Eddie checks his turkey and they sit around the dining table, drinking beer.

"You want to stay the night?" he asks.

A smile. "That's why I came."

Adjourning to the bedroom, slowly stripping one another, Eddie vaguely conscious of the fact that he has yet to ask her name. Forget it. Tangled in the sheets, their bodies joined, identity has no significance at all.

And then, the darkness.

"Somewhere in the middle of our making love," Cole says, "the booze kicked in, or else my mind went blank—I can't say which. I've experienced blackouts before, drinking and afterward finding myself in strange surroundings, uncertain how I got there. Understand, I'm not making excuses for what went on. It's simply a fact."

He wakes at sunrise on Thanksgiving Day, the sheets and mattress fouled with human waste. Beside his bed, the blonde's red dress and underthings lay scattered with his own familiar clothes. Cole makes it to the kitchen, where a slice of meat he can't identify is lying in a skillet, on the stove. Another piece, all cut up bite-size, occupies a lone plate on the dining table.

Snack time.

Instinct draws him toward the bathroom, searching, more or less convinced of what he'll find before he steps across the threshold. Pinkish water pooled on the linoleum, with darker clots of blood smeared on the tub itself. The blonde reclines in bloody water that would probably be ankle deep, if she were standing up. Long past that now, with both feet and her right arm severed, tongue protruding from the stranglehold that took her life. Blood leeches from her buttocks, where a hefty slice of flesh has been removed.

The skillet.

Eddie backtracks to the kitchen, checking the refrigerator. Feet and arm accounted for, the ultimate in cold cuts.

With a flair for understatement, he recalls "That day was something else." Disposal is his first priority, Thanksgiving and the turkey dinner shot to hell. He goes to work with kitchen knives, remembering his old Jeff City training as a butcher when it comes to separating joints. The mangled parts fill heavy-duty garbage bags, and Eddie turns his hand to scrubbing up. The bathroom first, proceeding to the kitchen, where he cleans the frying pan and plate, his silverware, refrigerator shelves.

He lugs the trash bags out and piles them in the woman's car. A cautious tour of the city, dropping off his bundles in commercial Dumpsters, sometimes miles apart. When he is done, Cole parks her car downtown, wiped clean of fingerprints, and leaves the keys in the ignition. If a thief should happen by, so much the better. Let somebody else get busted with the lady's wheels.

Tanya comes home that night, repentant, drunk, and sniveling. Cole takes her back, and hates himself for doing so.

"She should have been the one who died," he says. "She represented everything I despised, while the blonde was unmarried as far as I know, and she seemed fairly nice. Just dumb luck, I suppose."

*****

The building site started laying off its temporary employees in December, forcing Cole to think ahead. One of his fellow workers, also slated for the ax, described the oil boom going on in Denver City, Texas. Rumor had it skilled employees were in short supply, the company reduced to canvassing in bars and bracing total strangers on the street. Eddie was skeptical, but he had nothing to lose. With Tanya and his co-worker's girlfriend, they took off for Amarillo and points south, driving in shifts, stopping only for gas and cheap wine.

It wasn't quite the boom town Eddie's friend had prophesied, but Cole soon landed a position driving diesel tankers, hauling slag water and brine for an average monthly wage of $1,500, with overtime. It was the best job of his life, and things were looking up …if only he could get rid of Tanya.

As luck would have it, Denver City was "dry," forcing Eddie to drink at Higginbotham, in neighboring Gaines County, when his thirst got the better of him. Driving back to Denver City with a major buzz on Tuesday night, the twenty-fourth of January, Eddie stopped on Highway 83 to catch a nap. It seemed like only moments later when he woke up with a flashlight shining in his eyes, a sheriff's deputy inquiring whether he could stand up straight and touch his fingers to his nose

So much for Eddie's night out in the sticks.

A standard check for wants and warrants did the rest, uncovering his latest federal charge as a probation violator. One week after his arrest, Cole headed back to San Diego, wearing chains.

FOURTEEN

Eddie was booked into the Metropolitan Correctional Center on February 2, following stopovers in Lubbock and Los Angeles. Signing into the joint, he named sister Nancy, in Richmond, as his next of kin, to receive his effects in the event of death. Diana Cole was named as his wife on the booking sheet, but Eddie made no move to get in touch.

On Monday, March 6, he was back in court with Attorney Frank Gregorcich for a "show cause" hearing. There was no defense against the charge of skipping out on his probation, and U.S. District Judge Leland Nielsen sentenced Eddie to six months in the MCC, with three years probation contingent on fulltime employment and participation in an alcoholic rehab program. Simple.

Eddie settled in to do his time, initially impressing his keepers as a model prisoner. An evaluation from March 20 describes his work performance as "excellent," with the supervising officer adding a note that "Inmate has a good attitude, is no problem to unit staff."

That changed on April 7, when the clock officially began running on Eddie's six months. The same day MCC's warden received a detainer notice from the North Las Vegas Police Department, staking a claim to Eddie on the September 1977 bail-jumping charge. On Monday, April 10, the jailhouse lawyer reared his head with a new "request for administrative remedy."

I hereby protest the biasness shown the black & white inmates in this institution in favor of the exicans. Anything the mexicans want they get.

One classic example is last year when I was released from here on probation, I was released wearing jail clothes with L.A. County Jail stenciled on the back of the legs. This was after I put in a request for clothes & gratuity. Both were denied me. I've yet to see mexicans released without clothes & gratuity. Subsequently, I was met by S.D.P.D. a half block from this institution and my ribs were broke because they thought I was an escapee. C. Ortega and R. Castillo were to blame.

Furthermore, I protest my legal mail being opened in the

mail room without my presents.

Four days later, while the warden was digesting his complaint, Cole found new cause for outrage.

On April 10, 1978 I request administrative remedy on favoritism toward mexican inmates and the opening of my lawyer/client legal mail other than in my presents. No action has yet been taken.

Now on April 14, 1978 another lawyer/client letter has been opened other than in my presents.

This has gone on long enough. I have an active case in the court and I will not have my legal mail tampered with.

This time I have notified my attorney and anticipate legal action to be taken.

On April 19 Cole was interviewed by Officer M. E. Hoover, in response to his complaints. Hoover found him "still very bitter" about the tampering with his legal mail, though Eddie had no estimate of how many letters were actually opened. As for the charge of racial "biasness," Hoover noted: "This seems to be paramount in his mind. He just plain does not like Mexicans. He wants to keep accusing others of not helping him. Everyone else is to blame, not him."

A second interview with Cole on April 21 produced the following memo from personnel officer D. M. Roily to Associate Warden L. G. Kincaid.

During the interview, it appeared that [Cole's] main concern was that his legal mail had been opened. I discussed this with Mr. Motter and found it to be true. Apparently, the personnel in the mailroom have been somewhat lax in checking for legal mail prior to running the envelops [sic] through the opener. Mr. Motter has spoken to the staff about this on several occasions and hopefully they will be more careful in the future.

[Cole] is bitter about the Mexican Nationalists being released with clothing and money. I do not believe he understands that most of them are indigent when they are received here. It is also quite apparent that he doesn't care; he just wants to complain about something and has picked this area to base his complaints on.

And complain he did. On Monday, April 24, still without an answer from the warden, Eddie filed a new four-page chWalter Lumpkin, case manager Carolyn Ortega, and counselor Ron Castillo as the "defendants" responsible for "not only cruel and unusual punishment and treatment, but physical as well as mental suffering. And above all humiliation." All things considered, Eddie thought a quarter-million dollars in compensatory damages would make the problem go away.

But he had other problems in the lockup, too. As a separate document from April 24 explains—

There is open hostility between one other inmate and myself. He has gone out of his way to provoke a fight. Mr. P. knows of this hostility. He is putting out a snich jacket on me to other inmates, provoking me by name calling and flipping me the finger. And in all ways instigating me to action that is at this point critical. To avoid unnecessary bloodshed I request transfer to another floor. If this request is denied, I request that the reason why & explanation be incerted in my file.

Cole got his transfer, but it was a minor victory at best. Warden Lumpkin's April 27 memo scuttled Eddie's dreams of instant wealth.

Investigation has disclosed that in the past some legal mail has been opened inadvertently. Staff have been cautioned pertaining to the proper procedures in opening of legal mail. There is no evidence of discrimination between ethnic groups of inmates found to exist on your housing floor. Pertaining to clothing, you requested and were permitted to have your brother bring trousers and a shirt for release clothing on November 17, 1976. This clothing was received on this date and entered on your personal property form. However, at the time of your release on April 4, 1978, you chose not to wear this clothing.

As for any clothes lost in Los Angeles, Cole was advised to take it up with the staff at the L.A. County jail.

Of course, the news wasn't *all* bad. On May 9 his fortieth birthday, North Las Vegas announced dismissal of the bail-jumping charges, leaving Eddie a more or less free man when he finally hit the street. Emboldened by success, Cole sat down on the morning of May 10 and wrote a long-winded appeal of the warden's decision, addressed to the regional director for the Federal Bureau of Prisons. Modesty and a broken zipper had prevented Cole from wearing the pants his brother delivered, Eddie's probation officer adding insult to injury when he "sujested I go to a thrift store to buy clothes." It was too much for one man to bear, and Eddie closed with a plaintive note that "I still ask $250,000 for damages for the wrongs done me."

Good luck.

Regional Director E. O. Toft fired back on May 30 with a two-page response that read, in part:

> You state that upon your release from MCC you immediately reported to the Probation Department and showed them the pants that you were wearing which were coming apart. You state that after leaving the Probation Office you were forced to change your pants and put on pants with "L.A. County Jail" stenciled on the back legs [sic]. As a result of wearing this clothing, the San Diego police stopped you, handcuffed you and broke your ribs.
>
> In checking your allegations with the U.S. Probation Office, their records indicate that you did not report to that office until three days after your release from MCC. In addition, we were advised by the San Diego Police Department that they have no record of any contact with you during 1977 and that an incident such as you have described would certainly have been recorded.
>
> In conclusion, you were provided with clothing which had been supplied by your family, you were not forced to wear L.A. County Jail clothing out of the institution, you were not provided with a gratuity in view of the fact that you possessed $204.03 of your own money at the time of release, your statement that you reported to the Probation Office on the day of your release is not supported by documentation at the Probation Office, and any

altercation which you may have been involved in with the San Diego Police Department is not reported in their records and is certainly out of jurisdiction to remedy.

Attorney Frank Gregorcich showed no inclination to pursue a quarter-million-dollar lawsuit on the basis of a broken zipper, leaving Eddie to digest the latest setback on his own. With "good time," Cole was scheduled for release on June 16, and he decided to abandon his pursuit of the elusive trousers. This time, well before he hit the street, the staff at MCC made sure Cole understood his obligation to report immediately for an interview with John Salcido, his probation officer. It was a four-block stroll, beneath the interstate, but Eddie figured he could handle that.

Besides the money in his pocket at the time he was arrested, Eddie left the lockup with another bonus from the IRS, $300 refund on another bogus tax return. It was enough to set him up at Papa Smitty's, a hotel on Fifth, but Cole had no intention of abiding by the terms of his probation. Steady work was definitely not on Eddie's list of things to do, and he preferred a quiet bar to A.A. meetings, anytime. Five months of celibacy was enough for any man, and once he had the room nailed down, Cole started looking for a place to dip his wick.

As usual in skid-row neighborhoods, he didn't have to look too far for women on the make. There was Joann, who tended bar and gave him freebies, while Billy Jo competed for his interest at another bar, wearing Eddie's ring around her neck. When he got tired of Papa Smitty's, Cole moved in with Betty Lou at the St. James Hotel, stealing away when he could for an overnight with Margie. "Occasionally I also made it with a stray who came around," Cole said, "but these were the main girls I played around with." When the women came to blows, he sometimes had to hide from all of them, but he was not averse to sleeping on the roof from time to time, cherishing his new reputation as "Fast Eddie."

Life was almost good enough to quell his morbid fantasies.

Almost.

*****

Green's Bar, at Fourth and Elm. Cole meets a foxy blonde who doesn't look quite old enough to drink, much less hang out in sleazy joints and drive the old men wild. They talk a little, shoot some pool. Come midnight, Eddie volunteers to walk her home and they slip out the exit, arm-in-arm. Still joking as they move along the sidewalk, with the blond fox giggling when he starts to feel her up. No protest. Two blocks down he steers her into a commercial parking lot. All dark, the only car in sight an ancient clunker, parked way back, against the chain-link fence.

"I brought her here to do one thing," says Eddie, "feeling she was just a tramp playing around on her old man. I was going to kill her."

Eddie walks her right around the car, a perfect gentleman. She steps in front of him, and Eddie has an inspiration. Why not try the choke hold he has seen police and jailers use so often, maybe give his hands a rest? One arm around her neck, the other braced in back to close the noose, and Eddie gives it everything he's got.

No good.

Some kind of faulty execution, with the blond fox wriggling in his grasp and screaming now, as if she barely feels his grip at all. He makes his mind up in a heartbeat, switching to the old two-handed grip and takes her down. They wallow on the ground behind the junker, Cole still choking her, until the sound of her pathetic whimpering cuts through the crimson fog inside his skull.

Incredibly, illogically, he lets her go. An awkward moment, facing one another in the dark, before he offers her a hand. They spend the next half hour sitting there, while Eddie tells her all about his violent urges, going back to childhood. When she asks pointblank if he has ever killed a woman, Cole denies it, doing everything he can to put the fox at ease. She tells him he should get some help, and Eddie nods. How true. He winds up flagging down a cab and sends her home.

Strike one.

Another night at Patrick's, one block north at Fourth and Fir. Cole singles out a young Italian woman, instantly impressed with her appearance: long, dark hair, a clinging sweater, skintight jeans. Up close, he notes a shiner hidden by cosmetics, and she tells him of her latest battle with a brutish husband. Three days on the street, without a decent place to stay. She makes it clear that anybody with the price of dinner and a room can name his own reward.

Cole volunteers and checks them into a hotel, nearby. Upstairs, the woman barely has her sweater off when she collapses on the bed, passed out. Cole strips without delay and rolls her over, straddling her hips, both hands around her neck.

"She flopped around like a fish out of water," he recalls. "I guess my heart wasn't in it, because I backed off and released her."

She leaps out of bed, frightened and excited, all at once. Instead of bolting for the door, she finishes undressing, telling Eddie that he doesn't need the macho act to turn her on. They wind up staying for a second night, Cole slipping out for burgers in between their sweaty couplings. When he comes back with supper on the second day, the woman tells him she has spoken to her husband, and he wants her back.

"Going out the door, the bitch asked me for twenty dollars," Eddie says. "She was lucky to get out of there alive."

Strike two.

Another night, with Betty Lou asleep in bed, Cole hits a tavern down the street from the St. James. He spots a cute young woman drinking by herself. When drunks come on to her, she puts them off with style, no gutter mouth. No wedding or engagement ring, but there is something in her eyes—or maybe in the air— that tells Cole she must die.

The target finishes her drink, slips out the side door, Eddie following. He keeps it casual, a midnight stroll up Sixth, in the direction of Balboa Park. At Grape she veers across a vacant lot, toward yet another cheap hotel. No streetlights here. Cole sees his chance and hurries to catch up.

"She saw me coming," he recalls, "and stood there with a blank look on her face, maybe shock."

Converted into panic as he rushes her and locks both hands around her throat, momentum dropping both of them into the litter and the dirt. His lips are drawn back in a snarl, his victim frothing at the mouth, her body jerking as she tries to take in nonexistent oxygen. So close ...and then his goddamn hands begin to cramp.

He shifts positions, covering her nose and mouth with sweaty palms to smother her, but she won't die. At last, exhausted, Eddie takes a break, checking the action as several men emerge from a deli across the street. The woman comes up screaming like the blonde in *Psycho,* Eddie bolting as a mob of strangers gallop to the rescue. He is leading when he snags his foot on something, sprawling on his face, and then they have him, one arm twisted painfully behind his back. A squad car pulling up as they return him to the scene, his victim standing there with other men surrounding her, the tracks of fresh tears on her face.

Strike three, and there is nothing left to do but lie his ass off.

Thinking fast, he tells the story that has saved him once before. The woman and her boyfriend ganging up on Cole, a mugging, Eddie fighting back. The other man too quick for Eddie, but he has the woman dead to rights. A clear-cut case of self-defense.

"I bluffed it out again," he says. "I don't know what the woman told them, but the two cops didn't buy it. Instead of taking me in, they drove me back to the St. James and dropped me off with a warning to be careful around strangers."

Eddie gives the officers his word.

His mother may have raised a monster, but he would not be mistaken for a fool.

*****

A few days later Diana got word that Eddie was back and started calling around, trying to find him. One call, to the Gaslight Tavern, resulted in Billy Jo returning his ring, but Eddie had a few days grace before Di found him in a bar on Sixth Street, killing time with Betty Lou.

"Just my luck," he recalled, "she saved me from my sordid life downtown and took me back to an apartment she had on Louisiana Street, in North Park."

Diana looked better than Eddie remembered, almost a sight for sore eyes. She had been sober for a while, seeing a doctor about her cirrhosis, and she quickly laid down the law: No booze in the apartment, under any circumstances. Cole was skeptical, but he agreed. When he got thirsty, he could always take a walk downtown.

"We got along fine," he said, "but I was sleeping on the couch for several days, until she finally invited me to join her in the bedroom."

Wedded bliss.

Diana was living on Social Security, and Eddie soon went back on welfare, drawing a monthly check in addition to food stamps. He had yet to visit his probation officer, much less seek steady work or check into an alcoholic rehab program, but it did not seem that anyone was working overtime to track him down.

Bureaucracy is good that way, until you stub your toe.

On Wednesday, October 25, Cole was arrested by San Diego police on a charge of public drunkenness. A quick computer check turned up some traffic tickets he had never paid ...and his current status on federal probation. By Friday he was back at MCC, with his probation officer intent on sticking Eddie for another violation. Surprisingly, the magistrate set bail at $2,000, and Eddie hit the bricks on Halloween, John Salcido fuming as he watched another scofflaw wriggle through the system's gaping cracks.

With one bloodshot eye on the future, Eddie applied to the California Department of Vocational Rehabilitation for training in air-conditioning and refrigeration, but the class had no openings until January. While he waited, Eddie found a part-time janitorial position at the San Diego School of Pathology, neglecting to inform the welfare people of his job. That way, the monthly checks and food stamps kept on rolling.

Slick.

Cole's supervisor on the new job was a young woman named Sharon. In fact, except for another maintenance man, the whole staff was female, a situation designed to provoke Eddie's anger and lust.

"It wasn't a bad job," he explained, "but it was risky for all concerned. I had thoughts of calling the girls downstairs one by one, to kill them, maybe picking off the female couriers who sometimes came in through the basement on the night shift."

Dreamland, but he couldn't think of any way to hide his tracks.

Most evenings, after work, he made the rounds of favorite bars, still hunting. Once, he singled out a female bartender whose taste in clothing ran to sheer blouses with no bra, trailing her home one night after closing time, but other pedestrians spoiled the game. Another miss, his anger festering inside.

Cole logged another drunk arrest on Wednesday afternoon, November 8, but the police were either careless or forgiving. Eddie was released the same day, without another trip to MCC, and John Salcido never heard about the bust.

A lucky break.

Eddie started his air-conditioning class on January 5, and staffer Greg Anderson referred him to the county mental health service four days later. In an interview with Esther Salazar, Cole admitted his alcoholism and expressed a desire for counseling, Salazar noting that Eddie "does not consider himself a violent person unless provoked." Cole requested a male counselor and was referred to the University of California Medical Center in Hillcrest, on an outpatient basis. He kept sporadic appointments over the next two months, describing his main problem as barroom altercations, carefully omitting any reference to violence against women.

Eddie's class ran for three months, forcing him to quit his job, but he picked up the slack with unemployment checks to supplement the welfare. His academic grades were "nothing to boast about," as he preferred TV game shows to cracking the books. On the side, he continued to drink and carouse as before, sometimes sleeping over with Joann or Billy Jo for a change of pace.

Diana, for her part, was gradually slipping off the wagon, and Eddie was soon boozing at home, just like the old days. Di adopted a stray Siberian husky and named him El Lobo, relying on the dog for company— and later for protection, as her relationship with Cole degenerated into spite and violence.

In March 1979 Eddie was officially continued on probation, despite his October drunk arrest and frequent lapses in reporting to John Salcido. A few days later he and Diana rented a house on Forty-fifth, near University, in City Heights. For extra money Cole put his new training to work, repairing equipment and appliances at several bars and pool halls in the neighborhood. Come April he applied for a job at Sims Appliance, a few blocks from the house, on Fairmount, and the owners took him on as a repairman.

Maurice and Linda Sims befriended Cole, and Linda came to know Diana well in the ensuing months. Around the shop, Linda would later describe Eddie's behavior as "eerie," sometimes creeping up behind her silently, as if to take her by surprise. At other times, she had a sense of being watched and found him staring at her from across the room. At that, she got off easy. Eddie never made a move or threatened her in any way that she could specify. She once suspected Eddie or "another guy" of stealing from her desk, a pad of checks, but she decided not to push it and the mystery remained unsolved.

Aside from service and repairs, Cole's job involved delivery and

200

installation of appliances, sometimes accompanied by Maurice or other workers, sometimes on his own. In retrospect, with Eddie's murder confessions on file in Texas, Linda was relieved that there had been no incidents with any of her customers at home. Some of the housewives liked to tease deliverymen, and no one knew what they were playing with, where Eddie was concerned.

One incident that stuck in Eddie's mind involved a young, attractive woman whose purchases included a washer and dryer. Cole drove out with Maurice to make the delivery, and their customer met them in the kitchen, wearing a see-through blouse, no bra underneath. At one point she caught Eddie staring, flashed him a smile and arched her back, showing off pink nipples through the sheer material. Maurice got an eyeful, as well, but Eddie's mind was on the woman's husband, putting in another day at work to help support a bitch who flaunted her body at strangers in the family home. Cole's common sense and caution kept him from returning after-hours, and the smiling woman never knew how close she came to death that afternoon.

Diana had a caring friend in Linda Sims, and it was not unusual for them to spend an evening together, after work. Months later, reading the accounts of Cole's arrest in Dallas, Linda recognized Eddie's description of Di as a drunk, but she drew a blank when Eddie called his wife a tramp. According to Linda, Diana was "never flirty or anything like that" when they went out together, even though she had the opportunity. By that time, though, it hardly mattered. When he drank—and that meant every day—Cole's thoughts went back to Di's brief fling with Charlie, in the days before she was his wife. Conditioned to detest the infidelity of women, Eddie was unable to forget, unwilling to forgive.

While Di preferred the company of friends, Cole liked to prowl the streets and bars alone. He borrowed Linda's car sometimes, to look for women, picking up one semiregular in the saloon once owned by Essie Buck. It was a trip, revisiting his old haunts eight years later, wondering if Robert Ring had given up the ghost by now. The woman's name was Bunny, she was separated from her husband, and she welcomed Eddie to her bed. He thought of killing her each time they met, but managed to restrain himself.

It was a safer game with strangers, all around.

By all appearances, Cole's federal probation officer had given up when Eddie skated on the drunk arrest, in March. When Eddie showed up at the office smelling like a still or skipped appointments altogether, when he shunned the mandatory A.A. meetings, nothing more was said or done. The system missed another beat, and Cole went sailing through.

One evening a distraught Diana called on Linda and Maurice to help retrieve her husband from a local bar. Eddie was feeling no pain when they got there, and he gladly accepted Maurice's invitation "to a party." Even when they reached the county detox center, Cole was amiable, signing in and waiting for directions to his padded room. He must have changed his mind, though, and the detox center was not built for maximum security. Somehow, he beat Diana home to Forty-fifth Street, met her in the living room, relaxing on the couch with beer in hand, a sitcom on the tube.

If anybody bothered to report the incident, it never turned up in his file.

Some guys have all the luck.

*****

The night of Monday, August 27, Eddie drops into a bar on University, two blocks from home. He meets a short-haired blonde named Bonnie Sue O'Neil, and they begin to hit it off. A few more drinks, a game of pool, and Eddie doesn't mind at all when she suggests they try some other taverns in the neighborhood.

Bonnie Sue's reputation precedes her.

"In most of the bars," Eddie recalls, "she was treated like the plague. Everybody knew her as a rowdy, foul-mouthed drunk and whore."

His land of woman.

Eddie finally suggests that they go back to Sims Appliance, letting Bonnie Sue believe he owns the place. He has a key—a sign of trust, despite the unresolved suspicion of a theft—and there is no one to object as he shows Bonnie Sue around. She finds the bedroom on her own, a small apartment Linda keeps in back, complete with water bed and stove, while Eddie lingers at the desk, pretending to complete some urgent paperwork.

No rush. Good things take time.

"Come here a minute, will you?"

Bonnie tired of waiting for him, taking Eddie by the hand and leading him in the direction of the bed. It is his first time making love on water, and he will recall their tryst, years later, as "a night to end all screwing."

Well, not quite.

The clock is striking 2:00 A.M. when they come up for air and Bonnie reaches for the telephone, informing Eddie that she has to call her husband.

Click.

She makes the call, and Eddie listens to the brief, one-sided conversation, Bonnie nuzzling and playing with him all the while. At last she tells her husband she will be home soon and cradles the receiver, giving Eddie's cock a parting squeeze before she stoops to fetch her bra.

And he is waiting when she straightens up, hands clenching tight around her throat. He pulls her back down on the bed, waves rolling underneath them as he strangles her. No second thoughts or hesitation this time, nothing more to say. The phone call is her last good-bye.

When she is dead, Cole takes a moment to consider his dilemma. Fairmont is a busy street, with shops and homes together, and he has no car. That leaves the alley, still a chance of being spotted with the body, but he has no choice. He can't afford to leave her where she is.

Cole dresses quickly, leaving Bonnie naked like a cheap, two-timing slut deserves. He manages to hoist her in a fireman's carry, draped across one shoulder, hears the back door lock itself behind him as he takes her out. Dogs barking at him, lights in different windows as he labors down the alley, carrying his load of death. A block or so away from Sims Appliance, Eddie drops her in the shadows and begins the short walk home.

Next morning Linda finds the back room in a state of disarray, dried vomit on the floor, a smell of urine rising from the tangled sheets. Cole tells her that he had a fight with Di and went out drinking, coming here to spend the night in peace. But not alone, apparently, with women's garments scattered on the floor.

"What was she wearing when she left?"

Cole mutters something unintelligible, almost blushing.

"Anyway, I want this mess cleaned up."

"Okay."

He drops the clothing in a Dumpster, right out back, returns to strip the sheets and mop the floor.

One thing you have to say for Eddie Cole: He's not afraid of dirty jobs.

*****

Homicide investigator James A. Shively took the call on August 28. A nine-year veteran on the San Diego force, he had seen his share of corpses, and the stiff found in an alley behind 3625 Fairmont that Tuesday morning was nothing special. Caucasian. Female. Nude. No sign of any clothes or other personal effects around the scene. Without visible wounds, Shively did not even try to guess the cause of death.

Fingerprints made the ID, revealing Bonnie Sue O'Neil as a working prostitute with prior arrests, a.k.a. Bonnie Stewart, Bonnie Straus, or Bonnie Taylor. Take your pick.

Life has its dangers on the street. A lanky trick who likes his action rough. A pimp whose discipline gets out of hand from time to time. In Bonnie's case, perhaps a husband sick and tired of sitting home while she went out to make new friends and charge them by the quarter hour.

As it was, the medical examiner's report came back with a diagnosis of death by natural causes. Bonnie Sue's blood-alcohol level coincided with the pathologist's finding of advanced Laennec's cirrhosis, an ailment associated with acute, chronic alcoholism. In the coroner's opinion, Bonnie Sue O'Neil sat down and drank herself to death. As for her placement in the alley and the missing clothes, perhaps her final trick got nervous when she breathed her last and saw a chance to save himself some grief.

Case closed.

Remarking on the quality of San Diego homicide investigations, Cole's employer noted that detectives never questioned her or any other Fairmont merchants, never searched the alleyway for Bonnie Sue's belongings, never heard the tale of Eddie's one-night stand. In Linda's estimation, shared by others interviewed for this account, a victim "has to be somebody" —that is, someone well-to-do and worthy of respect— before police in San Diego will pursue a murder case with any zeal. A decade later, with the unsolved serial murders of forty-two prostitutes on the books, local authorities still maintained their traditional indifference to "low priority" victims.

*****

Cole's marriage was disintegrating through the latter weeks of summer, with Diana drinking more than ever, Eddie threatening her life on more than one occasion, sometimes choking her while they had sex. By August Di had confided in Linda Sims, describing her fear of Cole, the way she took El Lobo with her everywhere for self-protection, "even to the bathroom." Her doctor prescribed sedatives for Diana's nerves, but even with the booze they seemed to do no good.

Around the fourteenth of September, Di and Linda spoke to John Salcido, briefing him on Eddie's strange behavior, drunken binges, threats of homicide. Salcido listened, nodded sympathetically ...and told them there was nothing he could do. His hands were tied.

On Monday night, the seventeenth, Diana found her husband drinking with a slut named Bunny, in a bar not far from home. She nagged him into leaving with her, bitching at him all the way to Forty-fifth Street, Eddie finally telling her to can it, he was turning in.

Di joined him in the bedroom moments later, suddenly repentant, offering to make things right if he would only give her half a chance. They made love almost tenderly, the first time in a month of Sundays that the act had not been tainted with a stain of fear or violence.

And when they were finished, Eddie strangled her to death in bed.

The next few days, whenever Mama Joyce would phone the house, she found Diana "out," "asleep," or "in the shower." One afternoon she dropped in unexpectedly—to fetch a coat, she said—and Eddie told her Di was out. He didn't know exactly where, or when she would return. Cole hovered while she chose a jacket from the main hall closet. On the floor, a lumpy shape reclined beneath an old blue blanket, but if she saw it she apparently didn't have the nerve to ask, much less reach out and touch.

On Tuesday night, September 25, Cole's next-door neighbor called police, reporting Eddie scrabbling around beneath her house. Patrolmen found him in the crawlspace, working on a grave-sized excavation, and they drove him to the detox center. This time, members of the staff succeeded in confining Eddie overnight.

Next morning, bright and early, Joyce stopped by the house on Forty-fifth and found herself alone. A rancid odor led her to the closet, where a rumpled bedspread had replaced the blanket. Swallowing a knot of fear, she tugged a corner back …and ran to call police.

By sheer coincidence, Detective Shively caught the squeal on Eddie's second homicide within a month. He was examining Diana's decomposing corpse when Cole breezed in the back door, fresh from detox, and discovered uniforms inside his home. Without a second thought, he turned and ran, unnoticed, making for the Continental Trailways depot and the next bus out of town.

Las Vegas sounded right, for starters, Eddie certain there must be an all-points bulletin for his arrest by now.

In fact, Diana's autopsy revealed a blood-alcohol level of .42, more than four times the statutory limit for intoxication, and her death was ascribed to advanced cirrhosis, complicated by ethyl alcohol poisoning. Another diagnosis of "natural causes."

The only people looking for Eddie Cole, so far, were the feds. On September 27 Chief Probation Officer Sidney Sonnabaum appeared before Judge Leland Nielsen, requesting a bench warrant for Eddie's arrest on charges of breaking probation. Uncle Sam was pissed about his latest change of residence and failure to report for therapy.

As far as any murder charges, San Diego's finest were content to let it slide. Another pair of victims on the house.

FIFTEEN

Eddie's bus stopped in Los Angeles before the long desert run to Nevada, but the expected police dragnet never materialized. Once they were rolling east on 1-15, Cole let himself relax enough to risk a conversation with a young, attractive woman who was Vegas-bound to seek employment as a showgirl. She had all the right equipment, and they hit it off at once. The hour was late when they arrived, but there was little thought of sleeping when they checked into a cheap motel, downtown. It was a nice diversion, but when morning came, they went their separate ways.

"I couldn't afford another mouth to feed," Cole recalled, "and besides, I'd already gotten what I wanted."

A few days drinking at Dan & Ray's took care of his cash reserve, and Eddie started looking for a place where he could hide for free. He chose the A.A. house on Fourth Street, near Squires Park, and was accepted on condition that he go to meetings and abide by the prevailing curfew. Otherwise, the residents were free to come and go at will, presumably in search of jobs.

Work never rated high on Eddie's list of things to do, but the saloons in Vegas don't give credit, and his California welfare scam was shot to hell. He tried his hand at washing dishes, but it didn't take. At last, he went to work for another charity, a driving job, much like his former post with the Salvation Army. Eddie liked variety, and there was always something on the truck a man could use.

The warehouse staff included several handicapped employees, one of them a mildly retarded young woman named Sharla Floyd. Her dark hair and hourglass figure caught Eddie's eye, but Sharla remained aloof in those early days, a mixture of shyness and self-defense. Cole finally broke the ice by treating her to soda on a break one day, and they eventually grew closer, Eddie helping Sharla sort huge piles of clothing at the warehouse, in between his pickup runs. Their supervisor was a cagey profiteer who bilked his "slow" employees on the side, frequently paying them well below minimum wage. On one occasion Eddie got a look at Sharla's paycheck and discovered she was taking home the princely sum of thirty-four dollars for two weeks work.

"The boss did other asshole things, too," Eddie wrote, "but this was the main thing that pissed me off. After awhile, it got to be a regular thing, me ragging him about the way he took advantage of the retards. There was no love lost between us, but he kept me on the job."

With a couple of paychecks in hand, Cole decided it was time for a break. He told the boss and new acquaintances about a family emergency in California. Any luck at all, a week or ten days max should see him back. Cole's supervisor didn't care if it was true or not. Experience had taught him that your average driver hears a different drummer marking time, the music frequently a marching song.

All set.

Cole wasn't going back to California, though. Not yet.

He reckoned he could find most anything he wanted right downtown.

*****

Saturday night, November 3, he wanders into Dan & Ray's, half-potted as it is. An empty bar stool beckons, and he plants himself beside an aging redhead, checking out her wedding ring. No man in sight, and Eddie sizes up his prey. He pegs her age at fifty, give or take. The freckles and her slender body take a few years off, but you can see hard living in her face.

They let it go with first names, Eddie and Marie. Two strangers in the night. Their conversation has no fixed direction, drifting on a tide of alcohol. Cole has no interest in the woman's life beyond its final moments. In his pocket, coiled and waiting, is a length of nylon cord, fresh-cut to serve as a garrote.

It never hurts to be prepared.

An hour slips away before he feels the old man watching them, approaching cautiously. Gray hair, a sunken chest, and haunted eyes.

"Marie," he says, "I want you to come home."

She swivels on her stool to face him, her expression scornful. "No. I'm staying here, with *him.*"

The old man stares at Eddie for a moment, deadpan, clearly wishing there was something he could do or say. Instead, he turns and walks away, defeated. Eddie has a brief glimpse of his father slipping out the door ... or is the blurry profile closer to his own?

Marie explains. The old man is her husband of a year, but she regrets the marriage now. Security is one thing, but a man should also satisfy his wife in bed or stand aside while someone else fills in. She thinks of leaving him from time to time, but a divorce means she would have to get a job.

"I had already planned to kill her if we left the bar together," Eddie says, "but this removed all doubt."

Another thirty minutes, more or less, and Eddie sees the old man coming back with reinforcements. Number two is somewhat younger, slightly larger, but they don't know who they're dealing with. If it comes down to brawling, Eddie figures he can take them both, but he prefers to sip his beer and listen, let Marie decide her own fate for herself.

The old man pleads and argues, seeming on the verge of tears. Marie stands fast, demanding time alone—or with a friend. Cole wants to slap the old man's face and wake him up, remind him where he is with drunken strangers viewing his humiliation, but it is not Eddie's game. Marie is filling in the blank spots on her own death warrant, signing it in bitter gall.

At last, the old man gives it up, his friend providing silent comfort as they leave together. Eddie drains his beer and orders up another, killing time.

He has all night.

Marie has somewhat less.

By midnight Dan & Ray's is crowded, noisy to the point that Eddie feels a headache creeping in behind his eyes. He does not argue when Marie suggests they take a walk and find someplace to spend a quiet night alone.

The Casbah is a block away on Lewis Avenue. A smaller bar, less frequented by drop-ins from the neighborhood. Cole knows it well and is relieved to find the tavern sparsely populated as they enter. They are barely settled at a corner table when Marie suggests that he go on ahead and rent a room.

The night clerk takes his money, handing him the key to number 215. Cole fabricates a name and signs the register. Marie is working on another drink when he returns. He lets her finish it and takes her up the back stairs, so the clerk won't have a chance to see the two of them together.

In the room Cole suddenly decides to bathe before they go to bed. The night has left him feeling soiled, unclean, and there is worse ahead. He fills the tub, reclining in the water while Marie takes time to rinse her blouse and underthings in the sink, draping them over the towel rod to dry. Naked underneath the pitiless fluorescent lights, her heavy breasts sagging, she looks every day of her fifty-odd years.

Cole braces himself as she joins him in the bathtub, shifting so that she can kneel between his legs. Without preamble, she begins to stroke him, bending down to take him in her mouth. It seems a practiced gesture, no real passion to it. Eddie feels the room begin to spin.

"Oral sex has always disgusted me," he recalls, "and I made her stop—but gently, not wanting anything to interfere with my plans."

In bed they rut until exhaustion overtakes them, lying tangled in the sweaty sheets. Relaxing afterward, Marie suggests that they move in together, keep a good thing going. Or, if Eddie would prefer, she can continue living with her husband, slipping out to see him on the side. It makes no difference, either way.

Blind fury chokes off Eddie's answer as he rises, kneeling in the middle of the bed. Marie misunderstands, her fingers milking him, prepared to start from scratch. Cole shoves her hand away and straddles her, arms pinned against her sides. Confusion melting into pleasure as he starts to stroke her breasts, hands slowly working upward, toward her neck.

Unconsciousness comes swiftly, Eddie backing off to scramble for his slacks and find the nylon cord. A twist around each fist and once around her neck before he draws it tight, her body lapsing into mute convulsions as she dies. He keeps the pressure on for several moments longer, making sure his work is done before he rolls away.

No hurry, but he does not feel like using her again. Her body holds no secrets for him now, and he has done his best to show her for the sleazy, cheating tramp she is. The old man will be better off without her, when he stops and thinks about it.

No one *really* misses a deceitful bitch.

He dresses quickly, drunk enough to overlook his jockey shorts, still lying on the bathroom floor. Her body looks revolting to him now, the pale legs splayed. Before he leaves, Cole steps back to the bed and pulls the sheet up to her chin. Downstairs, he circles past the registration desk to get his key deposit back.

A penny saved...

*****

A maid at the Casbah discovered the body at half past noon on Sunday, and police were summoned to the scene. Detective Karen Good had close to fifteen years of service on the force, five spent investigating homicides, and in Las Vegas that means she had seen it all. Since January, Metro had been averaging one murder every five days, regular as clockwork, and they still had far to go before it made a record year.

The woman had no handbag, no ID of any kind. Her blouse and underthings were drying in the bathroom, slacks tossed carelessly across a chair, but they were all anonymous, no monograms or labels to identify their owner. Ditto for the Jockey shorts, which were routinely bagged and tagged. When Good removed the sheet, she had no trouble picking out the livid marks of strangulation on their victim's throat.

"Jane Doe."

In Vegas, as in other cities with a large-scale transient population, many victims wear that tag forever. Bodies dumped in alleys, sometimes curled up in the trunks of old, abandoned cars. The desert yields its share, most of them withered by the sun and gnawed by predators. This time, the good guys caught a break when a description of the corpse was published Monday morning and a friend came forward with her name.

The corpse from 215 was Marie Cushman, a.k.a. "Marie Powers" or "Marie Stoddard." She had been picked up for prostitution in her time, but luck had intervened before they had to work the print files, doing it the hard way.

With a name in hand, Detective Good pitched in to look for witnesses. She turned up Joseph Walsh, a patron at the Casbah Bar who told her he had seen Marie and a companion—male Caucasian, forty-five to forty-eight years old, brown hair—come in and take a seat. The man had ducked out moments later, pausing long enough to kiss Marie goodbye. A quarter hour passed before he came back in and said, "I have a room." They left together, shortly after 1:00 A.M., and that was all. The rest was history.

Or should have been, until the case took a peculiar turn. On Friday afternoon, November 9, the *Review-Journal* published a composite sketch of Metro's suspect, describing him as "an unidentified fifty-year-old man," five foot two, 120 pounds, gray hair. According to the article, the Casbah's desk clerk also saw a second man duck into Cushman's room, around 2:30 in the morning. The elusive second suspect was described as "an Indian in his thirties, about six feet tall, with short, wavy black hair." The late arrival had been driving a nondescript Chevrolet, with California license tags.

*****

The phantom Indian puzzled Cole, but he lost no sleep over Metro's composite. They were looking for a suspect nine years older, five inches shorter, and forty pounds lighter than Eddie, with gray hair instead of brown. Unless he bungled it beyond all comprehension, he was home and dry.

Everyone seemed glad to see him back at work, and Sharla most of all. She introduced Cole to her mother, and he picked up on the bad vibrations right away. With fifteen years between them, Sharla just turned twenty-six, her mother's doubts were understandable. She had new questions every time they met, exploring Eddie's past, but Cole could hold his own with experts when it came to lying, making up the details as he went along.

The first time he made love to Sharla, Eddie checked them into a motel, away from prying eyes and questions at the A.A. home. By this time Eddie heard talk at the warehouse that she may not have been a virgin, but he liked to find out for himself.

Eddie wrote, "I reasoned that she may have been taken advantage of, since she was retarded."

In any case, he felt no urge to kill her at the moment, and it seemed that their relationship was blossoming. A few more sessions in the sack, and Sharla started talking marriage, with her mother standing firm in opposition to the whole idea. Around the warehouse, friends fell out on either side of the debate, while Eddie started feeling cornered, less than eager for another fling at matrimony. Twice a widower—and once deliberately—he had no urge to play the old, familiar scenes again.

On Saturday night, December 15, Cole set out to drown his misgivings in liquor. He was well on his way to oblivion when he phoned Sharla from the Four Queens casino downtown, rambling, semicoherent at best. She rushed to join him, sensing trouble, drawing Cole outside. Before they traveled half a block he broke down, crying like a baby, begging her to let him go and save herself. Unable to explain, he finally gave it up as Sharla checked them into a motel, her simple hunger overriding Eddie's short-lived good intentions.

They were married Sunday morning, by a justice of the peace. It was a shock to Sharla's parents, but the deed was done.

The next thing Eddie needed was a change of scene.

His one-time foreman at the trucking company in Denver City, Texas, liked Cole well enough to hire him back, despite his prison record, and a phone call set it up. Sharla's father chipped in $500 for a used car, and the newlyweds left Vegas on December 20, driving east.

In Denver City they found a small room at the Hilltop Hotel, Eddie working hard and keeping his nose clean. Forty-one is late for starting over, but he thought it might not be *too* late. And if it was ...well, there would always be the highway, leading somewhere else. New faces. Variations on a waking nightmare.

Christmas that year was the best he could remember, since his mother's venom always spoiled the holidays in childhood, beer and whiskey blurring out the rest. It felt to Eddie like he had the makings of a family. If he could just hold on . . .

A few days after New Year's he was stopped by the highway patrol for driving with expired license tags. Cole didn't have a Texas operator's license, either, but he got off with a warning, telling the patrolman he had left his California license at the house. Computers shafted him again, revealing his most recent federal warrant, and he was arrested two days later, Sharla in hysterics as patrolmen led him to the car. Once all the paperwork was finished, Texas gave him to the feds and he was locked up at La Tuna, outside Anthony, New Mexico.

For Eddie Cole, it felt like coming home.

*****

La Tuna's celebrity inmate was Billy Sol Estes, a bosom friend of ex-President Lyndon Johnson's, then serving his second term for white-collar fraud, and Eddie had a chance to meet the grinning con man before he was flown back to Terminal Island, at San Pedro, California. There, he sat for six days, awaiting the return trip to San Diego's Metropolitan Correctional Center. In the meantime, Sharla had gone home to her mother in Las Vegas, selling off their car to cover bus fare.

Eddie was booked into MCC on January 17, with Attorney Craig Fenech appointed to handle his case. Cole's only visitor, aside from Fenech, was his old probation officer, described by Eddie as "a real asshole" who despised Eddie because "I wouldn't kowtow to him." Apparently, it never crossed Cole's mind that his contempt for John Salcido and the whole probation system might discourage friendly feelings in return. On this occasion he described the officer as "gloating," quizzing Eddie on his movements since the latest flight from San Diego, working back inexorably to the topic of Diana's death.

"Quite suddenly, he asked me if I killed her," Cole recalled, "and I said no. He said her body was found in the closet at our rented house, and that she died under mysterious circumstances. Also, he suggested the police would probably be coming by to see me in a day or two."

There was still no sign of homicide detectives by February 25, when Cole and his attorney stood before Judge Nielsen. Convicted of violating his probation a second time, Eddie was sentenced to the maximum one-year term for a misdemeanor, returned to MCC to start serving his time.

San Diego had him worried now, with the specter of a murder charge shadowing his every move. If the police started digging on Di, who knew where it would end? For all Cole knew, the sheriff's office might still have an eye on him for Essie Buck. And there was always Bonnie Sue O'Neil, if Linda started talking to the cops downtown. California had lately reinstated the death penalty, after a lapse imposed by the U.S. Supreme Court, and while the state showed no inclination to actually execute anyone, the mere prospect was bad enough.

Whatever lay in store for Eddie Cole, he didn't plan on sucking gas in the green room at San Quentin. Not if he could find another way to go.

The notion of a transfer piqued his interest, banking on the rule that someone out of sight is also generally out of mind. He filed for relocation to the federal pen at Englewood, Colorado—known within the system as "a pretty good place" to serve time—and his request for transfer got a thumbs-up at the end of April. Nothing from the local cops before his keepers moved him back to Terminal Island on May 10, parking him there for ten days in preparation for his final move.

Cole got to Englewood on Tuesday afternoon, May 20, but his reputation had preceded him, sounding alarms in the warden's office. A memo of that date advised that

> Subject's case has been reviewed and determined to be totally inappropriate for Englewood due to psycho-sexual problems and violent assaultive behavior. Subject requires in-depth mental evaluation and treatment. Serious history of assault upon females. Subject is redesignated to MCFP Springdfield [sic] for evaluation and treatment.

At Englewood Eddie went straight to the hole, a counselor and the assistant warden dropping in to tell him why he couldn't stay. "I'm pretty used to this reaction," Eddie wrote, "but the rejection still rankled and I told them to go fuck themselves, adding a few more choice insults as they left the cell."

Scheduling Cole for a transfer to Springfield was one thing; getting him there was another. Instead of going straight to Missouri, Eddie was routed back to La Tuna, where he remained through June 4. On the fifth he was moved again ...back to Englewood. After eight more days in the hole, he was shipped back to La Tuna *again,* this time cooling his heels till July 7.

Despite the Keystone Kops rendition of a Chinese fire drill, Eddie knew where he was going. To seasoned inmates, the Medical Center for Federal Prisoners at Springfield, Missouri, is known as "The Pits," made infamous by rumors of harsh treatment, electroshock therapy, and tough guards. Such stories frequently consist of one part truth and nine parts bullshit, but he had no wish to find out for himself. On the afternoon of June 29, he sent an urgent letter to the central regional office of the Federal Bureau of Prisons. It read:

> To whom it may concern,
> I am inmate Carroll Edward Cole, 35045-098, who are presently serving a sentence of one (1) year for parole violation. I'm presently being heldover at FCI La Tuna, Texas, enrote to Springfield, Mo.
> During the time of my iccorceration I have been designated

to Springfield, Mo., and Englewood, Cor. I only have approximately four (4) months to go before my mandatory release date.

My release plans are to live in the Ft. Worth, Texas, area and seek job assignment through CTC [the Community Treatment Center] immediately after getting there.

I am an inmate of the age of forty two (42) years of age and have been incarcerated for a period of time through the years. I feel that by me being confined in institutions with only four (4) months to go on my one year (1) sentence if I remain within institutions it will only restore me in possibly committing a crime immediately after me being released from custody to get self support in which I do not want to do therefore, I request CTC immediately.

It was a risky proposition, trying to wangle release with threats of future crimes, but Eddie figured it was worth a shot to miss out on The Pits. In case somebody overlooked his not-so-subtle message, Eddie typed a second document and sent it with the first.

DECLARATION OF INMATE CARROLL EDWARD COLE

I, Carroll Edward Cole, being first duly sworn hereby states the following as true for the purpose of his future.

1. I hereby states that I am an inmate of the age of forty two (42) years of age.

2. That I am presently serving a federal sentence of one (1) year for probation violation. Sentence began 12/31/79.

3. That I am a poverty person and needs federal officials full support and are requesting immediately CTC release.

4. I states that by me being confined to another institution will only possibly restore me to committing a crime shortly after release for my support if I'm not sent to a CTC immediately in which I do not want to do.

5. I now feel that crime is not my future and I am depending on this office for full support in keeping me from committing another crime.

6. I states that I don't have anyone to give me support once released from custody therefore I am depending on CTC immediately.

7. My request is a very important one within the special jurisdiction of this office.

8. Wherefore, because of the foregoing facts and reasons I am a poverty person it is highly prayed that this office will grant me the remainder of my one (1) year sentence in a CTC in or near Ft. Worth, Texas. Affiant Further Saith Naught.

Respectfully submitted

Carroll Edward Cole, 35045-098

Eddie's keepers were no more impressed with his threats than his grammar. Booked overnight at El Reno, Oklahoma, on July 8, he was finally sent on to Springfield the following day. His preliminary screening described Cole as "very evasive" when interviewed, closing with an ominous notation that "Englewood states he should be isolated from female staff."

The net result was confinement to what Eddie called "the nut ward," officially designated as "administrative detention," where Cole would remain under close guard through July 24. As Cole recalled the unit, "We had guards who took special delight in driving inmates until they did something to warrant a beating —and sometimes they dished out the lumps regardless, without reason."

The way things were going, Eddie was worried about receiving a "P number"—the technical designation for a patient that gave the green light for heavy medication or worse. "I started behaving myself," he recalled, "did what I was told, took their stupid tests, and only told the doctor things he would consider normal. Of course, he diagnosed me as perfectly rational and recommended me being placed in general population."

The record tells a somewhat different story, as reflected in a memo filed on July 22, by clinical psychologist Daniel Taub.

When I interviewed this man on July 17, 1980 he indicated that he did not know why he was taken into this service. I was able to get his general cooperation and was able to give him a Rorschach Inkblot Test. By way of psychiatric history he said that he had been in Napa, Atascadero and Stockton State Hospitals. He added that he supposed "they just didn't want me at

Englewood." He said that he received no medication while on the way here.

His Rorschach responses suggest a character disorder, not a psychosis. There is a suggestion of evasion in the protocol, but not any clear evidence upon which to base suggestion that he might be having some adjustment problems on a recurring basis. It would seem appropriate to consider him for transfer out of MCFP as not requiring hospital care.

Either way, it was good enough to spring Eddie from lockdown on July 24, though he still remained on the psychiatric wing. Five days later he formally refused to sit for any further tests. His reason: "Been designated. No point as results will be to [sic] late." An August 13 memo claimed that Cole "has now completed treatment" and was scheduled for transfer to the general inmate population. He made the move two days later, with a parting diagnosis of "passive-aggressive personality."

By the time Cole arrived on the Springfield main line, unit manager Paul Macias had been forewarned by a memo from Medical Director A. E. Miller and psychiatrist Theodore Trusevich. It read, in part:

Initially, the correctional staff voiced serious concerns about placing Mr. Cole in open population. Consequently, he remained on lock status for about 1 week [sic]. It should be noted that he handled the frustration involved very well. He was eventually released to open population and has had no difficulty adjusting to that situation. His conduct with both male and female staff has been very appropriate. Interpersonally he has tended to be a loner; however, he could also be described as very cooperative. He was assigned to Mechanical Services and has worked in their refrigeration department. Since that assignment, we have two requests from Mechanical Services that he remain at this institution. He is apparently a very fine worker. During his time here, *he received no formal psychotherapy.* [Emphasis added.]

There is no evidence of psychosis or neurosis in Mr. Cole. Diagnostically he may be described as a character disorder. It is unlikely that major personality changes will occur. He does not appear motivated for any sort of treatment at this time.

It remains unclear what sort of "treatment" Eddie had completed by mid-August, if he received no psychotherapy and flatly rejected all diagnostic tests after July 29, but the Springfield doctors apparently felt they had done their job. As long as Eddie wasn't physically assaulting staff or other inmates, everyone was satisfied.

Diana's ghost might still come back to haunt him, though, as noted in a classification study dictated by case manager E. L. Horton on August 29. A two-page summary of Eddie's life includes the observation that

> Cole has been legally married on at least 3 separate occasions. His third and most recent spouse [sic] was found dead on September 26, 1979, in a dwelling occupied by the couple. Her body was discovered in a closet but was so badly decomposed that an official cause of death could not be established. An effort was made to charge Cole with the murder of his wife but the charge could not be pursued due to the decomposition of the body and the lack of accumulated evidence.

Horton's source of information on the case remains anonymous, and his summary flies in the face of official statements from San Diego. Three months *after* this report was filed, with Cole's confession in their hands, police still blamed Diana's death on a combination of long-term cirrhosis and ethyl alcohol poisoning. As late as 1985 no effort had been made to charge him with a California homicide.

Cole never saw the Horton memo, but it might have put his mind at ease. Salcido's warning of potential prosecution haunted Eddie every day at Springfield, marking time and waiting for the San Diego dicks to drop by for a chat. When word came down that he was scheduled for release on Halloween, Cole started looking for a way to shave more "good time" off his sentence—and he found it in a class on auto air-conditioning.

It was a squeaker, even so. Eddie started the class on September 18 and graduated on October 1, just under the wire. With his accumulated good time working for him, Eddie was released on October 4, at 7:15

A.M. In parting, he received a one-way bus ticket to Dallas and a hundred dollars, courtesy of Uncle Sam, to "aid in facilitating Mr. Cole's reintegration into society."

Predictably, reintegration did not figure into Eddie's plans that Saturday.

He had his mind on raising hell.

SIXTEEN

EDDIE'S TICKET WAS A THROUGH-FARE TO DALLAS, but he stopped off in Tulsa regardless, to check out his old haunts from 1967. Most of skid row had been demolished, part of a late-blooming urban renewal program, and the only familiar landmark was one bar where he used to kill time, sandwiched in between flophouses with derelicts slumped on the sidewalk.

Times change.

He spent the better part of Saturday drinking to forget—or was it to remember? Eddie wasn't certain, and the more he thought about it, he was pretty sure it didn't matter, either way.

The next bus out to Dallas rolled at half past ten, arriving in the predawn hours. Cole had blown a fair chunk of his hundred dollars back in Tulsa, but he didn't want to risk a vagrancy arrest this soon, for sleeping in the terminal.

"I was still paranoid," Cole explained, "feeling hunted even after my release from Springfield."

Instead of waiting for the beat cops to arrive and check him out, Cole walked a few blocks north and found a cheap hotel on Main Street, shelling out twelve dollars for the night. At that, he barely had a nap, for Sunday would not be his day of rest. Cole had to get his act in gear and find a better, cheaper place to stay. A source of income.

Back at Springfield, Eddie's forwarding address was the Salvation Army dorm on North St. Paul, but he was not expecting any mail and he did not intend to waste time at the "Sally" if he had a choice. Priorities in order, Eddie hit a few bars first and tried to track his brother down. The word came back that Richard was divorced from Mary, paying through the nose for child support, his whereabouts unknown.

So much for family ties.

By Monday street talk turned him on to Linda Bishop's Way Back House, on Lemmon Avenue. He called ahead for an appointment, offered up a *Reader's Digest* version of his background, and they took him in. His introduction to the other members of the staff included Becky, described by Cole as "a young girl with a terrific body who loved to draw in her breath and stick out her tits when the guys were around."

Old home week.

Linda Bishop handled job placement for the Way Back residents, and she soon put Eddie in touch with Joe Andretti, a contractor looking for grunt labor on a new job, digging drainage ditches around a site near Dallas. Eddie was first on the list of applicants, so he became the crew chief by default.

It should have been a two-week job, but Joe was in the middle of a tough divorce, developing a tendency to knock off work early and hit the bars. He liked to take Cole with him, which was fine with Eddie, since he kept on getting paid, regardless.

At the Way Back House, his room and meals cost forty dollars for the week, and every resident was forced to keep an in-house "bank account" to get them started when they finally struck off on their own. No sweat, since Joe Andretti wasn't holding any taxes out of Eddie's pay, and Cole had ample drinking money on the side.

Too much, in fact.

He began hitting the neighborhood bars on his own, whether Andretti was buying or not. The Way Back had a curfew, but increasingly it slipped Cole's mind. In fact, it seemed his mind was slipping, period.

"I started blacking out more often," Cole recalled, "sometimes turning vicious toward people I knew. One night, while I was drinking at a bar on Cedar Springs, I began insulting my friends from the halfway house and cursing the bartender, who was always real nice to me. When these spells came on, I was often totally incoherent. It got to the point where people hated to see me coming."

Linda Bishop sensed trouble, trying to draw Eddie out, but he put her off with lies and vague excuses. His job with Andretti Construction was finished, which meant no more paychecks, but Eddie was tired of the half-assed routine. On Sunday, November 2, he cleaned out his "savings account" and left the Way Back House with no destination in mind. Instead of looking for another room, he opened bars and stayed until they closed, sleeping in parks and alleys when there was no place else to go.

It might not be rock bottom, yet, but he was on his way.

*****

The bars open at noon on Sunday, and Eddie finds himself a seat in

Charlie's Place by 12:01. The owner recognizes him despite the changes wrought by time and jail, a trick bartenders learn to make the booze hounds feel appreciated. Dallas Cowboys up against the New York Giants on the tube, but Eddie barely notices, catching up on old times and drinking steadily, pacing himself, with one eye on the goal of oblivion.

Outside, the sun goes down, but Eddie doesn't care. His stool is comfortable, and the television's background noise relieves him of the need to organize coherent thoughts. He puts off wondering where he will sleep tonight. The problem always takes care of itself.

A new arrival on the stool to Eddie's left strikes up a conversation, introducing herself as Dorothy King. She isn't much to look at, early fifties, flat-chested, but Eddie is running on fumes by now, the hunter's reflex kicking in. He can play this game in his sleep. If the bitch is that anxious to die . . .

1:30 A.M. Half an hour till closing time. Cole doesn't argue when Dorothy asks him to walk her home. A stroll up Gaston Avenue, the woman hanging on his arm to keep from staggering. The neighborhood is mostly Mexican, and Eddie stays alert, prepared for anything. He barely hears the woman going on and on about her worthless life.

Too late to save it now, in any case.

Her small apartment sits well back from the street, at the rear of the complex. Inside, it is stifling hot—a defective thermostat, she explains—and Dorothy leaves the front door ajar to cool things down. She fetches beer and settles on the couch beside him, snuggling close.

"She asked me to stay the night," Cole recalls, "and I leaned over to kiss her. It was cold, like kissing a fish."

He grabs her by the throat and shoves her backward, knocking off her wig. She does not struggle, alcohol and shock defeating any hope of self-defense. She is unconscious by the time Cole suddenly recalls the open door.

He drags her upright, one hand still around her throat, a simulated lover's clinch. As if on cue, another tenant passes by, a quick glance toward the couple on the couch before he moves along. Cole keeps the pressure on, makes sure that she is dead before he leaves her long enough to close the door.

"Returning to the couch," he says, "I started ripping off her clothes. The poor thing had no breasts at all, but what the hell."

He carries her to bed, retrieves a washcloth from the bathroom to wipe between her legs, where she has soiled herself in death. He pauses, halfway through the job, to vomit on the floor. No matter. When he mounts her, there is only rage and the perverse excitement he derives from heaping further shame on lifeless sluts.

Cole sleeps beside her corpse that night, awakened several times by murky, troubled dreams. Each time, she helps him back to sleep, a mute receptacle for the accumulated poison of a lifetime. She is finally the perfect woman: silent, unresisting, willing to accept the punishment they both know she deserves.

He takes the key next morning, spends the whole day drinking, finally wanders back to the apartment when the bars close down. She welcomes him to bed, no awkward questions or incessant nagging. Dorothy accepts him just the way he is, without complaint. It doesn't even matter that he hates her.

Tuesday morning, Eddie knows that it is time to go. The heat in Dorothy's apartment will be ripening her corpse before much longer, and a man can only take so much. He needs a drink—a lot of drinks—to wash the taste of death away.

No problem.

Darkness finds him in Pauline's, on Bryan, killing time. He never sets out with specific prey in mind, the way some hunters do. It is a woman's fate to cross his path and make herself available, give off the proper signals that will trip his switch and seal her doom. Predestination or coincidence, Cole doesn't give a damn.

This night, he rescues pretty Wanda Roberts from the Mexicans and she invites herself to Eddie's place, a chance to show her gratitude. In fact, he has a seedy room on Gaston, but they never make it. Eddie walks her south on Bryan, to a dark, deserted parking lot, and finishes his business there. Rent money wasted as he huddles in a nearby stairwell, passing out.

Awake at dawn on Wednesday, Eddie wanders aimlessly along skid row, waiting for the bars to open. A brutal hangover saps his energy, and he considers turning himself in to the police, finally dismissing the notion as too much trouble. If the lawmen want him, let them earn their salaries like anybody else.

He calls Linda Bishop that afternoon, and she agrees to take him back, starting from scratch. His old room is waiting, a new bunkmate fresh out of Huntsville. Bright and early Thursday morning, Eddie buys himself a paper, clips the article on Wanda's death, and hides it underneath a corner of the carpet in his bedroom.

Memories are made of this.

Over the next week, he tries to keep his nose clean, showing up for A.A. meetings, calling Sharla several times in Vegas. Every time they talk, she pleads for money, just enough to catch a bus and join him, but he puts her off.

"I always made some excuse for refusing," he recalls. "The real reason was that I feared for her life if she came back to Texas."

Linda finds a part-time job for Eddie, stacking crates at Toys "R" Us. On Sunday night, November 30, he stops off at the Club DeVille to have a drink and watch some football. Sally Thompson catches Eddie's eye, invites him home. Before they leave, he makes another call to Sharla, putting Sally on the phone. A stranger's voice tells Sharla that Eddie talks about her constantly. It must be love.

The rest is history.

By Monday night he has confessed nine murders to Detective Robinson. On Wednesday Joe McGuckin flies in from Las Vegas to confirm the Blum and Cushman homicides. Art Terry makes the trip from Casper on December 10 and wraps the Tepee Hamer case.

The news hits hard in Vegas, Sharla's parents too surprised and horrified to play I-told-you-so. By February Sharla has decided it is time to cut her losses. Eddie raises no objection when she files the papers for divorce. Their marriage formally expires on Monday afternoon, the twenty-third of March. Two weeks and one day later Eddie is convicted on a triple murder charge. The judge says twenty-five to life.

Cole figures he can do that standing on his head.

A few days after his conviction, Eddie hears from Richmond, where a heart attack has claimed his father's life. "The family blamed me for his death," Cole says, "with the embarrassment and shame of my arrest. For all I know, they may be right."

His sister breaks the news. Eddie's mother has nothing to say.

*****

Official transportation to the pen at Huntsville is the "Bluebird

Special," a bus manufactured by the same company that outfits most American school districts. The design is modified, of course, with wire mesh on the windows to prevent escape and other special "extras" for security. The Bluebird Special's passengers ride two abreast, each handcuffed by his right or left wrist to a long chain running down the center aisle. If anyone attempts to flee, he has to take the others with him, or prepare to leave a portion of himself behind.

Unless the guards screw up.

The morning Eddie left for Huntsville, he was waiting with a dozen other inmates when he noticed that his cuff was loose. So loose, in fact, that with some effort he could slip his hand out, sacrificing just a bit of skin around the knuckles.

Perfect.

He was in a curious position now, lined up to board the prison bus, his fingers looped inside the empty cuff to make it look Like he was still securely chained. Their route of march between the jailhouse exit and the bus was lined with concrete pillars, and he noted that civilian rubberneckers were collecting on the street, to see the convicts off. If Eddie timed his move precisely, taking full advantage of the cover and the crowd, he thought the guards might be afraid to use their guns. The rest of it came down to fate or pure dumb luck.

They set off for the bus, Cole keeping pace, and he was halfway there when sudden paranoia overtook him. "Call it a sixth sense or whatever," he wrote, "but something told me not to run. It just didn't make sense for my cuff to be so loose, when others around me were bitching that theirs were too tight."

He smelled a setup, mounting the steps and taking his place on the bus. When everyone was seated, two guards in standard prison khaki came aboard, one of them walking straight to Cole. The guard's expression was a mocking sneer, almost a challenge. Reaching for the empty cuff, he placed it back on Eddie's wrist and this time clamped it tight enough to cut off circulation in his fingers.

Eddie's hand was numb and useless by the time they reached the Huntsville lockup, hours later, but he offered no complaints. All things considered, he was lucky just to be alive.

And there would be no need for manual dexterity, the next few weeks. "Receiving" at a modern prison means a great deal more than passing out striped suits and Ming empty cells with bodies. There are diagnostic tests and interviews involved, no end to paperwork and lectures, classifying inmates as to risk of violence or escape, ensuring that the new "fish" know the rules. It is essential for the prison staff to demonstrate control at once, before an inmate starts to look for loopholes in the system.

Huntsville, with its reputation for brutality, introduced new arrivals to the harsh realities of prison life in no uncertain terms. Rookie inmates and returning veterans were treated to a nonstop flow of epithets and insults from the moment they arrived, locked down except for interviews or tests designed to show which prison unit they should occupy.

"Most of the abuse was mental, rather than physical," Cole recalled, "but they let you know you were the lowest form of animal life. At Huntsville, a beating means you're beaten to the point of death, so I did my best to avoid trouble."

Even so, he blew it, in the final week of his receiving period. A group of inmates were dispatched for "counseling" on rules concerning visitors and correspondence, Eddie forced to tag along despite his written statement that he had no family or friends. He spent all morning on a hard bench, waiting for his turn, while other cons were jumped ahead of him in line. At last, in early afternoon, he gave it up and went back to his cell, but he would not escape the ritual that easily. Two hours later four guards came to fetch him for the mandatory interview. Inside the private office Eddie peevishly refused to answer any questions, glaring at the "so-called counselor" across his desk and standing mute.

"Of course, they beat the shit out of me," he said, "but I never gave them the satisfaction of making a sound. I've been beaten by experts."

With Eddie's track record and triple murder conviction, he was a natural for maximum security at Ellis Unit #1. If possible, the prison camp outside of Huntsville was considered even tougher than the Eastham Unit where he served his time for arson, and the normal atmosphere of brooding menace found in any prison was exacerbated by an incident that took place shortly prior to Cole's arrival. As the grapevine ran it down, the Ellis Unit's warden and a major on the staff were taking a disruptive inmate on a one-way trip to the nearby riverbed, when the con got his hands on a gun. When the smoke cleared, the major was dead of bullet wounds, the warden drowned outside the prison in a decorative fountain, and the FBI was poking into everybody's business, trying to determine what the hell went down. It made for tense relations in the camp, but Cole regarded that as simple status quo.

Officially received at Ellis on July 16, 1981, Eddie was assigned to share a six-by-ten-foot cell with two other inmates, the crowding relieved by twelve-hour shifts in the fields. At night, he woke screaming from nightmares, angering his cellmates as they tried to sleep. Requests for transfer followed, a half-dozen cons bailing out on Cole before he grew despondent enough to attempt suicide that December.

The self-destructive effort got him moved to the Ellis hospital wing, where a staff doctor found him "interesting," and Eddie spent the next eleven months in virtual isolation, locked in a Spartan cell between tests and interviews. Aside from the doctor and a trusty who brought his meals, Cole's only companion was a jumping spider he trained to take flies from his hand. Near the end of his hospital stay, Eddie developed a case of claustrophobia that pushed him to the verge of a nervous breakdown. More time lost, before he was judged fit for release.

Back on the mainline in November 1982, Cole began plotting an unscheduled exit from Huntsville. "By now," he wrote, "escape was my only thought, and I began to put an elaborate plan in effect."

Assigned to the prison wood shop, Cole took his first step toward freedom by manufacturing several slingshots. Next, he stole bottles of food coloring from the kitchen, planning to dye a set of conspicuous prison whites before he made his break. Tabasco sauce was the final touch, meant for dousing Eddie's shoes to throw tracking dogs off the scent.

His plan involved a transfer to the garden crew in spring, a single mounted guard assigned to watch the older inmates as they cultivated vegetables. With some audacity and luck, Cole reckoned he could use a slingshot to disable the guard, grab his sidearm, and run to the nearest highway before someone raised the alarm. From there, he had to keep his eyes peeled for a passing vehicle and try to flag it down.

The risks involved in breaking out were high. Around the time of Eddie's suicide attempt, an inmate had escaped from Ellis, but a search team later found him floating facedown in the Trinity River. "Accidental drowning" was the verdict, but inmates claimed it was a deliberate execution by some guards, aimed at discouraging future escapes.

In any case, Cole thought it was worth the risk. Living at Huntsville was no kind of living at all.

By early March Cole had his slingshots hidden at strategic points around the camp, prepared to make his move. The warden was considering his bid for transfer to the garden crew, while Eddie kept his fingers crossed. Rejection meant that he would have to start from scratch, an all-new plan.

The problem, finally, was not Cole's preparation but an unpredictable event. Since being discharged from the hospital, he had been taking daily doses of Prolixin, to control his moods. "Although I functioned fairly well, with no visible effects," Cole wrote, "I sometimes tripped out unexpectedly, while doing simple chores."

On Thursday afternoon, March 17—St. Patrick's Day—Eddie "tripped out" in the wood shop. He was running a circular saw at the time, ripping six-foot boards, and he barely felt it when the blade sliced a seven-inch gash in his left forearm. Blood everywhere, shock setting in as he was driven to "The Walls," in downtown Huntsville, for emergency treatment. On from there to the medical unit at Galveston, where surgeons reattached the severed tendons in his arm.

And Eddie watched his best-laid plans go down the crapper.

He was back at Ellis Unit #1 by June, but he decided to postpone his bid for freedom. Whether it was simply nerves or something more, Cole managed to convince himself that dogs could track him better in the summer heat. There were also "too many people around," increasing the risk of swift capture. It would be a good idea, he thought, to bide his time and wait for fall.

"In the following months," Eddie wrote from death row, "I saw killings galore, one being over a Scrabble game. Some guy got pissed at being caught on a phony word he made up, and he went back to his cell to get a homemade knife. Coming up behind another player, he plunged the damn thing into his neck. The poor bastard bled to death before they could even get him to the infirmary."

And it was just another day at Ellis, marking time.

As summer faded into autumn, winter coming on, Cole grew increasingly depressed by the pervasive violence that surrounded him, provoked by petty jealousy and childish temper tantrums. He came to hate his fellow inmates, with their selfish attitude of "Do Unto Others,

But Not Unto Me." Every con in the joint was a weasel looking out for Number One and shafting everybody else.

"The worst thing," Eddie wrote, "was that in most respects, this was my attitude, too. I got to thinking long and hard about my past life and the murders I committed. Wasn't I taking lives without any regard for the victims? None of the women I killed had ever hurt me personally. I came to see that my attitude was no better than the bullshit I despised in others."

Increasingly, Cole felt that he should die for his crimes. Texas had resumed capital punishment in December 1982, with the execution of Charlie Brooks for killing a Fort Worth mechanic, and Eddie knew there were other cons stuck on death row for crimes that paled in comparison to his. Ironically condemned to live, he saw his options narrowed down to suicide or breaking out to kill again.

In January 1984 Cole got a letter from a California lawyer, informing him of his mother's death, two months earlier. A copy of her will was enclosed, along with a dollar to cover his share of the family inheritance.

At last.

He had expected something more, on learning of her death. The woman who had trashed his life was gone, but Eddie felt no urge to celebrate. How many times he had imagined strangling her, killed others in her place, and now it all came down to nothing.

So much wasted time.

The years he pissed away were Vesta's parting shot, her final victory.

On Wednesday, February 15, Texas prison officials received a detainer notice on Eddie Cole, announcing Nevada's intent to extradite and prosecute him for the Blum and Cushman murders. The D.A. in Las Vegas would be seeking death.

Cole saw his chance and took it, waiving formal extradition. Back at The Walls on March 30, to wait for his transfer, he was in time for the execution of "Candy Man" Ronald O'Bryan, sentenced to die for poisoning his own son's Halloween candy. He was still waiting on April 1, when serial killer Christopher Wilder blew through Las Vegas on his dead-end run to nowhere, snatching seventeen-year-old Michelle Korfman from the Meadows Mall. Six weeks would pass before her body was discovered in the California desert, and another month before the pitiful remains were finally identified.

On April 9 detectives from Las Vegas came to fetch their man. By that time, Eddie Cole was more than ready to oblige.

He had been waiting all his life to take that ride.

SEVENTEEN

FROM HUNTSVILLE, EDDIE'S ESCORTS DROVE HIM SIXTY MILES due south, to Houston, where they dropped him at the Harris County jail. His flight back to Las Vegas would not leave until the early afternoon of April 10, but Eddie was exempt from formal booking as a prisoner in transit. As it was, the jailers parked him in a barren cell, no furniture except the toilet, leaving him to curl up on the concrete floor if he got tired enough to sleep. His only meal that day was a bologna sandwich, but he wasted no time on complaints.

His mind was on Nevada and the future. What was left of it.

At 10:00 A.M. on April 10 his escorts came to fetch him for the drive to William Hobby Airport. There, they left him in a holding cell until they were an hour short of flight time, finally coming back to take his shackles off when Eddie promised not to run. In fact, he had considered trying to escape while they were at the airport, dodging through the crowd, but it was too much trouble, so he settled for a cup of coffee and a jelly roll.

The flight was uneventful, handcuffs and an unmarked cruiser waiting at McCarran International. Booked into the Clark County jail, Cole requested a psychiatrist on April 11 and was interviewed by a nurse the following day. She found him "very irritable," noting for the record that Cole "insisted to be put in isolation—afraid he will hurt himself or somebody else." On April 13 psychiatric counselor J. Phifer found the prisoner "moderately depressed," but noted that Cole was also "oriented as to time, place and situation. He does not appear psychotic at this time." Eddie's daily dosage of Triavil was continued from Huntsville, an appointment with the staff psychiatrist scheduled for April 17.

Dr. F. J. Acosta was the first Nevada psychiatrist to examine Eddie since the Sparks debacle, ten years earlier. His report includes the following remarks:

> Patient is alert, oriented x 3 with no gross memory deficit. He appears to be pleasant, cooperative, and was straightforward in giving his history without being guarded or suspicious. No delusions were elicited at this time and he denied any perceptual

disturbances though he stated that he used to hear voices and the last time was one year ago. He denied any suicidal or homocidal [sic] thoughts at this time, but he claims he had violent tendencies in the past. Patient was given diagnosis of Schizoaffective disorder with depressed feature when he was in Huntsville, Texas. At this time he does not appear depressed. His mood is neutral and his affect is appropriate. My impression of this case is of Schizophrenia, chronic, undifferentiated.

Eddie's next visitor was Attorney Scott Bindrup, appointed by the court to defend Cole in his forthcoming murder trial. Already briefed on Eddie's attitude, Bindrup approached his new client with some apprehension. Once they were formally introduced, he asked his first question of Eddie: "What are you doing, trying to get the death penalty?"

When Cole replied in the affirmative, Bindrup refused to take him seriously, running down their options and avenues of resistance. Only two condemned inmates had been executed west of the Rockies since 1977, one of them Nevada's own Jesse Bishop. In both cases, the men had waived their right to appeal and actively sought execution, a move that Bindrup regarded as suicide once removed. Eddie's Dallas confessions were a handicap, going into the trial, but with the proper effort and organization, Bindrup felt sure they could still cheat the Reaper.

Suddenly frightened, Cole went along with Bindrup's plan to plead not guilty by reason of insanity at his preliminary hearing. Once the plea was filed, however, Eddie found he could not sleep. He *wasn't* crazy, damn it, and he had not made the trip from Huntsville for another double term of life.

This time, it would be all or nothing.

A few days after the preliminary hearing, Joe McGuckin got a call from Eddie Cole, inviting the detective for a visit at the county jail. Cole had another statement that he wanted on the record, and it just might make McGuckin's day.

Arriving at the lockup with his partner as a witness, McGuckin repeated Cole's Miranda rights, advising him that any further statements could be lethal. Eddie shrugged it off and waived his right to silence, waiting for McGuckin to set up his tape recorder on the table between them. Eddie's statement, brief and to the point, confessed premeditation in the Blum and Cushman homicides.

At one stroke, he had wiped out his defense.

Scott Bindrup heard about the interview and rushed to see his client, pleading once again for Eddie to abandon his pursuit of "legal suicide." Opponents of capital punishment picked up the refrain, but Cole remained adamant in his desire to die. He tried to plead guilty at his next court appearance, but Bindrup rose to object, the proceedings degenerating into an argument between Eddie's unwelcome defender and prosecutor Dan Seaton, who suddenly found himself supporting the man he hoped to execute. Bindrup finally prevailed to the extent of scheduling a psychological exam before Eddie's next day in court.

Enter Jan Bruner, a Ph.D. in psychology, whom Eddie would later describe as "a real doll." She met Cole in the Clark County jail's "contact visit" room, Eddie arriving in shackles and belly chain, one hand left free for writing. The tests continued over several meetings, and while Eddie recalled "getting quite friendly" with Bruner, her results provided no ammunition for an insanity plea. Before his next court date, Bindrup and Bruner played their trump card, asking Cole to resist death for the good of society, submitting himself as a subject of study on the causes of serial murder.

"They almost convinced me," Eddie recalled, "but then I thought about the press and public, what a field day they would have. I told them to forget it, find themselves another guinea pig. I was committed."

At Cole's next hearing, Bindrup sought permission to withdraw from the case, noting irreconcilable conflicts with his client. Cole wanted to defend himself, but Judge Myron Leavitt had reservations, calling for a fresh battery of psychiatric tests to determine Eddie's competence.

Dr. Rosalinda Rueca was first up at bat, on May 28. Cole opened the interview with an admission of thirty-five murders, but Dr. Rueca had little interest in the specifics of his case. Her focus was restricted to the legal definition of sanity-that is to say, whether Eddie understood that killing women was a criminal offense. Apparently, he did. Rueca found no impairment of judgment or insight in her subject, crediting Cole with "normal mental status and a sociopathic personality."

Cole's second diagnostic interview, on July 24, was conducted by Dr. Franklin Master. This time, Eddie avoided specific body counts, but voiced a fear of future slayings if he was allowed to live. As Master noted, "[Cole] plans to plead guilty and very firmly states that he knows that in Texas in five years time he will be eligible for parole and that it is also possible for him to escape from Texas and that he knows that if he is on the street again, he will kill again." Master's final diagnosis was another vote in favor of the prosecution.

My clinical impression is that of antisocial personality in an individual who is competent to assist defense counsel. He is also competent to make his own decisions in the judicial process. At the time of the alleged offense he was able to distinguish right from wrong. Should this individual make a decision to plead guilty and to ask for the death penalty, he would be mentally competent to be making that decision, despite any personal opinion that any of us might have on the merits or lack of same of death penalties.

Dr. William O'Gorman rounded out the trio on July 29, with Eddie repeating his reference to "a total of thirty-four or thirty-five" murders. According to O'Gorman, Cole sought execution "because he does not have the courage to take his own life." In reference to Cole's background, O'Gorman noted that "The onset of his peculiar [sic] sex interpretation began in early life with autoexoticism [sic] and in order to achieve an organism [sic], he would have to think of a woman being strangled." That aside, O'Gorman found Cole legally sane and competent to manage his own defense.

In retrospect, Eddie was unimpressed with the psychiatrists, whatever they might think of him. "Of the three," he later wrote, "only Master conducted any worthwhile examination or devoted adequate time to the interview. The others were in and out quickly, with little to say."

They weren't the only doctors keeping watch on Eddie Cole, however. At the county lockup, Dr. Ivan Aralica examined the prisoner on May 15, noting the prior diagnosis of schizoaffective disorder, boosting the prescribed dosage of Elavil and adding Trilafon in response to Eddie's "increasing agitation since he was transferred to a different cell." On June 7, Cole complained of stomach pains and vomiting, convinced that he was suffering from ulcers. Twelve days later Dr. Aralica increased the Elavil dosage once more and noted Cole's continuing preoccupation with death.

He is less irritable, however, he still has desires about being shot by the state or he might try his best to provoke other people to kill him. Yet, during todays [sic] interview, he smiled and was quite friendly. He denied any hallucinations. I see no evidence of delusions, however, the time that I spent with him was limited and in my experience with similar individuals in the past, this man would be a bit psychotic. At present time, my impression remains the same. Major depression, probably recurrent with mild mood congruent psychotic features.

On August 9 Cole complained that his new medication repeatedly caused him to wake in the night, disoriented and hallucinating. Dr. Aralica returned five days later, pronouncing Cole "better." As the psychiatrist observed, "He is able to smile, a bit more relaxed, less depressed but still tired. My impression is that we need to continue Elavil but it could be decreased to 200 mg at bedtime, take blood Elavil level and then when levels are back, I'll be in touch with nurse and will decide then if I need to see Mr. Cole again."

First, though, Eddie would be going back to court. On Thursday, August 16, he appeared before Judge Leavitt and pled guilty on two counts of first-degree murder, with "standby" Attorneys Frank Cremen and Tom Pitaro watching from the sidelines. Pitaro later told the press he felt obliged to investigate Eddie's "attempt to commit legal suicide." Frank Cremen seemed a bit more confused, telling newsmen, "I'm not sure what he's doing." Dan Seaton, meanwhile, rose to Eddie's defense, proclaiming him "lead counsel" in the case, advising Cremen and Pitaro to "hear his interests and abide by them."

After hearing Doctors Master and O'Gorman vouch for Eddie's sanity, Judge Leavitt granted Cole permission to defend himself. It was a victory of sorts, but Tom Pitaro was not finished yet. On Friday afternoon, September 21, Judge Leavitt appointed Pitaro as a "friend of the court," invested with power to search for mitigating circumstances in the case. In yet another press conference, Pitaro dubbed his crusade a moral issue, opposing Eddie's death wish on grounds that Cole had no right to determine his own punishment and thereby "undermine the integrity of the court."

Eddie's view was simpler, more direct. "I believe in capital punishment," he told reporters. "I don't see where [Pitaro] is going to come up with this stuff, because there's nothing good about me."

*****

The next step on Eddie's march to the grave was a penalty hearing, scheduled for Thursday and Friday, October 11 and 12. His case would be heard by a panel of three judges, including Myron Leavitt, Richard Legarza, and Norman Robinson. Dan Seaton appeared for the state, while Cole represented himself. Frank Cremen remained as Eddie's unwelcome standby counsel, while Tom Pitaro could barely contain his eagerness to speak as a friend of the court—or, more accurately, as a die-hard opponent of capital punishment.

Prosecutor Seaton opened with an admission that Cole was not eligible for death in the Kathlyn Blum homicide, which occurred two months prior to Nevada's enactment of a new capital punishment statute. Only the Cushman slaying was open to debate, and Eddie grimaced as he saw the odds against him cut in half.

Cole followed Seaton with a brief prepared statement, objecting to Tom Pitaro's "infringement on my constitutional rights," and Judge Leavitt ordered both attorneys to leave the defense table, retreating behind a waist-high wooden rail. Pitaro, for his part, deplored Cole's refusal to "play the game," reasserting his desire to present mitigating evidence and attack the state's presentation of aggravating circumstances— that is, other felonies—which supported a sentence of death.

"I have to get into it," Pitaro declared, "because the state is going to try to, in my opinion, bulldoze and offer—just dump on you evidence that I think is improperly before this court."

With Eddie's case, Pitaro had a public forum for his views on life and death, and he was not about to let it go without a fight.

Judge Leavitt initially accepted Pitaro's written brief on the case but granted Cole's request that the attorney be restrained from entering objections to the prosecution's evidence. Ten minutes later, following a recess, the panel changed its collective mind. Pitaro could object as often as he wished, but he would not be calling any witnesses or cross-examining those summoned by the state.

Seaton's first witness was Detective Karen Good, from the Las Vegas Metropolitan Police, presenting a basic description of her work on the Marie Cushman case. None of her testimony linked Cole directly to the crime, and Tom Pitaro contented himself with a single objection to her mention of barroom witness Joseph Walsh.

Joe McGuckin was next on the stand, describing the Kathlyn Blum murder, linking Cushman through Eddie's Dallas confessions, and briefly alluding to Cole's latest statement, taped in the Clark County jail. Pitaro interrupted repeatedly, scoring private points with his objections to the mention of collateral crimes—theft of money from Cushman and Blum, Cole's reference to Cushman being "drunk like all the others," his statement that he "might have" raped Blum's body after she was dead.

Herb Thomas was the third in line, representing Missouri's highway patrol with an overview of the Virginia Rowden case. By this time, Tom Pitaro was on a roll, moving to disqualify the witness on grounds that Eddie's 1967 arrest was capricious and arbitrary, his identification by the victim a result of a "suggestive showup." He also moved to block introduction of Eddie's Missouri prison record, contending that a five-year sentence for assault with intent to kill "doesn't prove the fact of the conviction." Repeatedly overruled by Judge Leavitt, Pitaro finally registered "a continuing objection so I don't have to keep jumping up."

Art Terry, lately promoted to chief of police in Mills, Wyoming, was number four on the witness stand, called to testify about the Myrlene Hamer homicide. Tom Pitaro was on his feet before Terry had a chance to introduce himself, winning a concession from Judge Leavitt that the Hamer slaying would not be considered as an aggravating circumstance, but merely evidence of the defendant's character. With that settled, Terry was finally permitted to describe Hamer's death and Cole's subsequent confession in Dallas. In regard to the latter, Terry testified that Cole admitted raping Tepee's corpse, a charge that Eddie would deny until his dying day.

Art Terry was the only witness Eddie chose to cross-examine, and their brief exchange had no apparent impact on the charges.

Q: Mr. Terry, was there any confession signed by me?
A: No, there was not.
Q: That's all I wanted to ask.

"I just left it there," Cole later wrote from death row "I would have cross-examined on the sex matter, but Tepee's mother was there in the courtroom, and I would have had to ask for her removal. I suppose it doesn't make much difference after all the other things I've done, but it was still not true."

In the end, it hardly mattered. The three judges returned from a ten-minute recess and officially rejected Terry's testimony, on grounds that no supporting evidence corroborated Eddie Cole's confession to the crime. With or without posthumous sex, Myrlene Hamer's death would not be considered in deciding his punishment for the Cushman homicide.

San Diego was represented next, with Robert Ring called to describe Essie Buck's murder and his July 1971 interview with Cole, including Eddie's admission of dumping the body after Buck died of "natural causes." Pitaro's motion to strike the testimony was denied, and James Shively took the stand, filling in details on the deaths of Bonnie Sue O'Neil and Diana Cole. Despite official disclaimers from San Diego, Shively described both cases as "homicide calls," but he offered no link between Cole and the women, aside from the obvious fact of Cole's marriage to Di.

Gerald Robinson took up the slack in that regard, flown in from Dallas as Nevada's final witness of the day. His testimony was the linchpin of the prosecution's search for aggravating circumstances, linking up three homicides in Dallas with confessions to the other deaths in San Diego, Casper, and Las Vegas. Dan Seaton was saving the best for last, and Pitaro knew it, punctuating the testimony with repeated objections. Dallas murders were irrelevant, since they fell *after* Cushman's slaying. (Overruled.) A Dallas court clerk's signature on certain documents appeared suspicious. (Overruled.) The Texas victims were identified by means of hearsay testimony. (Overruled.) Cole's confession to the homicides in Dallas was irrelevant. (Overruled.) Pitaro finally succeeded in barring testimony on Myrlene Hamer and Bonnie O'Neil, in the absence of physical evidence linking Cole to the murders, but seven other cases passed the test of scrutiny.

Before the court adjourned that afternoon, Pitaro made another bid to corner the defense, renewing his plea for the right to call witnesses on Eddie's behalf— whether Cole desired it or not. If allowed to proceed, Pitaro said, he would call Jan Bruner and California psychologist

Donald Lunde to describe Eddie's unstable mind, along with unnamed religious spokesmen "to testify as to the morality of the death penalty."

Before the hearing reconvened on Friday, Eddie had another court date, picking up a term of life without parole for killing Kathlyn Blum. An hour later he repeated his objection to Pitaro's mitigating evidence and told the court he wished to testify. His statement, under oath, was brief and to the point.

"Well, Your Honor," Cole began, "the attorneys, my records and everything like that shows some hospitalization for me trying to get help for many years. Well, what I want to say about that, they tried to help me but I didn't receive the help. I didn't do what I was supposed to did and I want the court to know that I didn't have to kill nobody.

"I was drunk, but that's still no excuse. I was in my right mind. I knew exactly what I was doing, and I'm not sorry for what I did and I have no remorse.

"Also, I'd like to explain to the court that within about five more years I would be eligible for parole from Texas Department of Corrections. If not that, I got very ample chances to escape from the Texas Department of Corrections and I thought the court should know this here facts. That is about all I can think of that I wanted to say, Your Honor."

Dan Seaton rose to cross-examine Eddie, leading him through confirmations of three murders in Dallas, two in Las Vegas, the slayings of Essie Buck and Diana in San Diego, his assault on Virginia Rowden. In all, Cole admitted nine killings with bodies recovered, moving on to describe the Oklahoma City case and his murder of two Mexican women outside San Diego. The Dallas arson and his federal time were also tacked on, for dessert.

"Just one last question," said the prosecutor. "Is it really true that you have absolutely no remorse for any of the crimes that you've committed."

Eddie's face was deadpan as he answered. "That's really true, yes."

In essence, it was over. Tom Pitaro filled another dozen pages of the transcript with a list of things he would have done, if Cole had not opposed his efforts, but his monologue was strictly sour grapes. Dan Seaton summed up for the state, trying to dispose of the "legal suicide" argument once and for all.

Gentlemen, the only decent act that I have seen out of this defendant is the fact that he has recognized his need to die. But I am going to ask you, do not sentence Carroll Edward Cole to die because Carroll Edward Cole wants to die. That would be a wholly improper reason. I agree with Mr. Pitaro throughout, that no defendant should be able to legally commit suicide. No.

If you're going to execute him—and I urge you in the strongest possible terms to do just that—execute him because it is the wishes [sic] of not Carroll Cole, but the community. It's not only the wishes of the community, it's the need of the community. This man, should he ever be on the streets again, will kill again. Do we know anything if we don't know that?

For once, Eddie had the last word, telling Judge Leavitt: "Your Honor, I agree with Mr. Seaton and that I am a danger to society."

The judges agreed. At the end of a two-hour lunch break, they returned and sentenced Eddie to die for the murder of Marie Cushman.

He was on his way.

*****

On November 6 Cole began his trek to the Nevada state prison at Carson City. Ironically, that Tuesday morning also brought word that the state's death chamber—out of service for the past five years—was once again open for business.

Capital punishment in Nevada, as in most states, has evolved over time. Hanging was the rule from statehood, in October 1864, through early 1912, but statistics are vague since individual counties conducted their own executions before 1905. In 1912 the Silver State introduced its unique "shooting gallery"— three .30-30 rifles mounted on an iron frame—but only one inmate was shot before Nevada lapsed into a twelve-year moratorium on executions. In February 1924 Nevada pioneered in using a gas chamber to dispatch Chinese gunman Gee Jon. Thirty-one others would follow his lead, the last being Jesse Bishop, gassed for killing a bystander during a bungled robbery at El Morocco Casino. In custody, Bishop claimed eighteen previous contract murders, but none were documented when he went to his death in October 1979. By then, after fifty-eight years, the gas chamber was showing its age,

and Prisons Director Charles Wolff expressed a fear of deadly leaks
in future executions. Bids for the repair work averaged $20,000 mini-
mum, whereas the double chairs could be removed, a table bolted in
their place, with plastic tubes and a syringe installed for something like
a thousand dollars. Cost-conscious legislators got the message in 1983,
voting to adopt lethal injection as a "more humane" technique.

As the new kid on the condemned men's unit (CMU), Eddie was
exempt from the normal, longwinded diagnostic procedures reserved
for incoming convicts. There was only one place he could go, no pretense of a rehabilitation effort, but even condemned inmates require
psychiatric screening, to avoid potential conflicts on the cell block. On
November 8 a Dr. Knapp filed the following report of Cole's condition.

> Psychological evaluation (based upon psych test plus inter-
> view): passively suicidal plus mentally ill. (A) His suicidal ide-
> ation is topped off (100th centile [sic]) on the CAQ test but I am
> not ordering a suicide watch as the interview indicates that he
> will not actually attempt suicide. He stated that he "tried to kill
> myself a few years ago but I found that I couldn't do it—I'm not
> brave enough." The psych test results agree that he is "not brave
> enough." (B) Severe psychoneurosis/borderline schizophrenic
> psychosis is indicated on the test.
>
> He came here from Clark County jail on 2 medications:
> Elavil (anti-depressant) & Trilafon (antipsychotic). Recommend
> renewal of the Elavil but not the anti-psychotic. Will observe him
> for possible psychotic symptoms. Notified CMU Sr. CO (Mont-
> gomery) of Cole's mental status.

On December 12, Dr. Theresa McNeil found Eddie "alert, cooperative, talkative. Feels a bit depressed because his sisters won't com-
municate." His claustrophobia was back, as well, but it subsided when
he made his move into the general population on death row.

A sterling cast of characters was waiting for him in the CMU.
Henry Deutscher had the most time in, sentenced in December 1977 for
beating a Las Vegas woman to death and gnawing on her corpse. Serial killer Gerald Gallego had been extradited from San Quentin's death
row, his trial for a Nevada double murder financed by unprecedented

public contributions. John Olausen and Edward Wilson were cop-killers from Reno. Patrick McKenna and Jimmie Neuschafer had been serving life for rape and murder, respectively, when they were sentenced to die for killing other inmates. John Mazzan stabbed a Reno judge's son to death. Ronnie Milligan used a sledgehammer on his seventy-seven-year-old female victim. Kenneth McKague was in for killing a husband and wife, while Mark Rogers had wiped out a whole family in rural Pershing County. Cary Williams came to the row for the torture-slaying of a pregnant nurse and her unborn child. Robert Farmer, Gregory Collier, and Samuel Howard all killed during holdups. Thomas Nevius was trying his best to rape a Las Vegas woman, when her husband came home and took a bullet in the head. Robert Miranda, part of the Cuban Mariel boatlift in 1980, was ironically sentenced for stabbing an illegal alien. Ricky Sechrist beat two schoolgirls to death in Reno. James Hill's victim was a paraplegic woman, fatally injured when Hill rammed a stick into her vagina. John Snow accepted a murder contract on a Las Vegas saloon owner, but forgot to cover his tracks. Robert Jones shot his opponent in a barroom brawl, while Tracy Petrocelli used a car to flatten his teenage girlfriend. Robert Ybarra's promise to fly right and study for the priesthood failed to impress jurors who convicted him in the rape-slaying of a sixteen-year-old girl.

A shopping list of human toxic waste.

Of the lot, only serial killer Thomas Crump shared Eddie's attitude toward death. Convicted of one murder in Vegas and three in New Mexico, with others suspected, Crump told the world that he would be "relieved" to face immediate execution. It was not the kind of attitude that wins friends on death row, where most inmates are committed to extending their lives by any means available, from endless, frivolous appeals to feigned insanity. A convict with a death wish is the enemy, perceived by fellow inmates as a threat to *them,* as well as to himself.

Cole went into the CMU expecting trouble, and he was not disappointed. There were threats and scuffles, broken up by guards, more than one inmate suggesting that Eddie should take his own life, perhaps stage a breakout and let the guards shoot him, if he was so anxious to die. His laundry started coming back with items missing, others shredded, his complaints ignored by the administration to the point that Eddie started shaving hand soap in his cell, to wash the few things he had left.

When Cole began to write his story down, he started having "friendly" visitors who stopped to chew the fat, distracting him as much as possible from his appointed task. Cole singled out two of the inmates as the ringleaders of the harassment, arming himself in case they tired of games and tried the more direct approach.

Resentment from the cons was one thing, but Cole was unprepared for the treatment he got from prison guards, some of whom went out of their way to deliver insults and snide remarks. Again, it was not Eddie's crimes that seemed to piss them off—the child and fourteen women he had killed—but rather his continuing refusal to "play the game" by appealing his sentence.

"I would've thought the guards would be on my side," Eddie wrote from prison, "just as glad to see me go, but many of them seemed to think I should appeal and drag things out. It goes to show you how fucked up some people are."

The tension worked on Eddie's nerves and on his stomach, bringing back the pain and vomiting that he attributed to ulcers. Beginning on March 5 he filed repeated pleas for Maalox, the administration stalling to the point where anger and frustration finally overcame Cole's physical discomfort. On May 24 he penned a final message to the staff physician.

> To: Doctor (Quack) Subject: Deniel of medication From: Carroll Edward Cole #20163 CMU
>
> Unfortunately I'm unable to tell the doctor? what I think of him because of your *gutless* reprisals. However, the medication that Dr. O'Neil [sic] has prescribed for me I will no longer take nor request any other form of assistance from you or your medical staff, from this point on as to do so will avail me nothing no matter what.
>
> All you are is a Quack!

The nurse dispatched to visit Eddie found him "very uncooperative," but noted that he "seems perfectly normal physically." If nothing else, the venting of his rage helped Eddie focus on the task ahead.

He felt the jailhouse lawyer coming back.

Cole's hassles with the prison doctor were a sideshow to the main event, his hot pursuit of death. The original execution date had been set for January 7, but the Nevada Supreme Court issued a stay on Christmas Eve, to permit a review of the case. On January 27 Eddie wrote an affidavit authorizing Attorney Frank Cremen "to file any motion or plea he deems necessary to the State Supreme Court to stop any automatic appeals or arguement [sic] so affiant may be put to death promptly and without undue delay." Two months later, on March 23, he followed up with a personal letter to the court, waiving his right to appeal of the sentence.

Judges have no concept of haste, and it was April 25 before the state supreme court remanded Cole's case to Las Vegas, commanding that a lawyer be appointed for the limited purpose of verifying Eddie's waiver. On April 30 Judge Leavitt picked Edward Marshall out of the grab-bag, with orders to investigate Cole's case and report back inside of thirty days. It was May 9 before Marshall got around to writing Cole, expressing his personal doubts on the ease.

> I understand that you have heretofore stated clearly your desire to die and not to be involved in any criminal court appeals. It would help me greatly if you would write me indicating *WHY* you feel this way. Everyone understands that this is your sentiment. No one really understands why and that would shed some light on this entire problem.

On Monday, May 20, Marshall and Dan Seaton spent an hour with Cole at Carson City, Eddie repeating his wish to die as soon as possible, his fear of killing again if he ever hit the street. Nine days later Marshall informed the state supreme court that Cole "desires execution of the death penalty upon him at the earliest moment possible, avoiding any and all further delays for any and every cause whatever." It took Seaton's office another three weeks to respond with a seven-page brief in agreement with Marshall's conclusion. Three months later, on October 22, the high court finally affirmed Eddie's death sentence, noting Ed Marshall's observation as the last word.

> I am now in my 27th year of practice of law before the Nevada bar, including wide experience in numerous homicide

cases. Never before had I seen or *known* a man who so justly deserves to die or who so completely wants and desires to have the penalty of death executed upon him, as punishment for his crimes generally and more specifically for the murder he committed in this state.

Cole was back in Las Vegas on Wednesday, November 13, to hear Judge Leavitt set his new execution date for December 6. If all went according to plan, he had just over three weeks to live.

Before the long ride back to Carson City Eddie sat for another battery of psychological tests, dropped off at the county jail by Jan Bruner. He also agreed to posthumous examination of his brain by Vegas neurosurgeon Lonnie Hammargren, in an attempt to locate any abnormalities. In Hammargren's theory, childhood trauma or progressive disease might produce lesions in the brain's so-called "rage centers," prompting impulsive or violent behavior. Eddie's gallows humor was showing as he expressed his only concern with the test: His brain should be driven to the lab instead of flown, he suggested, because "I get airsick.

*****

As the clock runs down in Carson City, liberal and religious groups suddenly make themselves scarce. Nevada's Episcopal Diocese had gone to the mat for Jesse Bishop in 1979, over Bishop's strenuous objections, but a spokesman for the church refutes any plan to demonstrate for Eddie Cole. Even the vociferous ACLU backs away from Cole's case, saving its energy for killers with a wish to live. Reno Rabbi Myra Soifer is a lone voice crying in the wilderness, branding executions immoral under any circumstances.

Nobody is listening …except, for once, to Eddie Cole.

"Everything is in motion and I'm not changing my mind," he tells the press on Saturday, November 30. "That's not to say I'm not scared, don't get me wrong. I don't consider myself brave or courageous or noble. In my own way, even though I'm scared and nervous, I'm sort of at peace, too. I just messed up my life so bad that I just don't care to go on."

Following a last interview and visit with friends on December 4, Eddie is moved to the "last night cell," a seven-by-seven cubicle furnished with a cot, toilet, and washbasin, located some twenty paces from the death chamber. A twenty-four-hour suicide watch is imposed to keep Eddie from cheating the state, special dispensation required to get him a pencil and paper for some last-minute correspondence.

By Thursday, December 5, his neighbors on death row are showing signs of major stress. That afternoon, condemned inmates Cavanaugh, Wilson, and Olausen file an appeal to the state supreme court on Eddie's behalf, declaring Cole "legally insane," but their petition is rejected in a special night session. Meanwhile, too little and too late, San Diego County dispatches an investigator to quiz Eddie on his California murders, finding Cole less than cooperative after five years of being called a liar. Eddie skips lunch on Thursday afternoon, saving room for a dinner of Boston clam chowder, jumbo shrimp, tossed salad and fries, with Valium for dessert. When Ed Marshall checks in by phone, at 8:30, Cole tells him "all systems are go."

In his final hours, Eddie Cole seeks comfort in the religion of his youth, confessing his sins to a Catholic priest and keeping the padre around to play cards afterward. At 12:20 A.M., he receives another injection of Valium, though he hardly seems to need it.

At half past twelve, a tiny band of demonstrators gathers in the prison parking lot, shielding candles against a brisk wind and shivering as the temperature dips below twenty-five degrees. Guards armed with riot batons keep them away from the gates, news cameras picking out the only protest sign in evidence: WHY DO WE KILL PEOPLE WHO KILL TO SHOW THAT KILLING IS WRONG?

All things considered, it is the best Myra Soifer can do.

Spectators begin arriving for the execution at one o'clock, including nine official witnesses and seventeen reporters. They assemble in a recreation room and sit on folding chairs while Prison Director George Sumner delivers his opening remarks. From there, it is a brisk walk through the glaring television lights, past chain-link gates, to mount an outdoor stairway leading to death row. En route, they pass the execution chamber, with its airtight door and wheel lock, reminiscent of a diving bell. The viewing room is small, uncomfortably close. It seems to take forever, standing there and peering through a plate-glass window at the padded table, waiting for the guest of honor to arrive.

Eddie makes his appearance at 1:43 A.M., shoeless, wearing shackles and a belly chain, escorted by four burly guards. The narrow door will only handle one man at a time, an awkward moment as Eddie steps across the elevated threshold in his irons. Once everyone has squeezed inside the chamber, guards remove his chains and Eddie lies down on the table, no expression on his face as padded cuffs are buckled on his wrists and ankles, straps secured around his chest, waist, hips, and knees.

Despite the magnifying window, Eddie suddenly looks small.

Thin drapes are drawn across the glass while guards roll Eddie's sleeves up and insert the needles in each arm, unbuttoning his shirt to attach electrocardiograph sensors. They have a doctor standing by, but he will not participate directly in the execution. Rubber tubing snakes across the curved, beige-painted ceiling, through a hole drilled in the wall. Outside, their anonymity secure, two executioners stand by with their syringes, ready to proceed.

The state refuses to discuss its choice of poisons, but the standard killing recipe begins with sodium thiopental, a massive dose of anesthetic that renders the subject unconscious in seconds flat. That done, a mixture of Pavulon and potassium chloride is introduced, simultaneously shutting down the heart, lungs, and brain.

Better dying through chemistry.

The curtains open at 2:05 A.M., time enough for Eddie to smile at a couple of friends beyond the glass and tell them "It's okay." Offstage, George Sumner signals to the executioners, and they hit their plungers in unison. Cole's eyelids droop, his body going slack. At 2:07 he convulses twice, chest heaving, fingers curling into fists. At last, the hands that have extinguished fifteen lives relax in death.

Flat line.

The prison doctor makes it official at 2:10 A.M.

Outside, George Sumner tells the press that Cole was really dead inside of twenty seconds, give or take. Dan Seaton has a bright smile for the cameras, all those voters sitting snug and warm at home. "It is enjoyable," he says, "to see the system work."

Unfortunately, in the case of Eddie Cole, it took four decades, sixteen wasted lives, and countless dollars to complete the job.

But what a job it was.

EPILOGUE

IT WOULD BE COMFORTING TO THINK that Eddie Cole was a peculiar aberration, his case a unique example of the psychiatric system's failure to identify and curb a violent individual. Unfortunately, nothing could be further from the truth. From coast to coast, time after time, the story is identical: sadistic rapists, child molesters, and killers released to the streets with a clean bill of health from the "experts." In fact, the system fails so frequently, at such a cost in human lives, that failure almost seems to be the rule.

Cannibal-slayer Albert Fish provides a classic case in point. A veteran killer by the time psychiatrists had their first crack at him, in 1930, Fish was released after two months of observation, the official diagnosis reading: "Not insane; psychopathic personality; sexual type." A year later, found with torture instruments when police nabbed him on a charge of mailing obscene letters, Fish spent a mere two weeks under psychiatric scrutiny before he was discharged. When the depths of his depravity were finally exposed in 1935, New York psychiatrists closed ranks to help the prosecution make its case for sanity and death, explaining to jurors that Fish's compulsive coprophagia [eating his own excrement] was "socially perfectly all right."

James Lockhart was marking time in a Georgia mental institution when his temper got the best of him and he murdered a fellow patient. State psychiatrists helped Lockhart out at the trial, calling him "a severe schizophrene with a very poor prognosis for marked improvement," and a jury found him innocent by reason of insanity. Four years later the same doctors approved Lockhart's release from custody ...and no one, presumably, was more surprised when he soon committed yet another homicide.

It was December 1973 when Richard Chase entered a Sacramento, California, hospital, complaining that someone had stolen his pulmonary artery, leaving him short of breath. On top of that, he said, his head was changing shape. Staff psychiatrists examined Chase, labeling him a chronic paranoid schizophrenic, but they grudgingly released him at the insistence of their patient's "highly aggressive, hostile, and provocative" mother. By April 1976 Chase was killing wild animals and drinking their blood, sometimes injecting it into his veins. Committed by his parents this time, Chase explained that he was "falling apart," a condition alleviated only by shedding—and consuming—blood. Released with a "guarded" prognosis in September 1977, Chase was at large barely four months when police picked him up for killing six persons and drinking their blood.

Another California native, Herbert Mullin, was twice institutionalized in his home state during 1969, diagnosed as suffering from severe paranoid schizophrenia and symptoms of drug abuse, but fiscal cutbacks imposed by Governor Ronald Reagan resulted in closure of several state hospitals, returning Mullin— and hundreds of other walking time bombs—to the street. Briefly hospitalized once more on a trip to Hawaii, in 1970, Mullin was back in California two years later, hearing disembodied voices that informed him random murder would prevent a catastrophic earthquake on the coast. Before police arrested him in February 1973, he claimed thirteen lives.

Arguably the most prolific serial killer of modem times, Henry Lucas started with the murder of his drunken, sadistic mother in 1960. Sentenced to twenty years, he spent the first six in a Michigan state hospital for the criminally insane and was paroled in 1970. The next time he made headlines, in 1983, Lucas was confessing to 360 murders of men, women, and children across the United States and Canada. Those confessions led to convictions, including one death sentence, and while Lucas now claims total innocence, police from coast to coast list him as the prime suspect in at least one hundred other homicides.

Philadelphia's Gary Heidnik spent a year in the army before he was discharged on psychiatric grounds, his mental state sufficiently bizarre to earn him a 100 percent disability rating. Over the next quarter century, he was repeatedly committed to Pennsylvania mental hospitals, sometimes remaining for months at a time, but none of the experts picked up on his morbid obsession with collecting female "sex slaves." Convicted of kidnapping and molesting a retarded woman, Heidnik served four years and four months in prison— with three side trips to mental institutions following repetitive suicide attempts. By 1986, when he began collecting slaves in earnest, killing those who failed to please, the state and its psychiatrists had seemingly forgotten Heidnik, letting him fall through the cracks.

Another military reject on psychiatric grounds was Donald Harvey, twice committed in Kentucky after suicide attempts, the recipient of twenty-one electroshock-therapy treatments that failed to reverse his grim preoccupation with death. Poor legislation, inadequate records, and negligent staff allowed Harvey to cover his tracks, obtaining responsible jobs—and killing eighty-seven helpless patients—at hospitals in two states.

No one in California tried to hide Ed Kemper's background. Locked up for butchering his grandparents at age fifteen, Kemper spent six years in therapy before he was discharged, over his own strenuous objections, to the custody of his carping, shrewish mother. Back in the same old environment, subject to his mother's whims and acid tongue, Kemper gave free rein to the necrophilic passions that had driven him from early childhood. Over a year's time, Kemper killed six college coeds, dragging their bodies home for bouts of posthumous sex. On one occasion, Kemper drove to visit his psychiatrist with a severed head in the trunk of his car. Finally, tiring of the game, he killed his mother and her best friend, dismembering their remains before he surrendered to police.

A known child molester from 1959, Charles Hatcher had already killed most of his sixteen victims when Iowa psychiatrists held him for two months observation in 1982. Upon release, he murdered yet another child and was finally arrested ...while checking into a Missouri state hospital. Jurors ignored his plea for the death penalty, imposing a sentence of life imprisonment, but Hatcher had the last laugh, hanging himself in his cell.

Erno Soto's disintegrating marriage, spurred by the birth of an illegitimate black child to Soto's Hispanic wife, produced erratic behavior that led to his commitment during 1969 and 1970. Soto's outpatient treatment continued sporadically over the next three years, but he derived his main relief from the murder and mutilation of young, dark-skinned boys. Three were killed and a fourth maimed by New York's "Charlie Chop-off," before Soto was captured ...and returned to the asylum.

Another New Yorker, Joseph Baldi, had a ten-year record of commitment to psychiatric hospitals before his June 1972 arrest on charges of killing four women. Investigation revealed that the murders occurred after Baldi was released from Creedmore State Hospital "by mistake," therapists overlooking the fact that he was confined on charges of trying to kill a policeman.

Joseph Bryan first ran afoul of the law at age nineteen, when he abducted two small boys, tied them to a tree, and sexually abused them. Committed to a New Jersey mental hospital, Bryan was diagnosed as schizophrenic, warning doctors that he liked to see young boys "tied up and screaming." It was strong stuff, but not strong enough to keep Bryan inside. Upon his release, he joined the navy, but was soon discharged after service psychiatrists saw through his mask of sanity. A term in state prison for burglary and auto theft left him hungry for action, killing three boys and abducting a fourth within three months of his parole.

James Ruzicka was facing a ten-year sentence on conviction for a double rape, when the court offered him an escape hatch. Checking into a sex-offender rehabilitation program in Tacoma, Washington, Ruzicka worked his way up to trusty status in record time, telling therapists and nurses everything they longed to hear. Hospital administrators thought enough of Ruzicka to grant him a forty-eight-hour furlough, from which he never returned. In four weeks at large, the "new, improved" Ruzicka murdered two teenage girls in Seattle and brutally raped another in Oregon.

Joseph Kallinger's first brush with psychiatry came in 1957, when he was hospitalized with a "psychopathological nervous disorder" stemming from the breakup of his marriage. Two years later he was committed to a state hospital following a suicide attempt. In 1972 a conviction on child abuse charges earned him four years probation, with a provision for mandatory psychiatric treatment. Kallinger kept his appointments, but therapists failed to pick up on his conversations with a disembodied head named "Charlie," which directed him to kill and mutilate his son, moving on from there to brutalize other victims in their homes. At this writing, Kallinger stands by his desire to kill every person on earth, at which point he plans to commit suicide and "become God."

Richard Biegenwald was first committed for psychiatric observation at age five, after setting the family home on fire. Four years later a series of electroshock treatments failed to curb his escalating violence, and Biegenwald set himself on fire at age eleven. Committing his first murder at eighteen, Richard was paroled in 1975, claiming six known victims before he was locked up again, in 1983.

Silent Rage

In early childhood, Harvey Glatman displayed a precocious obsession with autoerotic asphyxia—that is, self-strangulation during masturbation—but the family doctor advised Glatman's parents that Harvey would "grow out of it." In a sense, he was right, but the alternative was hardly preferable. By his teens, Glatman was assaulting females, forcing them to disrobe at gunpoint. Imprisoned for robbery in New York, Glatman was still receiving psychiatric treatment at the time of his parole in 1951. Back home in L.A., he murdered three women before a fourth intended victim disarmed him and called the police. Glatman's final therapy was administered in the San Quentin gas chamber.

Sacramento native Jeffrey Jones was attending college in Arizona when he "began to exhibit abnormal behavior" and counselors sent him home for treatment. Antipsychotic medication was prescribed after doctors diagnosed Jones as a chronic paranoid schizophrenic, but drugs had little effect. Charged with robbing a disabled victim in May 1984, Jones got off without jail time. A November probation report found him "stabilized," noting that "the probability of threat to others is not significant at this time." It became significant two months later, when Jones launched a one-man crime wave in the neighborhood, killing three men and critically wounding a fourth with his trusty claw hammer.

Gary Addison Taylor began assaulting women in his teens, first with a hammer, later in a series of sniping attacks. Shuttled from one psychiatric ward to another over an eleven-year period, Taylor attacked several more women during ill-conceived furloughs from custody. Despite his continuing violence and self-proclaimed "compulsion to hurt women," Gary was rated a safe bet for outpatient status in 1973, "as long as he reports to receive medication." When he stopped checking in, Michigan authorities waited fourteen months before listing his disappearance with the National Crime Information Center in Washington, D.C. In the meantime, Taylor had murdered at least four women in three different states; authorities believe his final body count may be closer to twenty.

Christopher Wilder's psychiatric problems surfaced at age seventeen, when he was jailed for his role in an Australian gang rape. The court-assigned term of one year's probation included group therapy and electroshock treatments, but all in vain. Similar sex charges dogged Wilder across the Pacific, earning repeated terms of probation with mandatory counseling. On one occasion, he confessed a sexual assault to his therapist, but the confidential statement was inadmissible at trial, and Wilder was acquitted on the charge. He was still on probation in Florida, and a fugitive from pending sex charges in Australia, when he launched his final murder spree across America in early 1984. His several therapists, from all appearances, were taken absolutely by surprise.

New Yorker George Fitzsimmons never denied the murder of his parents, but a jury found him innocent by reason of insanity. Four years later state psychiatrists declared that Fitzsimmons posed no further hazard to society, releasing him to the care of an aunt and uncle whom Fitzsimmons claimed to love "like his own mother and father." The analogy was apt enough, as demonstrated when Fitzsimmons stabbed the aging couple to death in their Pennsylvania home. Detectives later found that Fitzsimmons had named himself as beneficiary to the life insurance of all four victims.

Robert Liberty was serving time in a California mental institution when he struck up a relationship with fellow inmate Marcela Landis. On release, he strangled her to death and was declared insane, packed off to another state hospital for treatment. After three years of therapy, a panel of six psychiatrists pronounced Liberty "cured," and he was released to southern California ...where he killed another victim six months later.

Maryland native Arthur Goode agreed to voluntary psychiatric treatment in 1975, following his fifth arrest for child molesting, but the terms of his commitment allowed Goode to leave the hospital at will. Unfazed by fifteen weeks of therapy, he checked out of the asylum and hit the road, murdering two young boys in Virginia and Florida. At his arrest, Goode told police, "You can't do nothing to me. I'm sick." Florida jurors disagreed, and he was sentenced to die for his crimes.

Gary Rardon served four years on an Indiana manslaughter conviction before a prison psychiatrist deemed him rehabilitated, declaring that "the likelihood of further violence would be unusual." It took eight years to prove the doctor wrong, but Rardon did so with a vengeance, gunning down three Chicago victims in November 1974. Arrested two months later with one victim's credit card, Rardon drew a sentence of forty to one hundred years in prison on conviction for multiple murder.

In Washington state, Westley Dodd traced his sexual feelings for children to age twelve, attracting police attention and dropping out of two voluntary counseling programs by age fourteen. His first arrest for soliciting a minor was logged in 1980, and he continued the habit through two years of naval service, climaxed by a dishonorable discharge linked to accusations of child-molesting. Sporadic counseling sessions, some of them court-ordered, failed to prevent Dodd from murdering three boys around Vancouver, in 1990. Arrested that November, after trying to drag a six-year-old boy from a movie theater, Dodd confessed his murders and was sentenced to die.

California psychiatrists first diagnosed Lawrence Bittaker as a "borderline psychotic" in 1961, expanding their judgment a year later to note Bittaker's "poor control of his impulsive behavior." By 1969, Bittaker was receiving antipsychotic medication, but it failed to keep him out of trouble or out of prison. While serving time, in 1978, Bittaker met rapist Roy Norris, earlier discharged from the navy for "psychological problems" linked to a "severe schizoid personality." Norris was also a veteran of Atascadero state hospital, where he spent five years as a mentally disordered sex offender before doctors released him as "no further danger to others." Bittaker recognized a soul mate on sight, and the pair became inseparable, hatching a grisly plot to kidnap, rape, and murder teenage girls "for fun," as soon as they were freed. At least five victims took the one-way ride in Bittaker's van, nicknamed "Murder Mack," their screams recorded for posterity, before a survivor identified the predators in November 1979.

While serving time in the Oklahoma state prison, from 1977 to 1980, inmate Gary Walker made three separate trips to the state hospital for psychiatric treatment. On each occasion, doctors played the same refrain their counterparts in Reno used with Eddie Cole, describing Walker as a con artist who used the psycho ward "to hide from the police." Walker also served federal time at "The Pits," in Springfield, Missouri, where he was diagnosed as paranoid and schizophrenic. The finding still left him eligible for parole in February 1984, and he slaughtered five victims before his next arrest, four months later.

Our list of psychiatric "cures" and rejects represents the mere tip of a deadly iceberg. Only identified serial killers have been included, ignoring—as too many therapists are prone to do—the countless thousands of one-time murderers, rapists, child molesters, arsonists, and other predators who are released from custody each day, year-round, to victimize society once more. The case of Carroll Edward Cole is not a fluke or aberration; rather, it should serve us as a warning, sounding the alarm.

In such a case, The System fails not only Eddie Cole.

It fails us all.

NOTES

CHAPTER 1

Details of the 1980 Dallas murders were compiled from correspondence with Detective Gerald Robinson, Cole's exhaustive first-person account, selected media reports of his arrest and trial, plus testimony given under oath by Detective Robinson, appearing as a witness at Cole's Las Vegas death penalty hearing, conducted in October 1984. Detective Robinson's memory of events was remarkably consistent with Cole's account of the interrogation leading up to and including his confession.

CHAPTER 2

Las Vegas authorities declined to cooperate in my investigation of Cole's case. The facts of Detective Joe McGuckin's Dallas interview with Cole are drawn from McGuckin's sworn testimony, given at Cole's Las Vegas penalty hearing in October 1984.

*****

Twenty years after the fact, San Diego authorities still refuse to discuss Cole's case or release any documents related to their investigation of local homicides. Early reactions to Cole's 1980 confessions are drawn from reports published in the *San Diego Union* during December of that year. Robert Ring's interrogation of Cole in 1971, and his continuing suspicion of Cole in the murder of Essie Buck, are documented in Ring's sworn testimony at Cole's 1984 penalty hearing in Las Vegas.

*****

Art Terry—formerly a Natrona County sheriff's investigator, later appointed as chief of police in nearby Mills, Wyoming—initially agreed to cooperate with my investigation in 1985, offering to re-create his notes on the Hamer case "more or less verbatim." Stony silence ensued after Terry was advised that Cole disputed certain aspects of the ex-detective's testimony, and attempts to reestablish contact over the next five years were dismissed without the courtesy of a reply. Terry's 1980 interview with Cole is reconstructed from the officer's sworn testimony, delivered at Cole's Las Vegas penalty hearing in October 1984.

*****

Correspondence between Dallas authorities and the Medical Center for Federal Prisoners in Springfield, Missouri, was released by the Federal Bureau of Prisons in 1985, under the Freedom of Information Act.

*****

Cole's first interview with Dr. Griffith is reconstructed from the doctor's clinical notes, released in accordance with a notarized request from Cole.

*****

My correspondence with the district clerk of Dallas County, in September 1985, elicited the curious announcement that only brief "supplemental transcripts," totaling fourteen pages, now exist from Cole's murder trial in April 1981. With verbatim transcripts curiously nonexistent, the events of Cole's trial are reconstructed from Cole's memory and media reports published in the Dallas *Times Herald.* The description of Cole's second interview with Dr. Griffith derives from the doctor's dated clinical notes, released in accordance with a notarized request from Cole.

CHAPTER 3

Bizarre as it may sound, compulsory cross-dressing during early childhood has been documented in the cases of at least six other criminals whose twisted sexuality expressed itself in homicidal violence during modern times. In every case but one, the perpetrator of abuse has been a female relative or guardian, and while their motives vary, the results are strikingly consistent. An exception to the rule of torment by a brutal mother figure (and perhaps the most notorious of tortured children turned assassin) is Charles Manson, sent to elementary school in dresses by an uncle, with the sage advice that it would teach him "how to fight and be a man." Serial killer Henry Lucas—convicted of ten murders and suspected of more than one hundred others—was also sent to school in skirts and dainty curls, until administrators filed injunctions to prevent his mother from abusing him in public. It is curious—and probably irrelevant—to note that Manson and Lucas both suffered their peculiar torment in Virginia, through the early 1940s. Farther south and ten years later, in the neighborhood of Jacksonville, homosexual slayer Ottis Toole was dressed in petticoats and lace because his mother *wished* that he had been a girl. As an adult, ironically teamed up with Lucas for a murder spree that spanned the continent, Toole still dressed up in drag from time to time, when he was not consuming meals of human flesh. (Lucas, himself a bisexual, occasionally went to bed with Ottis "as a favor," but he stopped short of joining Toole's cannibal feasts. His reason: "I don't like barbecue sauce.") A wicked stepmother was the culprit in the case of Californian Rodney Beeler, her favorite dress-up "punishment" producing a serial rapist, presently sentenced to die for the one murder authorities are able to document. Another Californian, Gordon Northcott—hanged in 1930 for three of an estimated twenty homosexual slayings—was habitually dressed as a girl by his mentally unbalanced mother (herself convicted of murder) until age sixteen. And worlds away, in Ecuador, child-killer Daniel Barbosa bitterly recalls the way his mother dressed him as a girl to "keep him out of trouble" in the seedy barrio they occupied. Imprisoned for the rape-and-mutilation slayings of seventy-one young girls, Barbosa joins the rest as living proof of how impressionable twigs are bent and fashioned into deadly trees.

*****

My authority for Cole's delayed enrollment in school is his permanent academic record, covering grades seven through eleven, for the years 1951-56. While his elementary school records have not survived, the transcripts from Roosevelt Junior High School reveal that Cole entered seventh grade in September 1951, at age thirteen. Since California law permits enrollment in kindergarten at age five and requires first-grade enrollment at age six, a normal progression through the elementary grades should have placed him in junior high school by September 1950, at age *twelve*. Under questioning, Cole had no memory of repeating any elementary grade, and his performance in junior high—while undistinguished— was not suggestive of a student who has been held back for academic failure in the past. In recounting events from his childhood and adolescence, Cole generally covered this forgotten (or repressed) time lapse by dating school-related incidents a year before their actual occurrence. Thus, he described his expulsion from Roosevelt Junior High in the seventh grade (when it actually occurred in the second semester of *eighth* grade), and placed his departure from high school during his sophomore year (when, in fact, he dropped out on his birthday, in his *junior* year). I accept school records as superior to Cole's memory in this regard, and while he could not explain the obvious discrepancy, Cole granted that an age differential may well have encouraged students at Nystrom Elementary to tag him as "an oddball."

*****

I first learned of Cole's sexual experience with his female relative, carefully deleted from his lengthy autobiography, when author "Turk Ryder" published an article on his case in the August 1985 issue of *Official Detective*. In a letter dated July 13, 1985, Cole reluctantly admitted discussing the incident—"a very personal thing"—with author Genny McIlvaine, some months before he finally discharged her from his case.

*****

My efforts to identify Cole's childhood victim after forty years proved fruitless. Records of the Contra Costa County coroner and Richmond Police Department are routinely purged, and files relating to the 1940s were long gone by 1985. Newspaper morgues were likewise barren, Cole recalling that the local paper in the forties—long defunct— routinely buried news of children's "accidental" deaths. As Cole remembered Duane, "I only learned his name the day he died," his victim's surname long forgotten "if I ever knew it." To Eddie, he would always be "a real asshole who lived somewhere beyond the school." Without a surname for a starting point, obituary scans were hopeless, and the Richmond Yacht Club has "no detailed records of anything happening on the water" prior to its construction of private facilities in 1967. The district attorney's office was interested enough to scan their open files from 1945 to '47, yielding one report of a fifty-year-old "John Doe" fished out of the harbor on August 5, 1946. Again, the problem is that Duane would *not* have been a nameless "John Doe" corpse, nor would his so-called *accidental* death be listed in the records as an unsolved case. The trail is cold, but I remain convinced of Cole's sincerity, from his intense descriptions of the crime and lack of any motive for a fabrication in the case. The final answer, if it still exists, lies buried somewhere in the neighborhood of Richmond, underneath a headstone weathered by the years.

CHAPTER 4

Cole's performance in junior high and high school is documented by his permanent academic record from Contra Costa County, covering the years 1951 through 1956.

*****

The names "Rhonda Pearsall," "Ellie Roth," and "Randy Godwin" are pseudonyms, employed to protect the individuals' privacy.

*****

Cole's sexual fixation on the photographs in pulp detective magazines is not unique among serial killers. Ted Bundy and child-killer John Joubert shared a similar taste in adolescence, while Harvey Glatman took the game a step further, luring would-be models to their deaths with offers of jobs posing "jeopardy" shots for the pulps. Indeed, the wide variety of stimuli enjoyed by random killers is a telling argument against censorship as a cure for the problem, per se. In northern California, Leonard Lake was so taken with *The Collector,* by John Fowles, that he dubbed his own kidnapping effort "Operation Miranda," after the novel's female protagonist. In Germany, sex-slayer Heinrich Pommerenke committed his first murder after a screening of *The Ten Commandments,* which persuaded him that women were the root of all worldly evil, deserving a terminal "lesson."

*****

California juvenile records are sealed when a subject reaches adulthood. Cole's memory of teenage arrests was understandably vague, but his rough tabulation coincides with published estimates of his total arrests, when compared to adult records maintained by state and federal authorities.

CHAPTER 5

Cole's version of life in the brig was documented eleven years later in exposes that led to dramatic reforms in the system. For example, see Jack Fincher's "In a Marine Corps prison: The hog-tied brig rats of Camp Pendleton," *Life* magazine, October 10, 1969.

*****

For reasons of privacy, pseudonyms have been applied to Nancy's husband "Ronald," and to Eddie's girlfriend "Pat Morris."

CHAPTER 6

Cole's confidential files from Napa State Hospital were released to the author in accordance with a notarized request from Cole.

*****

Pseudonyms are used for Cole's Reno acquaintances, "Carla," "Lydia," and "Rick," in the interest of privacy.

*****

Cole's confidential files from Atascadero and Stockton State Hospitals were obtained by the author through a notarized request from Cole.

CHAPTER 7

Cole's patient files from Parkland Memorial Hospital were released in accordance with a notarized request from the patient.

*****

The pseudonym "Lucinda" has been used for Billy Whitworth's daughter, to protect her privacy.

*****

Cole met Jack Ruby once more, following the Oswald murder. While serving time for assault in 1965, Eddie was appointed as a trusty in the county jail, his duties including food service on Ruby's cell block. He recalled that Ruby seemed drugged, "out of it," but a guard noted Cole's expression of recognition and asked if he knew Ruby. When Cole replied in the affirmative, he was transferred to a different wing and never saw Ruby again.

*****

A pseudonym has been used for Billy Whitworth's sister, in the interest of privacy.

*****

The merger of sex and brutality in Cole's mind is common with serial killers. Ted Bundy also enjoyed some "playful" choking during voluntary intercourse, and Pennsylvania's Joseph Kallinger performed best with his spouse when he kept a knife clenched in his fist. As time goes on, playacting fails to satisfy, and violence escalates until we have a specimen like Lawrence "Pliers" Bittaker, incapable of sex without the grim accompaniment of dying screams.

*****

Cole's Texas prison files were released to the author before his execution, in accordance with a notarized request. The description of disciplinary techniques at Eastham is drawn from Cole's recollection, amply supported by independent published sources.

CHAPTER 8

A pseudonym has been employed for Eddie's Oklahoma City girl-friend, "Lisa," in the interest of privacy.

*****

Several years after the attempt on Virginia Rowden's life, Cole learned that his young victim had died in a car wreck. Her death, though not produced by any act of Cole's, occasioned deep remorse. It was apparently the one and only time that Eddie grieved for any of his victims, through the years.

*****

A pseudonym is used for "Roger," to protect his privacy.

*****

Cole's confidential records from the Nevada State Hospital were obtained with a notarized request, prior to Cole's execution.

CHAPTER 9

Cole's patient file from the San Diego Community Mental Health Center was furnished to the author under terms of a notarized request from Cole.

*****

A pseudonym was used for "Mrs. Baker."

*****

As previously noted, San Diego authorities declined to cooperate with my research. Robert Ring's involvement in the case of Essie Buck is reconstructed from his sworn testimony at Cole's Nevada death penalty hearing in October 1984, supported by Cole's own recollections and brief items published in the San *Diego Union*.

*****

Recalcitrant San Diego authorities still deny the existence of Wilma and Cole's third female victim, even though they sent an officer to question him a few hours prior to his execution in December 1985. Passage of time and the official ban on cooperation made it impossible to double-check missing persons reports from 1971, but I accept Cole's version of events in this regard, as he showed no interest in playing a "numbers game" with spurious confessions.

CHAPTER 10

Cole's murder of the two Mexican women was not included in the detailed autobiography he wrote for me in 1985. I first encountered the story while reading transcripts of Eddie's testimony at his Las Vegas death penalty hearing, a year after the fact. When I asked about the crime in September 1985, Cole replied that it was "something I made up in Dallas, on the witness stand," to divert attention from actual victims and thus repay detectives who were "screwing me around." Available records from Dallas, however, contain no reference to any such case or confession; indeed, Cole's Nevada testimony seems to be the one and only public reference to a double slaying, which he later denied. Finally, in an interview granted two days before his December 1985 execution, Cole admitted "there might be a couple more" victims besides the established thirteen. He claimed a lapse of memory and put the blame on alcohol. Despite a lack of corpses to substantiate the crime, I now believe Cole's sworn description of the double murder was essentially an accurate account of real events.

*****

A pseudonym has been employed for Diana Pashal's mother, in the interest of privacy.

*****

Cole never saw Jean again, but several years later he heard news of her murder at a tavern in Los Angeles County, near Edwards Air Force Base. The killer used a knife, and to the best of Eddie's knowledge, he was never apprehended by police.

CHAPTER 11

Cole soon forgot the young woman's name, if he ever learned it, but he recalled the near-miss incident six years later, when Las Vegas Detective Joe McGuckin flew to Dallas for a jailhouse interview. Among the open files presented for consideration was the 1974 murder of a female victim closely matching Cole's description of the woman from the Silver Slipper. "I was stunned," Cole wrote in 1985. "Of course, it could have been somebody else. I had no way of knowing, either way."

*****

A pseudonym has been provided for Diana's brother, in the interest of privacy.

*****

Pseudonyms have been used for "Tom," "Sara," "Ann," "Jane," and "Susan."

*****

Controversy endures over the precise circumstances of Myrlene Hamer's death. Testifying at Cole's October 1984 death penalty hearing in Las Vegas, Art Terry summarized the confession Eddie gave him in Dallas, on December 10, 1980. According to Terry's sworn testimony, Cole described the murder as occurring "on an early Tuesday or Wednesday morning"—that is, August 5 or 6—after which Cole reportedly drove around Casper with Hamer's corpse in his trunk until the predawn hours of Saturday, August 9. In his statements to me, Cole described the police version as "a bunch of shit," insisting that he met and strangled Hamer on the night of August 8. He also disputed Terry's statement alleging that Cole "had sex with her one or two times after her death." In an effort to resolve the matter, I wrote to Art Terry, then the police chief of Mills, Wyoming, in June 1985. His reply, dated July 24, closed with this offer of assistance: "I don't have access to the files. However, I can remember and almost quote you verbatim what happened, etc. Coupled with what you have, I think we could put it together." I then sent Terry a summary of Cole's account, including his denial of the alleged posthumous rape. Six years of stony silence ensued, with Terry ignoring my several attempts to reestablish contact. By the time he finally answered me again, in September 1991, Terry had retired from law enforcement and his memory of events from 1975 had faded in the stretch. Once more, he expressed a desire to be helpful and "contribute something to this book" …if only *I* could obtain the sheriff's file on Myrlene Hamer's death. Predictably, the Natrona County sheriff's office declined to share their files with a civilian, and there the matter rests, with vital questions forever unresolved.

CHAPTER 12

Eddie's confidential records from the Community Mental Health Center were released to the author in compliance with Cole's notarized request.

*****

Pseudonyms have been employed for "Sister Rachel" "Fred Warren," and "Macy," in the interest of privacy.

*****

Cole's inmate records from the Metropolitan Correctional Center were obtained with the help of a notarized request in 1985.

CHAPTER 13

"Tanya" is a pseudonym.

*****

Las Vegas authorities declined to cooperate with me in my research for this book. Detective McGuckin's background and participation in the case of Kathlyn Blum are reconstructed from the officer's sworn testimony at Eddie Cole's Nevada death penalty hearing, in October 1984.

*****

In the interest of privacy, pseudonyms have been employed for Carrie Chadwick, her children, and the Larsons.

*****

A pseudonym has been used for "Kathy."

*****

In his Dallas courtroom testimony, during April 1981, Cole described his Thanksgiving victim as a brunette, later correcting himself when he told me the full story in June 1985. The Dallas reference to cannibalism was a lie, he later insisted, contrived to support an insanity defense—but his description of the severed arm and feet, together with the meat found in the frying pan and on his dinner plate, was accurate. "I still don't know what made me do that," Eddie wrote, six months before his execution in Nevada. "There was never any thought of eating human flesh, before or after that. I can't explain it." No remains were ever found in Oklahoma City—not surprising, after three full years, when garbage is routinely burned or buried—and without the victim's name, police officially reject Cole's statement as a fabrication. After interviewing Eddie, watching him relive the crime, I am convinced that the events took place as he described.

CHAPTER 14

Eddie's inmate records from the Metropolitan Correctional Center were supplied by the Federal Bureau of Prisons, in accordance with a notarized release from Cole.

*****

Confidential patient files from the San Diego County Mental Health Service were released to the author in 1985, at Cole's request.

*****

Linda Sims was interviewed by telephone on October 25, 1985. She recalled that Cole often brought cans of soup to work and heated them for lunch, leaving one behind when he fled San Diego in September 1979. The soup was still around when his Dallas arrest and confessions made news in December 1980, prompting some anonymous wag to slap a new label on the can. It read: "This can of soup belonged to a man who killed nine women."

*****

San Diego police maintain a strict rule of silence where Eddie Cole is concerned. Detective Shively's involvement in the Bonnie O'Neil and Diana Cole investigations is reconstructed from his sworn testimony at Cole's Nevada death penalty hearing, in October 1984.

*****

My efforts to elicit comments from John Salcido—or any other member of the federal probation office in San Diego—were ignored. Salcido's reaction to complaints from Diana Cole is reconstructed from an October 1985 interview with Linda Sims, who witnessed and participated in the conversation.

*****

In October 1984, testifying under oath at Cole's death penalty hearing in Las Vegas, James Shively described Bonnie O'Neil and Diana Cole as murder victims. Even so, the original verdicts of death by natural causes remain intact, and details of the twice-solved cases are still officially closed to the public. In the words of SDPD's records supervisor: "We will release nothing."

CHAPTER 15

A pseudonym has been used for "Sharla Floyd."

*****

In the absence of cooperation from Las Vegas authorities, Karen Good's investigation of the Cushman homicide is reconstructed from her sworn testimony at Cole's Nevada death penalty hearing, in October 1984. The conflicting suspect descriptions—never officially explained—were published in the *Las Vegas Review-Journal* on November 9, 1979.

*****

My October 1985 interview with Linda Sims confirmed that Cole's probation officer believed him guilty of Diana's murder. Salcido allegedly told Linda as much, point-blank, but when she pressed him to initiate prosecution, she received the stock response: "My hands are tied." In fairness to Salcido, murder of a spouse is not a federal crime, and without proof to the contrary, we may assume the San Diego Police Department showed John Salcido the same brick wall of indifference they later displayed to Eddie Cole and the media.

*****

Confidential inmate records from the Federal Bureau of Prisons were obtained under the Freedom of Information Act, with a notarized request from Eddie Cole.

CHAPTER 16

A pseudonym has been supplied for Joe Andretti, in the interest of privacy.

CHAPTER 17

Medical records from the Clark County jail were released in accordance with a notarized request from Eddie Cole.

*****

Dr. Rosalinda Rueca was unavailable for comment during my research for this volume. Her findings of May 28 are summarized in a report filed by Attorney Edward Marshall, with Marshall's opinion that the document "leaves something to be desired." The July findings of Doctors Franklin Master and William O'Gorman were released in accordance with notarized requests from Cole.

*****

Eddie Cole supplied me with the transcript of his October 1984 penalty hearing, and all relevant quotations are drawn from that official record.

*****

After Cole's vehement denial of a sexual assault on Tepee Hamer, Art Terry broke off contact with me in 1985. By the time he consented to answer my letters again, six years later, Terry had "forgotten" all the details of the case he previously volunteered to "re-create verbatim" from his memory. No taped or written transcript of the Dallas interview exists, and the Wyoming autopsy report—sought by Cole to disprove the finding of semen in Hamer's vagina—remains unavailable today, with the Natrona County sheriff's office refusing to acknowledge my correspondence. Eddie could never say why anyone would want to fabricate a posthumous rape—if it *was* fabricated— though he once offered a curious suggestion that the added element in the story might have made "things easier on Tepee's mother." At this writing, the mystery remains unsolved.

*****

Eddie Cole supplied me with his prison file and legal correspondence, from which various quotations are drawn and events reconstructed.

*****

Dr. John Peacock was scheduled to remove Eddie's brain on December 6, but he missed the appointment. Instead, the operation was performed by David Melarkey, a pathologist from the V.A. Medical Center in Reno. Dr. Peacock did join Lonnie Hammargren for the posthumous examination, which revealed no evidence of trauma or disease. Jan Bruner's research bit the dust, but Dr. Hammargren didn't mind, telling the press, "It is good research, even if nothing comes of it." Unclaimed by his family, Eddie's remains were cremated at a Carson City funeral home.

AUTHOR'S NOTE

I FIRST SET EYES ON EDDIE COLE IN MID-OCTOBER 1984, when the Las Vegas CBS affiliate broadcast a jailhouse interview, with Cole reciting details of a tortured youth and blighted adolescence, ticking off the victims who had fallen prey to his abiding rage in later years. He spoke without remorse for those he killed or pity for himself, but I perceived a hint of sadness as he dwelt on the pervasive scourge of child abuse, his own example offered as a warning to the parents of tomorrow.

Instantly intrigued, I wrote to Cole in care of the Clark County jail, proposing that we work together on an article or book that would explore the details of his wasted life and share his message—if he *had* a message—with the world at large. His answer was immediate, polite ... and firmly negative. He had another local writer on the line, and he had promised her a fighting chance to make a sale before he took the story elsewhere.

I respected Cole's decision (and the risk of legal action if I interfered with an existing contract), moving on to other projects through that fall and winter, into spring. Meanwhile, unknown to me, the killer and his Boswell came to verbal blows with her submission of a lurid broadside to *The National Enquirer* and the publication of an article in a detective magazine that Cole perceived as grossly slanted and inaccurate. They parted company in April, and the letter I received from Cole that month inquired if I would still be interested in covering his story, from the trauma of his early years to his impending death.

I was.

From the beginning, Cole expressed predictable dissatisfaction with "the system" that had cycled him through juvenile detention, psychiatric wards and detox centers, jails and halfway houses, since his teenage years. His overall contempt for the police was nothing short of monumental, citing cases where patrolmen actually drove him home from two attempted murders, while detectives stubbornly ignored the evidence supporting his confessions to a string of "unsolved" homicides. I took Cole's allegations—and his evident concern for children—with a hefty grain of salt, reserving judgment until he had proved himself.

To that end, Cole provided me with notarized releases that unlocked the confidential files of lawyers and psychiatrists, the schools that he attended as a child and penal institutions where he spent so many of his adult years. While scattered agencies and individuals ignored the law, denying Cole's request for documents that focused on himself and no one else, the vast majority complied. Within Cole's final seven months of life, we managed to collect the records of his junior high and high school years in Richmond, California; prison documents from Texas and the federal government, in Washington, D.C.; the privileged files of mental institutions and psychiatrists in California and Nevada, Texas and Missouri; reminiscences from court-appointed lawyers, and a lengthy rap sheet from the FBI. In Carson City, waiting on death row, Cole penned his graphic memoirs of a life outside the law, encompassing 300 legal pages, better than 100,000 words in all.

At every turn, I found the public record generally supporting Eddie's version of events. His memory had gaps, of course—he never learned the names of several murder victims, for example—and the passing years occasionally blurred his recollection of a date or name. But for the most part, Eddie's memory for detail was remarkably precise. I read the transcripts of his interviews with doctors and attorneys; followed him through state and federal prisons via detailed, day-by-day reports; and marveled at the diagnosis of a "healer" in Nevada who prescribed Cole's psychiatric "treatment" as a one-way ride to San Diego, California —where he killed at least three women in the next six months.

At times, the very reticence of sources was enough to bolster Cole's account of some bizarre event. According to Cole, members of his family refute Cole's memories of savage and prolonged abuse in childhood, but attempts to learn their side of the debate were met with stony silence. Sealed lips, likewise, are the rule in San Diego, where police attribute one of Eddie's murders to "natural causes," ignoring his detailed confessions to blame the rest on unidentified pimps or "persons unknown." A homicide detective in Wyoming vowed to re-create his files "verbatim" on a local murder, later fading in the stretch and breaking off our correspondence after Cole disputed crucial points of his recorded testimony.

On the flip side, Cole's acquaintances, employers, and defense attorneys were cooperative and forthcoming, adding depth and color to the portrait of a tragic, barren life. Of Cole's three wives, one managed to survive him, and she granted me an obviously painful interview that added new dimensions to the man. In deference to her privacy and grief, she is protected by a pseudonym in this account. The only other persons so disguised include a handful of reputed lovers, acquaintances, or accomplices in petty crime whose real names have no solid bearing on the story.

My thirty-two-week odyssey with Carroll Edward Cole entailed a number of surprises, chief among them my attendance as a witness at his execution, in December 1985. A cryptic sideshow to the main event revolved around three letters Cole received within the last week of his life, which may have emanated from Seattle's notorious "Green River Killer." The author— who has managed to evade authorities since 1985— made note of his perceived resemblance to Cole and questioned Eddie on the means by which a random killer might avoid arrest, digressing to explain why "my own work" around Seattle and Tacoma was "important" to the cause of criminology. A shipyard worker, he eluded homicide detectives and apparently evacuated Washington ... around the time authorities in San Diego County, California, claimed Seattle's killer gravitated south to find himself a change of scene.

As noted, various officials and civilians have assisted me in the production of this book. Defense attorneys who provided interviews or excerpts from their privileged files included: Edgar Mason (Dallas); Frank Gregorcich (San Diego); Tom Pitaro, Edward Marshall, and Frank Cremen (in Las Vegas). On the other side, I received material assistance from Dan Seaton, chief deputy district attorney for Clark County, Nevada; A. Bruce Ferguson, referee of the San Diego Juvenile Court; John Fusselman, senior inspector for the Contra Costa County (California) district attorney's office; Joyce Ann Hudson, criminal justice specialist with the California Department of Justice criminal records security unit; Rosalind Johnson and L. Winters, deputy clerks in Dallas County, Texas.

Law enforcement agencies were not universally hostile in my quest for background information. Those who ultimately helped me trace Cole's criminal career include Detective Gerald Robinson, Crimes Against Persons Division, Dallas (Texas) Police Department; Geneva Watson, supervising clerk of the Records Division, San Diego County sheriff's office; Carolyn Gaspar, records supervisor for the Richmond (California) Police Department's Special Services Bureau; and Michelle

Gordon, supervisor of records and identification for the Reno (Nevada) Police Department. At the U.S. Postal Service, I was ably assisted by Chief Postal Inspector C. R. Clauson, Deputy Inspector J. Rosasco, and W. J. Maisch, postal inspector in charge of the Los Angeles division.

Eddie Cole spent much of his adult life in correctional facilities, and I am indebted to numerous officers for helping me compile a comprehensive, "rap sheet" on my subject. In Missouri, I received assistance from Bill Armountrout, warden of the state penitentiary at Jefferson City. At the Nevada State Prison, Warden George Sumner and visiting officer James McHugh facilitated my correspondence with Cole, later clearing the way for my attendance at his 1985 execution. From the Federal Bureau of Prisons, where Eddie was shuttled around like the proverbial hot potato, I am indebted to the following: Clair Cripe, general counsel; C. B. Faulkner, regional counsel for the north-central regional office; John Shaw, regional counsel for the western regional office; D. J. Southerland, warden of the federal institution at La Tuna, New Mexico; R. H. Bison, warden at San Pedro, California; L. E. DuBois, warden at Littleton, Colorado; and Patrick Whalen, associate warden for the Metropolitan Correctional Center in San Diego.

Cole's detailed medical and psychiatric records were furnished by the following physicians: Dr. E. Clay Griffith (Dallas); Dr. Franklin Master and Dr. William O'Gorman (in Las Vegas); and Dr. Harold Mavritte, for the County of San Diego Department of Mental Health. In Nevada, institutional records were also obtained from the Las Vegas Mental Health Center and from Sandra Quilici, in the medical records department of the Nevada Mental Health Institute, at Sparks. Julia Barajas, at Parkland Memorial Hospital in Dallas, furnished records documenting Cole's treatment in the mid-1960s and again, fifteen years later. In California, I am indebted to the following: Alicia Moran, medical records department, University of California at Davis; Louise Wada, supervisor of clinical records for the Stockton Developmental Center; the records department at Napa State Hospital; David Hamilton, assistant to the executive director of Atascadero State Hospital; Marilyn Haase, Virginia Padgett, and Betty Thompson, all employed in the medical records office at Atascadero State Hospital.

Information on Cole's spotty employment record was traced with the assistance of former employers. In that regard, I wish to thank Rev.

James Byrd, chaplain of the Green Oak Ranch in Vista, California; T. A. Morris, industrial relations manager for the Rheem Manufacturing Company in Richmond, California; Denise Mathey, payroll clerk at the Commercial Hotel in Elko, Nevada; Grace Alexander, in charge of personnel for the Salvation Army in Las Vegas; and the personnel department of the Western Linen Rental Company, also in Las Vegas. Cole's last employer in San Diego, Linda Sims, provided critical insight on local police procedures and the apparent apathy of probation officials, resulting in the murder of Cole's second wife.

General background information and assistance was provided by sources including the Dallas Chamber of Commerce; David Taylor, assistant superintendent for the Richmond (California) Unified School District; Otis Watson, principal of the Nystrom School in Richmond; Jed Crane, commodore of the Richmond Yacht Club; and Richard Campbell, manager IV with the California Department of Motor Vehicles, in Chula Vista.

I have shied away from secondary sources, for the most part, backing up Cole's memory of the events he caused or witnessed with excursions into the official record. Still, no author can be everywhere at once, and I am grateful to the media for covering some ground that I might otherwise have missed. In California, I consulted daily papers that include the Bakersfield *Californian,* the *Los Angeles Times,* the *San Diego Union,* and the San Francisco *Chronicle.* In Nevada, material was gleaned from the *Las Vegas Sun* and *Review-Journal,* the *Reno Gazette-Journal,* the *Nevada Appeal* and the *Nevada State Record* (both in Carson City). Supporting details of Cole's 1967 Missouri prosecution for attempted murder were obtained from *the Miller County Autogram-Sentinel,* in Tuscumbia. In Texas, sketchy information on his 1960s arson arrest and 1981 murder trial was provided by the *Dallas Times Herald.* Magazines generally ignored Eddie's case, but author "Turk Ryder" furnished a few useful details—among much sensational rubbish—in the August 1985 *Official Detective.* Two of my own contributions on the case were published in LV—*The Magazine of Las Vegas,* in November 1985 and January 1986, respectively. No book to date has given major coverage to the case, though Eddie rated four pages in *Murderers Die,* by Dennis Brian (St. Martin's, 1986), a short chapter in Cliff Linedecker's *Serial Thrill Killers* (Knightsbridge, 1990), and thumbnail sketches of the case are contained in two of my previous books—*Mass Murder* (Garland, 1988) and *Hunting Humans* (Loompanics, 1990).

While Cole was marking time in Carson City, waiting for the needle, a psychologist and neurosurgeon lobbied for the right to pick his brain, postmortem, in the hope that some genetic defect or disease might be conveniently determined as the trigger in a life of brutal violence. Eddie acquiesced with some misgivings, all the while maintaining that the key would not be found in any hormone, growth, or lesion. (He was right, in that regard; the test results were negative.) Rather, he insisted through his final months that a productive scrutiny should focus on his childhood, blighted by abuse. Cole offered up his life in that pursuit, as an atonement for his crimes, and as a bloodred warning sign to future generations, with their own domestic monsters waiting in the wings.

This story is his legacy. Too little and too late for Eddie's victims, it may still provide us with instruction in the workings of a homicidal mind, revealing clues or symptoms to assist police, psychiatrists, and social workers with their task of weeding out the other monsters in our midst.

The FBI estimates that random "recreational killers" like Eddie Cole will claim at least 3,500 victims in the next twelve months, with many of those murders remaining forever unsolved. If this account can some-how spare a single victim from addition to that roster, then perhaps Cole's life will not have been a total waste.

Please visit us at
TheWriteThought.com
for more exciting titles.

Also by Michael Newton

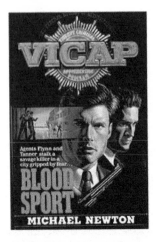

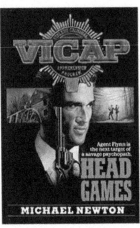

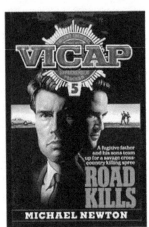

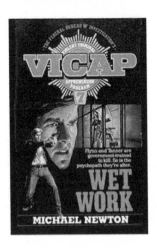

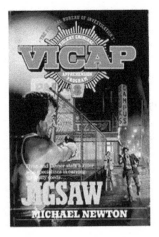

CPSIA information can be obtained
at www.ICGtesting.com
Printed in the USA
BVHW071733230119
538456BV00001B/55/P

9 781618 092045